FEMINIZING VENEREA

Feminizing Venereal Disease

The Body of the Prostitute in Nineteenth-Century Medical Discourse

Mary Spongberg

First published 1997 by
MACMILLAN PRESS LTD
Houndmills, Basingstoke, Hampshire RG21 6XS
and London
Companies and representatives
throughout the world

ISBN 0–333–63923–5 hardcover
ISBN 0–333–63924–3 paperback

A catalogue record for this book is available
from the British Library.

This book is printed on paper suitable for recycling and
made from fully managed and sustained forest sources.

10   9   8   7   6   5   4   3   2   1
06   05   04   03   02   01   00   99   98   97

Printed and bound in Great Britain by
Antony Rowe Ltd, Chippenham, Wiltshire

For Guy, Catherine and in memory of Mary

O Rose,
Thou art sick!
The invisible worm
That flies in the night,
In the howling storm,

Has found out thy bed
Of crimson joy,
And his dark secret love
Does thy life destroy.
                    William Blake

Pathology literally speaking is a flower garden. Syphilis covers the body with salmon-red petals. The study of medicine is an inverted sort of horticulture. Over and above all this floats the philosophy of disease which is a stern dance. One of its most delightful gestures is bringing flowers to the sick.

                    William Carlos Williams, *Kora in Hell*

Contents

List of Plates

Preface

When I first began working on this book William Blake's poem 'The Sick Rose' kept coming back to me as I burrowed through mounds of medical literature describing women's bodies. The book began as a text on prostitution in the nineteenth century, but as I became more aware of the AIDS crisis (both personally and politically) the book took on added dimensions. It became increasingly informed by AIDS-related cultural studies and criticisms of biomedical discourse. William Carlos Williams's *Kora in Hell* reminds me of the beauty of the men and women who inspired my interest and concern in this area and without whom this book would not have been written.

My first and most profound thanks go to my doctoral supervisor Barbara Caine, without whose help this book could not have been written. I would also like to thank my grandparents, Vic and Bess Spongberg and my parents Catherine and Donald Spongberg for their continuing interest in my work and their generous financial support.

I am very grateful to those people from the History and Women's Studies Departments of Sydney University who gave their time and attention to reading drafts of chapters, listening to papers and commenting on ideas. Special thanks go to Penny Russell, Pat Davies, Ann Mossop, Elizabeth Mossop, Thérèse Taylor, Carole Adams, Celia Roberts, Alison Best, Emma Grahame, Jeanette Joy Pritchard, Patty O'Brien, Sue Himmelweit, Jan Kociumbas, Sophie Watson and Judith Keene for their encouragement, support and helpful suggestions.

The staff at the National Centre for HIV Social Research and the School of History, Philosophy and Politics at Macquarie University provided an atmosphere that was most conducive to the completion of this book. I would like to thank Sue Kippax, Sonia Lawless, David McInnes, Catriona MacKenzie, Pam Stavoropolous, David Christian, Murray Chapple, June Crawford, Max Kelly, Gary Smith and Jill Roe for their interest and their humour.

I would like to thank Tom Laqueur, Martha Vicinus and Deryck Schreuder who read this book in manuscript form, for their insights, criticisms, comments and suggestions. Marilyn Lake, Joy Damousi and Judith Allen have provided me with both incisive criticism and much-needed encouragement. Michelle Lyons and Kim Wilson must also be thanked for their efforts in proofreading and indexing.

I would also like to thank the Wellcome Institute for the Study of the

History of Medicine for a travel grant to use their libraries in London and Glasgow, and who have generously allowed me to use illustrations from their Collection. I would particularly like to thank Chris Lawrence, Roy Porter, Sally Bragg and the members of the post-graduate reading group at the Wellcome, for their advice and criticism. I am also grateful to CARG who offered me a Post-Doctoral Fellowship that allowed me to work on the HIV/AIDS material.

My final thanks go to my husband Guy Fitzroy and my stepdaughter Hannah, who have put up with this book for what seems an eternity. Not only have they provided encouragement and support in ways too numerous to mention but they have shown me that there is life after the book.

Introduction

Falstaff: You make fat rascals, Mistress Doll.

Doll: I make them? Gluttony and Diseases makes them. I make them not.

Falstaff: If the cook help to make the gluttony, you help make the diseases, Doll. We catch of you Doll, We catch of you.

Shakespeare, *Henry IV, Part II*, iv, 45

On 21 April 1497, the town council of Aberdeen, Scotland, ordered that for protection from the disease of syphilis 'all light [loose] women . . . dicist from thair vices and syne of venerie' and work for 'thair [*sic*] support, on pain, else being branded with a hot iron on their cheek and banished from the town'.[1] The Aberdeen council believed it was necessary to stigmatize possible carriers of syphilis in this way, in order to differentiate fallen women from upright women. Such measures proved unsuccessful and after six months the Scottish Privy Council passed an edict ordering all syphilitics into banishment on the island of Inchkeith near Leith. While the state came to use less brutal means of dealing with promiscuous women, the need to brand or to stigmatize such women remained a central feature of public health policy. Some four hundred years later, medical authorities in Great Britain began to suggest that it was possible to distinguish likely carriers of syphilis and other venereal diseases by the way they looked; that is, that such women's bodies were inscribed with clear signs of degeneracy and subsequently these women could be shown to have an aptitude for prostitution and a capacity for disease. Public health officials, eugenicists, some feminists, social purity workers and certain members of the clergy used this information to lobby the government to create homes and 'colonies' for these unfortunate women so they would no longer be a threat to society.

These stories illustrate both the continuities and changes in the treatment and construction of ideas about venereal disease in Britain over time. The continuity is evident in that it was taken for granted that women were principally responsible for the spread of the disease and that it was by controlling the liberty of such women, by branding them either physically or metaphorically that the disease would cease to be a problem. The major change was that not all women were regarded as a possible source of disease, rather only those women who bore clear signs of physical and mental degeneracy were considered likely carriers.

1

The Aberdeen example is particularly pertinent because, as the Scottish historian Linda Mahood has pointed out, this Act was passed before any medical authority had ever connected the diseases with sexual intercourse.[2] Yet even without clear knowledge, promiscuous women were targeted as the source of the disease and it was hoped that by curtailing their activities its spread would cease. This idea that women were the source of venereal disease draws on a long tradition in Western thought in which women were seen as abnormal, deformed or diseased.

The idea of women as carriers of venereal disease was derived from more general views about the inferiority of the female body. From the earliest Greek medical discourse, women have been seen as inherently diseased. Certain doctors in the nineteenth century claimed that Hippocrates, the father of medicine, defined woman as 'disease'.[3] Recent work on the Hippocratic Canon has countered such claims, suggesting that it was later writers who conflated Hippocratic discussion of gynaecology with pathology.[4] Those medical writers who followed Hippocrates failed to make this distinction. Writing in the fourth century BC, Aristotle claimed that women were a 'deformity, though one which occurs in the course of nature'.[5] It was, however, the Graeco-Roman physician, Galen of Pergamum, writing in the latter half of the second century AD, who created the model of feminine inferiority that most shaped Western tradition.

Combining the views of Hippocrates and Aristotle, Galen developed a model of sexual identity based around the notion that women were essentially men in whom a lack of the 'vital heat of perfection' had resulted in the retention of the structures, that in the male are visible on the outside, inside the woman.[6] Temperature difference as means of defining gender difference was an article of scientific faith throughout the Classical period.[7] That is, Galen theorized that the vagina was an interior penis, the labia were the foreskin, the uterus was the scrotum and the ovaries were testicles. Women's sexual organs were merely considered the inverse of men's. Female genitalia were perceived to be a lesser form of male genitalia.

Thomas Laqueur has noted that this model of sexual identity was an hierarchical one, which was replaced in the eighteenth century by an oppositional model in which women were considered different from men in every conceivable way. Yet even before the eighteenth century, femininity was defined as oppositional to masculinity in many important ways. The male body was consistently represented as the healthy body, while the female body represented the diseased body.

For many centuries women's unique biological functions, especially menstruation, were represented as morbid and polluting.[8] The medieval imagination produced the idea that menstruation turned women into a 'machine' capable of producing a certain dose of 'poison' every month.[9] During the seventeenth and eighteenth century, attitudes that denigrated menstruation flourished. At this time menstruation was widely considered to be a putrefaction of the blood.[10] One of the earliest theories of the aetiology of syphilis suggested that the poison was introduced to men through menstrual blood.[11]

The idea that men acquired venereal disease from women is taken for granted throughout the medical literature on the subject. Men are consistently represented as the victims of disease, women as its source.[12] For the most part, medical advice was written for the male sufferer, with women being confined to the role of contaminator.[13] Bernard of Gordon in his *Lilii Medicinae Particula*, written around the beginning of the fourteenth century, wrote 'diseases of the yard are numerous, following lying with a woman whose womb is unclean, full of putrid sanies, virulence'.[14] Petrus de Argelata of Bologna made a similar claim, stating that 'the retention of the poisonous matter lodged between the glans and the prepuce, after a man has had to do with a foul woman causes the part to become black, and the substance of the yard to mortify'.[15] There is no suggestion as to how women became 'foul' or their wombs 'unclean'. Classical medical views of the uterus and the vagina emphasized the idea of women's devouring sexuality and simultaneously linked this with disease.[16] It was accepted both within popular culture and medical discourse that women could be exempt from the disease while passing it on to men.[17] This, of course, heightened the fear which women's bodies aroused and justified the notion that women's bodies were necessarily pathological. The female body came to be treated as the organic cause of the disease.

Gonorrhoea was considered a mild disorder and received little attention from the medical writers until it was confused with syphilis during the sixteenth century. Certainly, doctors believed that women were the source of gonorrhoea, in fact the slang term for the disease 'the clap' is derived from the Old English *clip* or *clap*, meaning to fondle or embrace and the Old French *clapises* or *clapiers*, referring to houses of ill fame. Men were advised that their symptoms were due to sexual excess and avoidance of women would promote cure. One doctor, Ambroise Paré, writing around 1575, went so far as to tell his patients that looking at pictures of women would inhibit the possibility of cure.[18]

Syphilis, then known as the Grand Pox, posed a much greater problem as its symptoms were both more severe and more obvious. The apparent introduction of the disease to Europe at the end of the fifteenth century created confusion and horror. Great medical minds of the time such as Gilinus and Torella believed that the disease had an astrological origin.[19]

At the time of the siege of Naples, astrologers had noted the ill-fated
appearance of five planets in the sign of the Scorpion, the zodiacal sign of
the genitals.[20] Other theories were more spurious. One held that it came
about after men had slept with monkeys although others, following
Fracastoro's poem (see below), suggested that it derived from men having
sex with pigs.[21] Certain theories related the outbreak specifically to the
siege. Fallopius, the Italian anatomist, believed it was introduced to Naples by the Spaniards who mixed lepers' blood with Greek wine. French
observers believed it was introduced to their society by treacherous Nea-
politans who put poison into their wells. Another theory suggested that the
outbreak was due to cannibalism as it was claimed French soldiers had fed
'universally upon dead men's carcasses'.[22] One advocate of this theory
constructed a series of experiments feeding a cow 'with a sow's flesh,
then a whelp and then an owl with flesh of its own kind'. According to the
experimenter, this resulted in the animals being covered with 'red and
yellow pimples' all over their bodies and other symptoms of 'the pox'.[23]

Xenophobia characterized the response to syphilis. Each newly affected
country blamed its neighbour for the disease: Russians called it the Polish
sickness, Poles the German sickness, the Italians blamed the French, the
French blamed the Italians. In Asia the Chinese blamed the Japanese, and
the Japanese called it the Portuguese sickness.[24] Moslems blamed Chris-
tians for its spread.[25] Throughout Europe sufferers were forced into exile.
In Lyons in 1496 anyone afflicted with 'the great pox' was expelled from
the city. The Moors were blamed in Spain and driven out in 1492. Several
years later in Geneva all foreigners with the disease were refused entrance
to the city and those within the city were forbidden to circulate. In 1496
Parisian sufferers were forced into an institution outside the city.[26]

For the next three centuries it was women, especially promiscuous
women, who were generally regarded within the popular imagination as
the source of the disease. It was the doctor poet, Fracastoro, who most
explicitly captured this sentiment in his poem 'Syphilis'.

> Blame not the stars; tis plain it neither fell
> From the distempered Heav'ns; nor rose from Hell,
> Nor need we to the distant Indies rome;
> The curst Originals are nearer home.
> But from the banefull source of all our wo?
> That wheedling charming sex, that draws us in
> To ev'ry punishment and ev'ry sin.

Medical opinion on the subject was however more ambiguous. Anna
Foa, writing on the origins of syphilis, has suggested that women were

blamed for transmission as those describing the disease merely borrowed from the Aristotelian language of generation. That is, women being mere vessels, conceived the disease in much the same way they conceived a child.[27] While it would seem most medical authorities were not opposed to the connection between women, sexual promiscuity and disease, they could find little evidence to confirm this assumption.

During the eighteenth century, doctors began to consider the precise ways in which women were transmitting disease. Many doctors came to believe that discharges from the female body were more important in the transmission of the disease than the obvious sores and pustules. The breakdown of the Galenic model of sexual difference facilitated this development. The new model of sexual difference was a model of biological divergence. Where earlier physicians had stressed the similarity in male and female bodies, doctors from the late eighteenth century onwards called for sharp corporeal distinctions between the sexes. In this model of sexuality, masculinity and femininity were constructed as oppositional. The male body came to represent the standard for health, the female body came to be seen as an aberration from the norm. The vagina and its secretions therefore were no longer merely considered the female analogues of penis and semen but somehow aberrant and diseased.

The confused knowledge of the symptomology of these diseases meant that earlier medical authorities remained somewhat vague in attributing the source of the disease to women. In the early 1800s, however, ideas about the nature and the spread of venereal diseases altered radically. This alteration was closely connected with new discoveries regarding gonorrhoea. That gonorrhoea was often asymptomatic in women had long confounded doctors. They found it impossible to explain why a disease that had such profound effects on men could appear so obscurely in women. By the end of the eighteenth century, however, several significant findings altered this perception. The breakdown of the duality of the viruses theory and the discovery that gonorrhoea could infect internal organs enabled doctors to recognize that women could be diseased without appearing to be diseased. The result of this combination of newly acquired information on the symptomology of syphilis and gonorrhoea and the new theories of sexual difference was to enhance the notion that women's bodies were a pathological terrain. Science appeared to confirm misogynistic assumptions. The lack of symptoms in women no longer meant that they were less dangerous but rather that they were more dangerous, because the disease was hidden.

The emphasis on the female body as the source of venereal infection meant that physicians paid far more attention to vaginal discharges as symptoms of syphilis and gonorrhoea than they had previously done. Prior to this, the scabs, sores, chancres and pustules that graced the penis had taken precedence in medical diagnosis. This was not entirely inappropriate as such symptoms were almost always connected to some form of venereal infection. Vaginal discharges, by contrast, occur naturally as a result of women's menstrual cycle and as the result of a variety of benign causes. Doctors of the period often failed to distinguish between minor infections such as thrush and the symptoms of gonorrhoea.[28] Unaware of their lack of precision in diagnosis, medical authorities came to argue during the 1830s that it was quite possible for all women to carry some taint of venereal disease.

By the early nineteenth century all venereal disease appeared to be sexually transmitted by women. As the incidence of these diseases increased markedly in the early part of the century, prostitutes became the main focus of a major panic about morals and public health. While doctors agreed that it was possible even for virgins to transmit venereal disease, it was the prostitute who was the obvious symbol of sexual excess and the easiest target for sexual regulation. That a prostitute could engage in the sexual act without any outward display of disease struck fear at the very heart of the medical profession. Hence prostitutes became a cause of ever greater concern in medical literature from the 1830s onwards. Medical anthropologists, such as Alexandre Parent-Duchatelet, attempted to define prostitutes in ways that distinguished them from all other women. Prostitutes came to be seen not only as sexual pariahs, but also as women exhibiting a variety of other forms of deviancy and excess, such as lesbianism, alcoholism and other forms of addiction. No longer could prostitutes be sympathetically viewed as frail women who 'fell' in a moment of moral weakness – rather, they became abnormal women who could be regarded as less than human. This of course created a gulf between the upright woman and the fallen woman. The prostitute's body continued to be seen as the representative sexualised female body, but it increasingly was also seen as a site of abnormal indulgence. Doctors began to look for physical anomalies to distinguish prostitutes from other women. Bodily differences, particularly those relating to women's sexual function, such as menstrual disorders and sterility, were highlighted to show the pathological nature of the prostitute. In this way the body of the prostitute came to be almost synonymous with venereal disease. The terms 'social disease', referring to syphilis and gonorrhoea, and 'social evil', referring to prostitutes, came to be used interchangeably. Prostitutes were seen as both physically and morally responsible for the spread of venereal disease. They were seen not merely as agents of transmission but as inherently diseased, if not the disease itself.

Legislative changes relating to the control of prostitutes, such as the Contagious Diseases Acts (CD Acts) enacted in the 1860s, reinforced the idea that the prostitute's body was an infectious site. The enactment of the CD Acts marked a definite shift in emphasis away from the idea that all female sexuality was inherently diseased to the idea that women were diseased by virtue of being prostitutes. In part, this relates to the impossibility of policing all women and, of course, to the moral outrage that would meet any suggestion that virtuous women were diseased. It also marks a shift in ideas about the spread of the disease. The evidence put forward by doctors at the committees held on the workings of the Acts and in their defence of the legislation stressed the uniqueness of the prostitute's body, implying that only such women could create 'true' venereal symptoms in men. This strengthened the conviction of medical authorities that prostitutes were innately different from virtuous women and thus should be treated only as a site of disease to be contained.

The failure of regulation meant that medical authorities sought different ways to deal with the threat of prostitution. Doctors found the most effective way of doing this was to incorporate the idea of congenital defect into the disease model. Prostitutes began to be considered as physically degenerate, the product of poor breeding. Such ideas had been in circulation since the 1830s. Doctors of the late nineteenth century took them one step further, listing and describing the distinctive physical attributes of the prostitute as a kind of catalogue which allowed them to distinguish those women who appeared to have a particular aptitude for prostitution. Throughout Europe this medical anthropology became a tool of public health officials. As evolutionary ideas spread, prostitutes began to be seen not merely as pathological females but as atavistic. Such a conception of prostitution combined well with new ideas of eugenics. By the end of the First World War medical authorities began to suspect that congenital syphilis was a causal factor in the making of a prostitute. Doctors related the moral degeneracy of the prostitute to the mental and physical degeneracy wrought by congenital syphilis. This connection further separated prostitutes from other women. Prostitutes were completely pathologized. By the 1920s it was impossible to consider the prostitute in any way a normal woman, but a woman who bore all the signs of a mental, moral and physical degenerate.

It is this progressive pathologization of the prostitute that is the subject of this book. In part this involves an attempt to reconstruct the body of the prostitute, largely drawing on medical and legal discourse. It also involves an examination of the changing ideas about the aetiology and pathology of syphilis and gonorrhoea. This book will argue that during this period, despite efforts on the part of doctors to treat medicine as a pure science, medical knowledge remained greatly influenced by cultural assumptions and social and moral codes. Medical discourse was granted considerable authority in creating definitions of prostitution and its relationship to venereal disease at this time. But such discourse did not exist in a vacuum and was greatly influenced by prevailing social, religious and cultural practices.[29]

This work draws on the extensive feminist critiques of Victorian medicine and science, particularly the works of Carroll Smith-Rosenberg, Elaine Showalter, Mary Poovey and Elizabeth Fee. Such writers have shown that during the nineteenth century science came to articulate the authoritative social discourse on the female body. More importantly, however, they have examined the ways in which scientific authority replicated cultural attitudes towards women.[30] Mary Poovey's work on the ideological construction of gender in the nineteenth century has been of critical importance to the methodological development of this book.[31] Unlike Smith-Rosenberg and Fee, who deal unproblematically with the connection between patriarchal values and medical discourse, Poovey's work indicates that those attempting to reconcile patriarchal norms with science created a model of femininity that was riddled with inconsistencies, ambiguities and contradictions. For instance, in her discussion of the mid-century debates around the use of chloroform in childbirth, Poovey shows that by rejecting the authority of the Church to construct a theory of sexual difference 'scientifically', medical experts opened a Pandora's Box of ideas about female sexuality. Poovey argues that the use of anaesthesia in childbirth made visible both the female organism's excitability and its susceptibility and, in so doing, disclosed the female body's 'problematic capacity to produce meanings other than and in excess of what was intended'.[32] Integral to her analysis is the conception of the body as social construct, yet at the same time she acknowledges the ways in which the biological body impinges upon the social order that has been composed around it. Moreover, Poovey recognizes that in attempting to justify certain medical practices or to account for physiologically unaccountable disorders, doctors drew on moralistic assumptions about women created in social and religious discourse that already had a history of contradictory meanings. This makes problematic any one-dimensional analysis of the conjunction of patriarchal and medical discourse.

This is particularly true of the construction of ideas about the prostitute in the medical discourse regarding syphilis and gonorrhoea. The prostitute can be seen as symbolic of all the contradictory demands of Victorian sexual ideology. Women were supposed to be innately pure and yet at the same time thousands of them were needed to be available to service the sexual needs of men. In order to account for this, prostitutes were treated as pathological, as women who could not control their sexuality. Yet, until a critique of male sexual privilege developed, no observer of prostitution could simultaneously accept the ideal of female sexual anaesthesia and the existence of mass prostitution without noticing the paradox involved.

The Victorian idea that women were innately pure was relatively new and highly contested. Until the mid-eighteenth century women were considered naturally depraved, they were 'the sex': sexual temptation personified. Male lust and lack of sexual control could thus be attributed to women's natural sexual depravity.[33] The spread of literacy, the growth of printing, the revival of evangelical religions and an enlightened interest in reformulating social systems and personal relations in natural and rational rather than spiritual terms meant changes in the prescribed role of women.[34] In a sense, the new role for women meant ceasing to think that women were naturally whores.[35]

This reconceptualization of femininity must be viewed in relation to the political, social and cultural development of the middle-class. The ideal of domestic harmony was the basis of middle-class men's demand for political power at this time and was dependent on the notion of innate female purity.[36] The political theorists of this class claimed that the excesses of the aristocracy had made them unfit to wield power. For the radical middle classes, political freedom and power became dependent on a prudish and rigid sexual ethic. In order to sustain this demand for political power, a reconceptualization of female sexuality was necessary. If all women were naturally depraved, then middle-class women could not hold up the ideals of sexual self-control and verbal prudery that distinguished the middle classes from the excesses of the upper and lower orders. If women were truly sexually uncontrollable this threatened bourgeois notions of property and legitimate inheritance. Evangelical and Protestant reformers came to argue that women were made for God's purposes and not man's.[37] Moral agency became linked to femininity.

New scientific theories helped to consolidate these ideas. One result of the rejection of Galenic medicine was the dismissal of the theory that female orgasm was necessary for conception to occur. Since the second century AD, female orgasm had been regarded as essential to the generative process. By the end of the eighteenth century it was believed that only male orgasm was crucial to conception.[38] The implication of this theory was that female sexual pleasure could be considered unnatural. Male sexual pleasure was recognized as being crucial to conception. If female sexual difference was to be defined as oppositional to men's, then it was a simple step to argue that sexual pleasure in women was abnormal. Such assumptions complemented the new theories of feminine virtue. Science confirmed the notion that women were not naturally depraved. Sexual pleasure in women came to be classified as unnatural in moral terms and this was shown to be a 'fundamental scientific truth.' Women who were seen to enjoy sex were thus regarded as aberrant and unnatural, further distinguishing them from pure women.

Conflicting discourses around female sexuality went hand-in-hand with conflicting discourses around male sexuality. In one way, the notion of innate feminine virtue served to calm masculine fears about female sexuality, while simultaneously the severe prescriptions of female virtue only seemed to heighten male concerns. The shift from seeing women as naturally depraved to seeing them as naturally asexual was not such a great one. It did not mean that women were no longer defined in terms of their sexuality, but rather they were defined in terms of their lack of it. Moreover, these ideals are not so far apart – the asexual Victorian woman representing a 'triumphant sublimation of the sexual anxiety' that women had previously generated.[39] This sublimation was not always successful and, as Carol Christ has argued, the 'Angel in the House' image of femininity, that was so popular with the Victorians, can also be read as anxiety-creating.[40] Christ suggests not only that considerable fear of female sexuality helped generate this ideal of womanhood but that it was matched and complicated by men's fear of their own sexuality. The Angel in the House ideal left 'the man who embraced it with an impossible dilemma' as the Angel became both a 'perpetual reproach and a perpetual temptation'.[41]

This dilemma was compounded by the conflicting discourses around male sexuality. The dominant discourse equated masculine social, economic and industrial vigour with sexual vigour. Despite a valiant effort from the evangelical middle classes to promote a masculinity based on self-control and sexual restraint, primacy was given to the idea of men's sexual uncontrollability. Moreover, economically, middle-class men had a considerable investment in the continuation and expansion of prostitution. Resorting to prostitutes was considered the solution for young men who were in no financial position to marry. This meant that men could relieve their 'uncontrollable' sexual urges and still make prudent marriages.[42] Middle-class men thus had an investment both in maintaining the notion of female purity and an investment in violating it.

Fear of venereal disease provided the framework both for articulating male sexual anxiety and for the nineteenth-century debate on prostitution by making it a health problem. This approach still allowed the idea that prostitutes were a necessary evil. On one level, this left the notion of women as innately pure untainted, by making the prostitute pathological. But on another level, it meant that all women were tainted because of the connection between venereal disease and femininity. The use of syphilis

as a metaphor for male sexual anxieties and loathing meant that any expression of female sexuality was viewed as pathological. This explains the
tone of hysteria and hyperbole found in discussions of women's sexuality
during the 1840s and 1850s. Men seem to have wanted to obliterate any
sense of female sexuality, making the act of sex for women seem a fate
worse than death. Yet prostitutes could not be whole-heartedly treated as
objects of disgust, any more than virtuous women could avoid the stigma
produced by the connection between female sexuality and disease. It was
impossible to have it both ways.

Competing definitions of sexuality, led to conflicting expectations around
sex. Men could not demand total sexual freedom for themselves and ex-
pect to be able to sustain a sexual ideology that was dependent on the idea
that women were innately 'pure'. The ambiguities and contradictions that
can be seen in discussions of prostitution during this period are the result
of the impossible demands the dominant sexual system placed on women.
Much of the medical discourse regarding both prostitution and venereal
disease can be read as an attempt to overcome these contradictions. By
pathologizing the prostitute, male responsibility for both the sexual exploitation of women and the spread of venereal disease could be conveniently
overlooked. Moreover, the suggestion of innate difference between prostitutes and other women calmed any doubts men might be having about
their wives or daughters.

The central aim of this book is to examine the medical literature on
syphilis and gonorrhoea and to show how this influenced the construction
of the prostitute as pathological female and contaminated other. This is a
very different approach from other histories both of prostitution and venereal disease during this period. Since the growth of interest in the history
of sexuality, prostitution in the nineteenth century has been examined as
a subculture, a profession, a form of sexual negotiation, a sexual deviation
and a paradigm of the oppression of women. Prostitutes have perhaps
received more historical consideration than any other group of women
during the nineteenth century. For the most part, however, histories of
prostitution have ignored the issue of venereal disease. Indeed, it could be
argued that many of the works published on the subject before 1980 have
been little more than an excuse for some historical 'slap and tickle'. With
the exception of Steven Marcus's ground-breaking work, most of the early
works on prostitution have merely attempted to recreate the world of the
'London Underground', relying upon pornographic and sensationalist texts
of the period, such as the work of the unorthodox venereologist William
Acton, to provide much of their evidence and replicating the values espoused in these works.[43]

During the 1980s the history of prostitution in nineteenth-century Britain began to receive serious consideration. Frances Finnegan's work on prostitution was perhaps the first major text to deal with the subject seriously.[44] Central to Finnegan's approach is a rejection of the validity of sources such as pornography and William Acton for a study of prostitution. Unlike her predecessors, who treated Acton's text *Prostitution* as the seminal work on the subject, Finnegan's work can be read as an attempt to disprove Acton's assumptions about the lives of prostitutes. Finnegan was one of the first historians to point out the internal contradictions in Acton's work and she depicts with depressing clarity the impossibility of his claims. Far from being the Amazons with 'iron bodies' depicted by Acton, the prostitutes that Finnegan recreates in her study are poor, ill-fed, drunken and diseased. Finnegan however goes little further than contradicting Acton's claims. There is little attempt to address other issues, such as how Acton's work relates to more orthodox medical writings or how the system of prostitution functioned within the broader sexual economy. Consequently her treatment of the relationship between prostitution, venereal diseases and the medical profession is little more than descriptive.

Paul McHugh's *Prostitution and Victorian Social Reform* and Judith Walkowitz's *Prostitution and Victorian Society*, both published in 1980, remain the two major works in the field.[45] McHugh's work is primarily a study of the machinations of the state in establishing regulation and in dealing with the opposition to the Acts. Walkowitz's work is more adventurous, examining the impact of the Acts upon prostitutes and on the subjected districts, exploring both the support for and the opposition to the Acts as a struggle for control over the policing of working-class sexuality. Unlike Finnegan, who views prostitutes as silent, oppressed women working within a system of sexual negotiation over which they have little control, Walkowitz portrays prostitutes as important historical actors, and represents their move into prostitution as neither pathological nor deviant, but as a rational economic choice.

McHugh's exhaustive knowledge of the personalities involved in the campaigns surrounding regulation and his analysis of the intrigues and struggles leading to repeal have proved of invaluable assistance to the construction of my arguments regarding regulation. Walkowitz's work has also been influential in its stress on the importance of a gendered analysis of the issue of prostitution and its locating the study of Victorian prostitution within a much broader social and political perspective. While Walkowitz has critiqued the double standard of morality that made possible such legislation, she has also tended to privilege a class-based system of analysis over one based on gender difference. This has obscured both the true nature of the Acts and the more pressing demands of feminist Repealers. Central to Walkowitz's text is her analysis of the ways in which the CD Acts professionalized prostitution. Her ideas about the professionalization of prostitution have been of great importance to the study of the history of prostitution, shifting the emphasis away from viewing the prostitute only as victim.[46] My interest in the CD Acts relates more to representations of the prostitute, rather than their reality. My analysis concentrates on how the medical discourse that informed the Acts manipulated ideas about venereal disease to present an image of the prostitute as necessarily diseased.

That is not to suggest that this will merely be an examination of how the medical profession treated prostitution. While the book offers a detailed textual analysis of the medical literature of the period, this is informed by a wider cultural analysis. Medical opinion on prostitution and venereal disease is not treated as an entity divorced from other influences. Medical discourse can be shown to have constantly borrowed evidence and ideas from imaginative literature and art in order to construct and articulate ideas about the prostitute. Throughout the nineteenth century the prostitute was a regular figure in popular journals, in art work, in romantic literature, in opera and theatre, religious works and cartoons. The construction of the prostitute in these texts has been treated by many medical historians and historians of sexuality as peripheral. Yet an analysis of these more popular forms of discourse is essential to a better understanding of its treatment in the more formal medical and legal texts. These specialist discourses were often dependent on ideas popularized through art and literature. The Victorian belief that art reflected life meant that many of the most important pieces on prostitution in serious journals were based on observations from favourite novels. The alcoholic prostitute in Mrs Gaskell's *Mary Barton* for example was often cited as proof that all prostitutes were drunken. Charles Dickens's Nancy from *Oliver Twist* was used as an example of the reclaimability of prostitutes. Doctors were just as likely to cite evidence from Alexander Pope, Alfred Lord Tennyson or Alexandre Dumas, as they were data from *The Lancet* or the *British Medical Journal*.[47]

It is the purpose of this book to examine the points at which these various discourses meet. The central aim of the project is to illustrate that medicine in the nineteenth century can not be simply viewed as the prefiguration of a 'rational science'. The history of medicine tends to be presented as a series of discoveries and 'breakthroughs', where superstition and misinformation give way to the onslaught of scientific reason. Yet in the case of syphilis and gonorrhoea the opposite appears to be the case.

While nineteenth- and early twentieth-century medical research provided significant breakthroughs regarding the aetiology and pathology of both diseases, medical opinion retained ancient fears and superstitions about female bodies and female sexuality. That is not to say that medical opinion on prostitution and venereal disease remained static during the nineteenth century. This is certainly not the case. What is traced in this book is the various ways in which medical opinion responded to new 'scientific' evidence about venereal disease and how such evidence was incorporated with archaic notions of female sexual pollution.

Thus there was a shift from the early nineteenth century when femininity itself was considered diseased. The practice of the CD Acts meant that it was expedient for only some women to be seen as diseased and by the early twentieth century the medical profession was advising that only certain women bearing visible signs of degeneracy were at risk. The purpose of examining the pathologization of the prostitute in this way is to show how it functioned to control all women's bodies and sexuality. This study will indicate how medical and legal discourse explicitly served the needs of men by protecting male sexual privilege and allowing the continuance of a sexual system that placed impossible demands on women. Fear of sexual disease represented a wider fear of women. Attempts to control sexual disease were ostensibly attempts to control women. I will argue that construction of the prostitute's body as pathological within medical discourse during the period must be viewed as a direct response to the contradictory demands which the dominant sexual system placed on women. Ideas about venereal disease were shaped in accordance with the fears and desires men felt for women. By pathologizing the body of the prostitute, doctors were creating a *cordon sanitaire* that differentiated good women from bad while, at the same time, rejecting any possibility of male responsibility for the sexual exploitation that prostitution entails.

Medical knowledge regarding the aetiology of syphilis and gonorrhoea can be seen to represent the unhappy marriage of the dominant ideology of male sexual uncontrollability and the no less powerful discourse of masculine sexual loathing and anxiety. The pathologization of the prostitute's body in medical discourse highlights the untenability of the system of sexual exchange that had developed since the mid-eighteenth century and serves to throw into question all that was held as naturally masculine and naturally feminine. Therefore the debates about venereal disease in the nineteenth century marked more than the struggle between men and women over the definitions of femininity and female sexuality and control over women's bodies: they did nothing less than subvert (perhaps inadvertently) the ideas of masculinity and femininity as 'natural'.

PART I
Feminizing Syphilis

With her much fair speech she caused him to yield,
with the flattering of her lips she forced him.
He goeth after her straightway,
As an oxen to the slaughter,
Or as a fool to the correction of the stocks.
Till a dart strike through his liver;
As a bird hasteth to the snare,
And knoweth not that it is for his life.
Harken unto me now therefore,
O ye children, and attend to the words of my mouth.
Let not thine heart decline unto her ways,
Go not astray in her paths.
For she hath cast down many wounded: yea, many strong men have
been slain by her.
Her house is the way to hell,
Going down to the chambers of death.

Proverbs, vii. 21–27

1 The Sick Rose

In this book I propose with God's help to consider diseases peculiar to women. And since women are, for the most part poisonous creatures, I shall proceed to treat the bites of venomous beasts.

Arnold of Villanova, *Commentaries*, Book One

Until the twentieth century, much of what was known about syphilis and gonorrhoea was based on myth and superstition. Gonorrhoea had been known to exist for many centuries before Christ. It has been claimed that Moses was referring to gonorrhoea in the fifteenth chapter of Leviticus, when he laid down the law for the government of those who are affected with 'a running issue out of the flesh'.[1] Others have suggested that Herodotus, the Greek historian, was referring to gonorrhoea when describing the punishment inflicted by Venus on the Scythians. He reported that when the Scythians invaded Palestine, raiding the temple of Venus, 'the angry goddess sent upon them and their posterity, the woman's disease, which is characterized by a running from the penis'.[2] The first detailed account of the disease was given by Aretaeus, a Greek physician, in the first century AD. He described the discharge as unfruitful semen that continued for days and nights.[3] Hippocrates in *De Locis Affectis* mentions this disease and suggests that the principal cause of the illness was 'excessive indulgence in the pleasures of Venus'. Celsus wrote of gonorrhoea in his *De Medicina*, claiming that it was due to an ulcer in the urethra.[4] Both Hippocrates and Galen are credited with coining the name gonorrhoea which comes from the Greek meaning 'flow of seed'.[5] Galen, like his predecessors, believed that gonorrhoea was an involuntary flow of sperm unaccompanied by an erection.

Little progress was made in the study of the disease until the Middle Ages. While doctors developed new treatments for the ailment they retained the ideas of the ancient writers, which treated gonorrhoea as the fermentation of the sperm or as the result of an ulcer in the urethra. In both ancient and medieval literature the sufferer of gonorrhoea was male. The treatments devised for gonorrhoea were, consequently, for ailments of the male generative organs, such as suspensory bandages for penises or the introduction of a live flea to the urethra. Because the symptoms of gonorrhoea manifested themselves as a discharge from the urethra it was considered a feminine affliction that occurred in men. Few writers recognized gonorrhoea as a problem affecting women and when it was noted it was described as a much milder disorder. It was unanimously agreed that sexual excess was the primary cause of gonorrhoea. Women were considered the source of the temptation and subsequently of the infection.

The origins of syphilis remain the subject of much speculation. Nineteenth-century historians of medicine have claimed that the Chinese Emperor Hoang-Ty referred to syphilis as 'pustules formed by a worm' and its treatment with mercury in his massive medical treatise written around 2637 BC.[6] It has also been suggested that syphilis was known in Old Japan.[7] Others refer to Biblical authority claiming that David caught syphilis from Bathsheba.[8] The condition described in Psalm 38, 'There is no soundness in my flesh . . . neither is there any rest in my bones, because of my foolishness . . . my loins are filled with a loathsome disease' could refer to the symptoms of syphilis. Hippocrates, Thucydides and Celsus are all said to refer to syphilis-like conditions.[9] According to certain authorities, the Hindus knew of syphilis around 1000 BC.[10]

The most widely accepted theory was the theory of American origin, which held that Columbus had returned to Europe with the disease. This theory was put forward some thirty years after the return of Columbus, by Oviedo, the comptroller of Spanish gold mines in the Darien.[11] The American theory was said to develop because of the use of Guaiac wood from the Antilles in the treatment of syphilis. Such ideas became widely accepted and were combined with other misogynistic and xenophobic myths. C.B. Godfrey, writing on the history of venereal diseases in the late eighteenth century, provides an interesting example of this by adding suggestions of witchcraft and menstrual pollution to his explanation of the American origin. He wrote:

Fernandez de Oviedo who accompanied Columbus on his discovery of the Antilles Islands, says that the women there from habitual nastiness, indolence, often lived on worms, spiders, serpents, bats, and on a kind of lizard palatable indeed, but poisonous to any but the natives; which induced Dr Lister to give a decided opinion that this was the cause of producing the Venereal poison in these islands and from which a rational presumption is drawn of their engendering in the very blood, a complicated species of poison; another circumstance he mentions and it is such, indeed as will apply to all women under the torrid zone, that in their menstrual state, they are so intolerably hot and so unusually indecent that they frequently lay in open highways, intreating and provoking indiscriminate connections with men, the hetrogenity [*sic*] of whole semen, co-operating in conjunction with the two causes mentioned, gave it that complexion it wore at its first introduction into Europe, by the soldiers of Columbus.[12]

Recent observers however are sceptical of the American theory, suggesting that Oviedo developed the theory to deflect European sympathy away from the Indians as victims of Spanish abuse. Placing blame on the Indians simultaneously located the disease as far away as possible, entirely within the realm of the other, the alien.[13]

Regardless of its origin, when syphilis made its appearance in Europe around 1495 it was treated as a new disease. It made little difference to the treatment of gonorrhoea as they were considered two separate diseases. But the aetiology of syphilis truly confounded the medical authorities. There was general agreement that the disease was a poison introduced to the body, but there was an infinite number of explanations of how the disease first evolved. It was not however until some time after the outbreak of syphilis that gonorrhoea came to be seen as a symptom of syphilis. The contemporaries of the first great epidemic of syphilis speak incidentally of gonorrhoea as a disease of antiquity, or they do not mention it at all in the treatises devoted to the new affliction.[14]

By the sixteenth century, several authorities claimed gonorrhoea to be a symptom of syphilis. The venereologist and surgeon to the King of France, Jean Astruc, claimed that James a Bethencourt, writing in 1527, was the first person to describe gonorrhoea as a symptom of syphilis. Paracelsus has also been blamed as he began to refer to syphilis as 'French gonorrhoea' around 1530.[15] In 1551, the Italian physician Antonus Musa Brassavolus in his text *Examen Omnium Loch . . . de Morbo Gallico Tractatus*, claimed that both gonorrhoea and chancroid were symptoms of syphilis. Indeed, he maintained that there were some 234 compound forms of syphilis. Other famous physicians, such as Gabriel Fallopius and Ambroise Paré, further confused syphilis with symptoms of gonorrhoea.[16] Such authorities were confused by the similarity of the anatomical sites involved and the obvious evidence that sexual intercourse was the mode of transmission and chose to consider them as symptoms of the same disease. At the same time, doctors confused non-syphilitic venereal ulcers with syphilis. Contagious ulcers of the genital organs (chancroid), which develop into suppurating buboes but do not develop constitutional symptoms, had been described by nearly all the Latin, Greek and Arabic writers.[17] Prior to 1495, all such ulcers of the genital organs were treated by local remedies and generally disappeared after a course of treatment. By the mid-sixteenth century a tendency developed amongst medical writers to confound the various venereal diseases. Such confusion continued until the middle of the nineteenth century.

Unlike gonorrhoea, syphilis appeared to affect both men and women with equal vehemence. Yet, as with gonorrhoea, the medical literature was written exclusively for the male sufferer.[18] The syphilitic was represented in religious and secular art as a male sufferer, the signs and symptoms of his disease were written on his body like the stigmata of a parodied Christ.[19] The iconography of the suffering male syphilitic was taken from the traditional representations of the leper. In the Middle Ages the leper had been a social text in which corruption was made visible.[20] By the sixteenth century the male syphilitic took over this role as an emblem of decay. The disease however, was generally personified in a female form. Women, who were rarely represented as sufferers, were ubiquitously represented as contaminators. By the eighteenth century, the image of the male sufferer began to disappear and women came to represent the syphilitic, but by this time the syphilitic had the dual role of sufferer and contaminator.

In most of the medical literature on syphilis and gonorrhoea from the sixteenth to the nineteenth century it was generally taken for granted that men caught the disease from women. Prostitutes especially were targeted. Many of the observations made by doctors in the sixteenth and seventeenth century would however eventually result in the belief that the female body, especially the promiscuous female body, was in some way the organic cause of the disease. This was not an entirely new idea, nor was it unique to syphilis. The female body had always been represented as an elusive terrain and many medical mysteries were explained in essentially gynaephobic terms. Doctors in the Middle Ages had suggested as much when writing on leprosy. Intercourse with a woman during menstruation was often believed to result in leprosy.[21] Both leprosy and syphilis had been related to certain humoral disorders in women. The Neapolitan physician Al Benedetti suggested in the mid-sixteenth century that the cause of syphilitic contagion was a 'venereal tint' [*sic*] which resulted from the change in humours exhaled by the generative organs of the woman during intercourse.[22] It was also believed that women could pass on these diseases while remaining immune to them. William of Conches explained this phenomena regarding leprosy:

> The hottest woman is colder than the coldest man: such a complexion is hard and extremely resistant to male corruption; nonetheless the putrid matter, coming from coitus remains in the womb and when a man penetrates her with his penis, made of sinews, enters the vagina and, by virtue of its attractive force, attracts this matter to itself (and to the organs to which it is attached) and transmits it to them.[23]

While few nineteenth-century doctors would have attributed such quasi-magnetic powers to the penis, the idea that a 'sound' man could engage in intercourse with a 'sound' woman and become syphilitic was still regarded as quite within the realms of possibility. Several doctors during the eighteenth century attempted to explain this phenomenon. Jean Astruc wrote that it was possible if a 'sound' woman 'had to do with a person infected, and has not washed the parts, since she has lain with him; for the remains of the putrid seed latcly received, adhering to the vagina, or womb, may infect the glans of the person last lying with her with a like disorder'.[24] Others suggested that the disease was caused by a mixture of different sperm in the woman which would ferment and infect other men.[25] Certain experts claimed that men could be affected and women remain untainted. The more men that a woman slept with, the more likely it was considered that she would pass on the infection but remain untainted herself. François Rachin, lecturer in Medicine at the University of Montpellier wrote in 1640:

> One should not lie for long with a fallen woman, and one should wash and dry one's member most carefully. For if one lies with such a woman for long . . . and the infected quality penetrates, there is no remedy. Some women are so easily polluted that their venom is easily communicated.[26]

From the late seventeenth century many surgeons and physicians began to record their clinical observations and have them published. In this way an abundance of material became available on the venereal diseases.[27] Around this time, doctors in England began to write their texts in English rather than Latin. This accessibility to English texts coupled with the growth of the printing industry meant that information about venereal diseases was more easily disseminated. The more systematized medical knowledge of syphilis became, the less doctors could definitively explain. By the beginning of the eighteenth century many doctors were discrediting the theory that gonorrhoea was caused by the corruption of semen. It was pointed out that the discharge expelled from the urethra was not sperm but a combination of pus and mucous. Other doctors claimed that the idea of the fermentation of sperm in the uterus was also an unlikely cause of gonorrhoea.[28] Gonorrhoea was also more frequently being reported in women. John Marten, English author of *A Treatise of all the Degrees and Symptoms of the Venereal Disease in both Sexes* (1708), and his contemporary Daniel Turner, author of *Siphilis* [*sic*], *a Dissertation on the Venereal Disease* (1717), both suggested that gonorrhoea may be equally virulent in women.

Such ideas were confirmed by the researches of the Italian anatomist Giovanni Battista Morgani who, through post-mortem studies, showed that women could be internally affected by chronic gonorrhoea. Morgani was also the first to show that the discharge was not due to an ulceration in the urethra, but originated from changes in urethral mucous membranes and not from the seminal vessels.[29] He was also one of the first researchers to establish that syphilis could affect the primary organs.[30] Morgani described syphilis of the lungs, including the complications caused by tuberculosis. He maintained that syphilis could affect the bones, the heart and the blood vessels and even the cerebral vessels. He made valuable contributions in distinguishing between syphilis and other local venereal diseases and by his studies of the sequelae of gonorrhoea, described cystitis, prostitis, cowperitis and most other complications of the genito-urinary tract.[31]

As more case studies of gonorrhoea were reported, there was extensive confusion as to its true cause. Far from making diagnosis easy, Morgani's findings only added to the perplexity surrounding the aetiology of gonorrhoea. Many doctors asserted that the disease was the result of the introduction of syphilitic matter into the urethra. The idea that gonorrhoea was a poison that was introduced into the body only explained certain aspects of the disease, leaving doctors bemused. Some physicians claimed that on occasion gonorrhoea appeared 'spontaneously'. Other doctors ascertained that men suffering from gout and rheumatism frequently suffered from a clap that had no 'venereal' origin. Certain doctors maintained that some men engaged in 'impure intercourse' and became diseased while their female partners showed no sign of the disease, either in the form of discharge or chancre. Some believed that certain conditions in women, such as menstruation and leucorrhoea, predisposed them to infect their sexual partners.

Such confusion led to the idea that there were several different forms of the disease. First, there was the simple gonorrhoea that arose spontaneously and was non-venereal. Secondly, there were two forms of venereal gonorrhoea. Both were believed to be the result of 'impure intercourse' and both were virulent. One however was considered to result from intercourse with women during their menstrual period or when they were labouring under inflammatory or diseased states of the vagina. It was maintained that such women furnished men with discharges of an acrid and irritating nature. They were unpleasant but not contagious. These discharges were not followed by constitutional symptoms, nor did they respond to mercury. The alternate form of gonorrhoea was considered the 'true gonorrhoea' and was passed on by a woman who was herself diseased.[32] Symptomatically it was almost identical to the other form of venereal gonorrhoea, except that it resulted in syphilitic symptoms if not treated. The terms 'true', 'simple', 'spontaneous' and 'venereal' were all used interchangeably and the distinctions made between them were based on spurious case studies rather than explicit diagnostic signs.

The notion that gonorrhoea and syphilis were twin diseases further confused the medical imagination. The view that a real case of gonorrhoea was a symptom of syphilis was particularly confusing. On the one hand, cases of gonorrhoea that were venereal but were unaccompanied by sores were not treated very seriously. On the other hand, cases of gonorrhoea that were accompanied by sores were always taken to be symptomatic of syphilis. During the course of the century, many physicians came to question the idea that gonorrhoea was merely a symptom of syphilis. William Cockburn, author of *The Symptoms, Nature, Cause and Cure of a Gonorrhoea* (1715) was among the first in England to promote the idea of the duality of the viruses. Hermann Boerhaave, a renowned professor of medicine at the University of Leyden, writing in 1753 pointed out from clinical observation that the symptomology of syphilis was changing and that gonorrhoea was being more frequently seen without syphilis. He insisted on the separateness of the two infections.[33] In describing the clinical course of syphilis Boerhaave anticipated by a hundred years the more complete work of Philippe Ricord. His claims were supported rather timidly by British doctors Francis Balfour in 1767, Hales in 1770 and Ellis in 1771.

In 1761 John Hunter, the eminent Scottish surgeon, anatomist, physiologist and pathologist, became interested in debates about the unity and duality of the venereal diseases. His contribution to the debate derived from an ill-fated experiment he performed upon himself to 'prove' that gonorrhoea was indeed a symptom of syphilis. Having collected venereal matter described as a gonorrhoea, Hunter made two small punctures on his penis with a lancet and inoculated himself with this pus. Both incisions were converted after a short time into pustules and superficial ulcerations that were accompanied by other inflammatory symptoms. These spots were then cauterized repeatedly and slowly healed. During recovery, swelling of the inguinal gland occurred and about three months later an ulcer appeared upon his tonsils, which was followed some three months later by a copper-coloured eruption of pustules. All these symptoms were quite correctly attributed to syphilis.

After his death John Hunter came to be referred to as the 'Shakespeare of medicine'.[34] He developed a 'sort of talismanic stature' upheld by medical historians since the end of the eighteenth century.[35] Hunter made no fundamental discoveries nor did he devise a therapeutic model. He did however change the face of British medicine in the eighteenth century by the development of research in all its branches. Hunter began a new era in surgery by the application of the principle of experimental verification. Before his time, surgery had been based solely on anatomy and little or no heed was paid to pathology, that is, the natural history of disease. Hunter's major achievement was that he showed first the importance of applying available knowledge to surgery and secondly of making experiments to try the accuracy of his conclusions. In so doing Hunter made clear the 'elevated, esoteric status of surgical science, furnishing an overlay of "scientificity" for the professional status of the elite surgeon anatomist'. Hunter's panegyric status proved very comforting to the ambitious Victorian medical profession. As Russell C. Maulitz writes, '[I]intellectually minded surgeons of the nineteenth century could mirror their own careers against the Hunterian hologram and come away with flattering reflections'.[36]

Hunter drew a wide variety of conclusions from his experiment. The most significant of these was his maintaining that a gonorrhoea may produce a chancre. His adventures in auto-inoculation were perceived as path-breaking experiments in that field and he received far more credit for this than his efforts really deserved. Due to his symbolic importance to British medicine he remained the great authority, although his findings were widely challenged. Until the 1840s most British doctors maintained a belief in the unity of the virus theory. There has been very little critical analysis of Hunter's actual contribution to debates on venereal diseases in the eighteenth century or of the impact his teachings had on the treatment of syphilis and gonorrhoea during the nineteenth century. His heroism in undertaking the experiment led others to revere him and amongst his panegyrists criticism of Hunter's findings on venereal disease is treated as akin to blasphemy. As late as 1967, the medical historian Michael Kelly launched a vehement attack on Hunter's contemporary F.X. Swediaur. Kelly wrote of Swediaur's quite appropriate criticisms of Hunter's cavalier attitude to patients with gonorrhoea who slept with their wives:

> The first time I read that chapter I hated Swediaur for his foul abuse; I had expected praise of Hunter and I was nauseated . . . Swediaur disappeared from the British scene and has hardly left a trace. Which is what we should expect from one who wrote so badly and with such venom against a great man.[37]

Those historians who write about Hunter's contribution to venereal disease tend to play down his influence and stress that most of his errors were redressed by the mid-nineteenth century. This is only partly true and ignores the fact that in the interim many people probably suffered as a result of the confusion caused by his addled logic. This was particularly true of his writings on 'true' and 'spontaneous' gonorrhoeas. Hunter was certainly amongst the first medical writers to distinguish between a 'venereal' and a 'simple' clap, but he failed to describe their different diagnostic signs. His ardent belief in the unity of the virus theory meant that Hunter really believed that the only significant diagnostic difference between the various forms of gonorrhoea was that true gonorrhoea left untreated would develop into syphilis. Armed with this knowledge and other observations picked up from his vast experience and further experimentation on his students, Hunter wrote the mammoth volume *On the Venereal Disease* which was first published in 1786.

In this work Hunter not only set out his emphatic belief in the unity of the disease theory but he made several other memorable errors: he denied the possibility of hereditary syphilis, he maintained that syphilis could not be transmitted through the blood, he believed it impossible to transmit syphilis to a suckling infant and he ignored the contagiousness of secondary lesions. He also believed himself to have been entirely cured after three years of treatment. He assumed that early treatment of syphilis with mercury would prevent any constitutional symptoms from developing. He never attributed his chronic bad health following the experiment to syphilis.[38] Nor did he ever suspect that his wife or his children could have been affected. Hunter would later die of an attack of *angina pectoris* which certain authorities have claimed was unquestionably related to his experiment with syphilis. Hunter's obvious mistake in his experiment was that he had inoculated himself with pus from a patient who had both gonorrhoea and syphilis. His later errors stemmed from his ardent belief in the unity theory and misplaced faith in his own ability to read his symptoms and to cure himself.

Hunter's writing style only added to the confusion. In the preface to the 1810 edition of *On the Venereal Disease*, the editor Joseph Adams apologized for the chaotic writing style of the author. He added that 'Mr Hunter found himself so frequently ill-understood that at last he was prevailed on to believe there must be some incapacity about him in the use of common language'.[39] Such self-doubt was entirely warranted. The first edition of Hunter's work was rewritten by two other doctors and most of the following editions had additional commentaries in order to clarify Hunter's ideas. This led to further confusion rather than clarification, as often the commentary text appears at odds with the main text.

That such clarification was necessary can be seen if one looks at his writings on the source of simple and true gonorrhoea. It would take a skilled reader to differentiate between the two. Hunter himself called his chapter on this question 'On the Difficulty of distinguishing the Virulent from the Simple Gonorrhoea' He began with a description of simple gonorrhoea:

The surface of the urethra is subject to inflammation and suppuration from various other causes besides the venereal poison. Such may be called simple gonorrhoeas, having nothing of the venereal infection in them; though those persons that have been formerly subject to virulent gonorrhoeas are most liable to them. It is given as distinguishing marks between the simple and the virulent gonorrhoea, that the simple comes on some days after, and gradually. But the simple is not in all cases a consequence of the man having had connexion with women, it does not always come on at once, nor is it always free from pain. On the other hand, we may see many venereal gonorrhoeas that begin without any appearance of inflammation; and I have been very much at a loss to determine whether they were venereal or not; for there are a certain class of symptoms common to all diseases of the urethra, from which it is difficult to distinguish the few that arise solely from the specific affection.[40]

It remained difficult for doctors to identify the different infections of the urethra until the late nineteenth century and Hunter was certainly not alone in being confused. For Hunter, such differentiation was not of real importance because of his 'unity of the virus theory'. From these findings, Hunter and those who have proceded him concluded that gonorrhoea could no longer be treated as an obscure disease in women. Hunter's findings implied that all discharges in women could produce disease in men. Such ideas reinforced the notion that women's bodies were not only different from men's but were somehow pathological, if not innately diseased.

Such ideas were instrumental in creating the belief that women were in some way the principal source of venereal disease. Hunter believed that discharge was essential for the transmission of venereal poison. He maintained that without some form of discharge or 'matter' from the urethra, the disease could not be passed on to another individual. He wrote '[I]t is the matter produced, whether with or without inflammation which alone contains the poison; for without the formation of matter, no venereal poison can exist'.[41] By stating this, Hunter could explain how some people engaged in intercourse with an infected person and became infected, while others slept with the same person and remained untainted. It also provided a seemingly logical explanation for the fact that one person would be seen to develop only a simple clap while another would develop the full symptoms of syphilis when infected from the same source. Hunter maintained that this was not much of a problem for men if they followed his treatment and wiped any offending 'matter' off the penis before intercourse. He argued the case as follows:

That venereal disease is to be propagated by matter is proved every day by a thousand instances. Married men contract the disease and not knowing they have caught it, cohabit with their wives, even for weeks. Upon discovering the symptoms of the disease, they of course desist, yet in all my practice I never once found that the symptoms were communicated under such circumstances, except where they had not been very attentive to the symptoms and therefore continued the connexion after the discharge had appeared. I have gone so far as to allow husbands, while infected, but before the appearance of the discharge to cohabit with their wives, in order to save appearances, and always with safety. I could carry this still further, and even allow a man who has a gonorrhoea, to have connexion with a sound woman, provided that great care be taken to clear all the parts of any matter.[42]

While this must have proved very convenient for errant husbands, it was of course a dreadful misconception that may have caused many women to be unknowingly infected by gonorrhoea. Moreover, given Hunter's inadequate diagnosis of the symptoms of gonorrhoea in women it is very unlikely that he would have recognized the symptoms in such women had they presented themselves to him. Hunter's ideas not only limited the responsibility of men for the spread of gonorrhoea, but his teachings positively encouraged the idea that women were generally responsible. The idea that 'matter' was necessary for the spread of gonorrhoea meant that more attention was paid to the discharges of the genitals. Such discharges occur naturally more frequently in women and most bear no relation to any venereal infection. Given Hunter's teachings, however, all these discharges became suspect. Hunter maintained that any change in the atmosphere of the vagina was likely to cause a gonorrhoea in man. This, he asserted, could happen with or without the woman being infected. The symptoms of gonorrhoea he considered were often only slight in women. This, he added, had little to do with the infection that they could transmit. He believed that the dose of clap produced in the man had more to do with the constitution of his sexual partner than on the 'poison' she could transmit.[43] In his opinion, the more accustomed to the disease the constitution became, the more it was immune to it.[44]

This had particular bearing on discussions about prostitutes as the source of the disease. A case study provided in the commentary of Hunter's treatise is particularly illustrative of this. Adams, his editor, wrote:

A young woman, who, though not on the town, was pretty liberal in her favours . . . . She had intercourse with many who were not delicate in their amours, till she became fixed in the house of a bachelor surgeon. This gentleman, naturally of a delicate constitution, had been for some time in a reduced state of health, during which he was nursed by the above female with much attention. The consequence of the convalescence may be easily guessed.[45]

The unfortunate surgeon soon presented himself to Dr Adams with several 'suspicious ulcers' on the glans of his penis. The girl, his only sexual partner, appeared in a state of perfect health. The amorous surgeon had examined her and found no sign of chancres. Adams however discovered that she was subject to a 'discharge'. He concluded:

> It was however discovered, that she had had, for a longer time than could be well ascertained, a discharge from those parts by which some of her lovers suffered, though others escaped probably in proportion as the parts were more or less habituated to the poison; and, perhaps, the surgeon might owe his greater susceptibility to his chastity during his previous illness.[46]

This idea that women of ill virtue were more 'poisonous' than other women was not based on the assumption that they were more exposed to catching the disease, but rather linked with the question of their immorality or their 'habituation' to sexual intercourse. Hunter did suggest that men also could become 'habituated' to the poison. But this was rarely taken up. Men, such as the ill-fated doctor in Adam's case study, were generally treated as hapless victims. The prostitute was the most visible emblem of illicit sexuality and to her was attached the idea that venereal disease was qualitatively connected with immorality.

This marks a shift in medical interest away from the symptomology of the disease to interest in its source. Discharges from the female body came to be seen as more important in the transmission of the disease than the more obvious sores and pustules. Prostitutes were especially shown to be a source of infection and throughout the nineteenth century doctors became more convinced that the body of the prostitute was in some way the organic cause of the disease. The findings of Hunter really meant that less, rather than more, was known about these afflictions. Yet these mysteries were quickly exploited. That venereal diseases, particularly gonorrhoea, were asymptomatic in women had long protected them from the finger of blame. By the end of the eighteenth century, lack of symptoms in women meant no longer were they less dangerous, but more dangerous because the disease was hidden.

The findings of the Swiss-French physician F.X. Swediaur further complicated the issues raised by Hunter. Although Swediaur was extremely critical of several of Hunter's ideas, he whole-heartedly endorsed many of Hunter's misconceptions. He believed that there were at least seven types of gonorrhoea. Only one of these types was from the same poison as syphilis. Like Hunter, he argued that gonorrhoea was a poison that seeped into the urethra. He proved experimentally that urethral inflammation could be produced by the injection of irritating chemicals. Swediaur injected ammonia into his own urethra with the result that he developed a violent urethritis which in its course and clinical symptoms closely resembled gonorrhoea. This misconception gave further credibility to the view that gonorrhoea was an introduced virus, not a discharge resulting from a deep-seated disease. In his *Practical Treatise on Venereal Complaints*, first published in 1785, Swediaur proposed that the term gonorrhoea be substituted by the term *blennorrhagia*, from the Greek, meaning 'discharge of mucus'.[47] Like Hunter, he also proposed that certain forms of gonorrhoea owed their origin to other acrimonious substances introduced to the urethra and also to certain forms of violent mechanical stimulation during intercourse.

Until the 1830s there was much debate over the question of the unity of syphilis and gonorrhoea. Benjamin Bell, a Scottish surgeon, was really the first to effectively challenge Hunter's reasoning. He was convinced that Hunter's findings were incorrect. In 1793 he published a *Treatise on Gonorrhoea and Lues Venerea*, in which he noted from clinical observation, that syphilis and gonorrhoea provided distinct clinical pictures and responded very differently to treatment. He asked, if they were the same disease, why did outbreaks occur at different times and places and never simultaneously?[48] He was also very critical of the way inoculation experiments were carried out. He claimed that in order for them to show any degree of accuracy they must be 'numerous' and 'repeated on a variety of patients'.[49] This was Bell's most telling criticism. Hunter's obvious mistake was that he had inoculated himself from a patient who carried both diseases. Had more experiments been carried out, the results would have been different.

In 1794, Jean-François Hernandez, Professor of Internal Pathology at Toulon, read of Bell's criticism and decided that an experiment should be run along the lines Bell had suggested. Hernandez believed that much confusion around syphilis was due to the presence of other diseases such as gout, scurvy and scrofula. Using a group of prisoners under his care he inoculated them with gonorrhoeal pus. This group was made up of three healthy men, two scorbutics, four men with scrofula, one man with gout and several with generally weakened constitutions. None of them developed symptoms of syphilis, although other diseases gave rise to the appearance of syphilis.[50] He published his results, *Essai Analytique sur la Non-identité des Virus Gonorrhéique et Syphilitique* in 1812. From this point onwards, the duality of virus theory began to lose credibility in France. In Britain, however, the reputation of John Hunter was such that most of the medical world maintained that his opinions were correct.[51]

Another legacy of Hunter's teachings was the confusion over syphilis and diseases that closely resembled syphilis. Hunter, in his characteristic paradoxical style, was the first to demonstrate that such venereal ulcers, though not 'syphilitic', would produce buboes and secondary symptoms resembling those of syphilis. Diagnostically these diseases were almost identical to syphilis with papular and pustular eruptions, the accompanying pains of the joints and temporary relief by mercury. The debate about 'true syphilis' and 'pseudo-syphilis' produced a variety of opinions, all of which added to the growing effort to pathologize female sexuality and feminize venereal disease.

The observations of Richard Carmichael in 1814 only served to further confuse the British medical profession.[52] Carmichael was the Superintendent of the Dublin Lock Hospital, a specialist venereal facility. He recorded that in his experience of venereal disease, there was a 'plurality of poisons'. He subdivided venereal infections into four major classes, each of which he maintained had a distinct exciting poison, a peculiar primary manifestation and a separate series of constitutional affections. From this he inferred that there were four varieties of morbid poison on which the existence of all these symptoms depended. He maintained that intercourse with a person with a sloughing sore would result in another case of sloughing sore; while intercourse with someone with a phagedenic ulcer would result in a phagedenic ulcer. Carmichael was correct in identifying that syphilis presented itself in many forms, both the primary and secondary lesions of syphilis can appear in one or in a variety of manifestations.[53] His theory about the plurality of poisons was however misdirected. Yet it might have proved quite an attractive idea to surgeons who were at a loss to explain the various manifestations of syphilis, except that in practice it was impossible to verify.

John Abernathy, a pupil of Hunter and the first Hunterian lecturer, entered the field of debate around the same time as Carmichael.[54] Unlike Carmichael, he did not divide syphilis into several distinct groups of poison but rather retained the division established by Hunter between 'true syphilis' and 'pseudo-syphilis'. Abernathy claimed that while there were many types of sores on the genitals producing secondary symptoms resembling syphilis that could be directly attributed to impure intercourse, only in certain cases were these, in fact, syphilitic. He claimed that such sores resulted from a variety of stimuli, especially uncleanliness, and asserted that it was possible that even discharges from the genitals of one person were capable of exciting ulcers in another.[55] Such findings were especially pertinent to prostitutes and Abernathy himself raised this point. He contended that pseudo-syphilis was a particular problem for women, as sores would frequently form as a result of 'diseased secretions from the vagina'. He added, '[S]ores, for instance, very frequently succeed to gonorrhoea in the lower class of females, who pay little attention to cleanliness, and do not abstain from sexual intercourse'.[56] Abernathy based his findings on spurious case studies. Like Adams, he used the example of a gentleman surgeon to 'prove' the story's credibility.

> A married medical man of more than forty years of age, connected himself with a married lady, his patient: she was also of an age in which the heyday of 'the blood is tame'. [sic] The act was punished by what he believed to be a most malignant clap, which continued on him with little mitigation, for more than a year. The patient had, however strictures of the urethra, of which he was not aware, and was readily cured after the period I have mentioned, by the use of bougies. Neither the female nor her husband had any disease, nor was there any previous connection.[57]

This is a fine example of the dubious logic upon which he built his claims, but it also shows the moral basis of his theory of disease. Abernathy believed that this case proved the spontaneous origin of pseudo-syphilis because his patient was a fellow doctor and one whose 'veracity . . . might be relied on'. He does not claim to have examined either the erring wife or her husband, and relies unquestioningly upon the testimony of a doctor who could not diagnose strictures in his own urethra.

The findings of both Abernathy and Carmichael are important not so much in and of themselves but because of the debate they created. Carmichael's teachings particularly roused considerable interest. It was not however the fact that doctors found them correct, but that they found them incorrect which raised so many issues. Most doctors found that from clinical observation it was impossible to determine what sort of sore would develop, even if they were treating both the sexual partners. Mr Evans, in his essay of 1813 on ulcerations on the genital organs, had already claimed that there was often a remarkable difference between the infected and those communicating the infection, which would tend to show how little influence any form of the disease has in propagating another of similar character.[58] Many medical writers claimed that often the most frightful cases of syphilis were caught from people with little sign of infection. Prostitutes were the most frequently cited as prime examples of this phenomenon.

Evans used the example of an examination of public women he had attended in France. He reported:

> At one [examination] which I attended, no less than 200 women of the lowest description, and of course, the most frequented by soldiers, were examined, and not one case of disease was found amongst them; nevertheless the military hospitals had, and continued to have, their usual number of venereal cases [ulcerations]. At an inspection I have since attended where 100 women were examined, only two were found with ulcerations. I noticed several with increased secretions, and one with purulent discharge, but these were taken no notice of by the attending surgeons, as they did not come sufficiently under the head of virulent gonorrhoea. That the two women above-mentioned as having ulcers infected the whole of the men diseased in the garrison during the preceding fifteen days, no one can admit as likely; but if it be allowed that an altered secretion be sufficient for the production of this disease . . . we shall at once have an explanation of how it happened that the military hospitals continued to have their usual number of venereal cases.[59]

There were of course any number of explanations for this, not the least being the inadequate diagnostic skills of the attending surgeons. Many of these men could have been suffering from secondary symptoms of syphilis after a period of latency, or could be suffering from other self-generating sores such as genital herpes, which the attending doctor failed to distinguish. Many of the women may have been suffering from syphilis but were at the time asymptomatic. Evan's conclusion, that syphilis could be generated in the male due to the altered secretion in the female partner, was widely accepted. This meant that more emphasis than ever was placed on vaginal discharges as symptoms of syphilis and gonorrhoea. Yet there was great confusion over what discharges were the result of a venereal infection and what discharges were the result of benign causes such as ovulation or menstruation. No medical practitioner of the time could satisfactorily differentiate between minor infections of the vagina, and often irritations such as thrush were confused with gonorrhoea.[60]

As a result, venereal disease came to be seen not only as far more common in women but, in fact, as a natural consequence of their reproductive systems. The combined impact of these teachings was to suggest that women could engage in the sexual act without any outward display of the disease. This created panic within the medical profession. Prostitutes as the most obvious purveyors of sex were, of course, the focus of much of this panic. The role of prostitutes in the spread of disease was addressed in one of the earliest editions of the *Medico-Chirurgical Journal*.

Dr Burder, writing on syphilis, claimed that '[I]t is well known that many unfortunate prostitutes although unconscious of being diseased, have infected numbers who have had commerce with them, with syphiloid diseases'.[61] Dr Burder persisted with this logic, observing that the root of the disease was the discharges of the prostitute herself. With great confidence he assured his audience that it was 'beyond doubt, that even the *natural secretions* of females who have promiscuous intercourse with men – who pay no regard to cleanliness and who destroy their health, strength, and life, by excessive drinking, become so acrid, that few can have commerce with them with impunity'.[62] In effect, Burder was suggesting that the body of the prostitute was itself infectious.

There were many horror stories of unfortunate men who engaged in intercourse with seemingly healthy women, only to be so badly diseased that they died or, even worse, lost their penis. The most commonly cited example of this was the story of a young opera dancer from Lisbon, first recounted by Dr William Fergusson, Inspector of the British troops in Portugal. Fergusson reported that this woman infected the officer with whom she was cohabiting with a phagendic ulceration so drastic that he lost most of his penis. She, however, continued to dance in the opera and received visits from other lovers. He argued that this would have been impossible had she too been suffering from a phagendic ulcer.[63]

Such speculation led doctors back to Hunter's suggestion that the 'venereal poison' was in some way dependent on the constitution of the woman. Carmichael too had hinted at this when he observed, 'I am perfectly aware how much the state of the human constitution will modify local diseases, and I am willing to attribute to a certain extent the great variety of appearances we witness daily in venereal complaints to this cause alone.'[64] There were considerable grounds for suggesting that certain conditions would cause the disease to be more severe in some cases and less severe in others. Patients suffering from poor nutrition, exhaustion, dissipation and general ill-health were more likely to experience complications. Yet, while some more humane doctors attributed the severity of certain forms of syphilis to these causes, it was generally assumed to be related to immorality. Prostitutes were considered to be both the principal victims and the carriers of the worst forms of the disease. Some doctors claimed that the constitution of the prostitute was so sturdy that she could pass on the disease while showing no symptoms of it herself. Other doctors claimed that the austere and irregular lifestyle of many prostitutes caused them to suffer most horribly.

There was a curious counter-argument to this. Some doctors suggested that certain constitutions, indeed even certain attitudes of mind, could protect one from syphilis. The story of the callous opera dancer from Lisbon who continued to dance on, while leaving a string of lovers with sloughing penises, is one such example. These stories were not all related to women of ill fame. Just as virtuous young surgeons seem to have been the most susceptible to the more serious forms of syphilis, medical reports suggest that particular types of men were immune to the disease. Mr George Morgan, in an essay critical of Carmichael's theories, reports the case of 'Dr Good's Friend' who claimed that 'for the sake of experiment' he had 'exposed himself to the infection of the lowest prostitutes, and yet escaped with impunity'. Morgan claimed that this was proof that the local application of the virus was 'inadequate to explain . . . the occurrence of primary syphilitic disease'.[65]

This growing emphasis on the importance of vaginal secretions as a source of venereal disease led medical authorities during the 1830s to argue that it was quite possible for all women to carry some taint of venereal disease. No secretion from the vagina was treated as innocent. Doctors went so far as to suggest that any discharge from the vagina could produce gonorrhoea. For instance, Mr Travers in the *Medical and Chirurgical Journal* of 1830 wrote that purulent discharge may occur independently of sexual intercourse. Even the 'vaginal mucus of a maiden woman' he charged may be converted into a 'puriform fluid'.[66] Moreover, the virulence of the taint seemed to be quantitative. Mr Eagle wrote in *The Lancet* in 1836 that prostitutes were the most likely source of infection, but he heightened masculine anxiety by claiming that such diseases might be picked up from any woman. He reported

> If delicate and modest females, whose habits of life are moderate, who are cleanly in their persons, and who have never been tainted by vene-real poison *can* inflict a gonorrhoea and sores, is it not fair, nay is it not an unavoidable conclusion that a 'woman of the town', labouring under high local excitement from venery, and high bodily excitement from drink would inflict a proportionably severe gonorrhoea and a propor-tionably severe sore, in other words, a venereal gonorrhoea and true chancre.[67]

Some went so far as to suggest that the secretions of an uninfected woman could produce a spontaneous dose of syphilis in a man. Sex during men-struation, too much sex, too little sex, sex with a woman after too much alcohol or asparagus, all were said to cause gonorrhoea in men, while leaving the woman unaffected. Some women were said to have vaginas that had an irritant character. The vagina became the source from which the disease sprang.

2 The Source

Prostitution is the great source of syphilis.

Etienne Lancereaux, *A Treatise on Syphilis*

From the 1830s onwards the female body came to be medicalized, not merely as a sexed body but as a diseased body – a space where disease could and did fester. This shift fitted in well to the newly emergent spirit of environmental and preventative medicine. Around this same time, public health was rapidly becoming an issue for the government. The publication of the 1831 Census with its mortality rates had caused some disquiet. The establishment of the Register-General in 1837 created further concern as it meant that for the first time reliable statistics were available on public health. An epidemic of cholera had struck the metropolis of London, with devastating results. These factors all worked together to confront the people of Britain with the appalling conditions that existed in their towns.[1]

These events were seen to necessitate state intervention in public health, and the medical establishment was fast to exploit what it considered its field of expertise in the service of the government. Since the early years of the nineteenth century there had been a growing call for some form of medical policing in Great Britain.[2] In this context medical policing had four broad meanings. First, the administration of public health and the well-being of the population. Secondly, the control of medical practice and practitioners. Thirdly, the development and control of legal medicine, that is, medical jurisprudence, and lastly, the creation of a science of hygiene.[3] By the 1830s this call was beginning to be answered. In 1838 the Poor Law Commissioners launched a small-scale inquiry into the relationship between urban conditions and disease. The report, possibly written by the sanitary reformer Edwin Chadwick, was published with three reports by physicians James Phillips Kay, Neil Arnott and Southward Smith. This was the first time doctors were employed formally by the government to gather factual information.[4]

This report and Chadwick's subsequent *Report on the Sanitary Conditions of the Labouring Population of Great Britain* pointed to a new direction in public health and medicine, that of preventative or environmental medicine. Ludmilla Jordanova refers to this as a 'crisis of conscience' in the efficacy of conventional medical practices, and in the rejection of 'curing' as the primary and paradigmatic medical task in favour of prevention. This search for alternative forms of practice was based on the conviction that many diseases had external, that is removable and controllable, causes.[5] Doctors increasingly came to believe that environmental factors such as bad ventilation, open drains and overcrowding were the real cause of most diseases. Although it was widely believed that certain diseases like small-pox had a specific cause, contagion theory had not yet received much attention.

During the next thirty years, the state and the medical establishment joined forces to campaign for moral reform. Venereal disease was only one of the many health issues that confronted doctors and politicians. Their reaction to the 'epidemic' of venereal disease in the context of moral reform is not very different from the reaction to cholera or typhus. Like typhus and cholera, they could find no specific cause for venereal disease.[6] It was known to be caused by an infection but not what caused the infection. Doctors were, however, quite certain of the circumstances under which it arose. No single authority ever questioned the fact that venereal disease was the result of promiscuous intercourse.[7] Thus, in the spirit of environmental medicine that prevailed, it came to be argued that to control the disease it was necessary to control women's bodies. Prostitutes were not only the most visible purveyors of illicit intercourse, they also appeared to be the source of the disease. The sexualized body of such women came to be perceived as a health problem and was viewed in much the same manner as a cesspool or a badly planned sewer.

It was in this spirit that the debate about prostitution and venereal disease continued throughout the 1830s and 1840s. The discussion was greatly influenced by developments in France, most especially the writings of Alexandre Parent-Duchatelet and Phillipe Ricord. Due to their authority, many doctors began to call for a system of regulation for prostitutes similar to those found on the continent. Parent's contribution to this discussion was the mammoth quasi-anthropological study of Parisian prostitutes, *De la prostitution dans la ville de Paris*. Parent began research for the book in 1828 but died before its publication in 1836. The work encompassed material taken from the police archives, hospital and prison records and Parent's own exhaustive enquiries. While the text provided extraordinarily detailed descriptions of the lives of Parisian prostitutes it was essentially a defence of the system of regulating prostitution.

The French system of mandatory examination of prostitutes was instituted on Christmas Eve 1810. Effectively, the system required every prostitute to be registered with the police. This inscription gave the prostitute the tacit approval of the law to carry on her unlawful profession, provided that she submit to regular medical examinations for venereal disease. If found to be diseased, the prostitute had to undergo a course of treatment at the prison hospital. The prostitute was arrested if she broke a regulation, failed to appear for examination or caused a disturbance.[8] Part of the rationale for the system was to protect prostitutes from undue harassment by the police but in practice it placed prostitutes outside the law, increasing their vulnerability to official intimidation and corruption. When the system was implemented, there was little discussion of the aims or implications of regulation.

It was not really until the publication of Parent's book that regulation had a theorist. His work lent prestige and professional approval to the policies of inscription, involuntary examination and administrative detention in hospitals and prisons.[9] His writings provided the regime of regulation with an acceptable rationale by explaining why such women must be separated from the respectable community. Parent showed prostitutes to be a class apart, outside civilization, 'differing as much in their morals, their tastes, and their habits from the society of their compatriots, as the latter differ from the nations of another hemisphere'.[10] For Parent, prostitution was a subterranean counter-culture that represented a moral, social, sanitary and political threat. The public hygienist compartmentalized those engaged in public prostitution into a variety of groups and subgroups. His descriptions of prostitutes were to be repeated until the end of the nineteenth century. The French historian Alain Corbin has suggested that this compartmentalization of prostitution helped to 'exorcise the anxiety aroused by the risk of social contagion'.[11] By categorizing prostitutes in a 'scientific' manner, Parent enabled doctors to present clinical solutions to the problems arising from prostitution.

De la prostitution dans la ville de Paris became the canonical text of the study of prostitution in nineteenth-century Europe. Parent's methodical analysis of the bodies and lifestyles of prostitutes set the pattern for subsequent studies. Parent's work became the model for the many studies of prostitution in the cities of the United Kingdom which followed the release of his book there.[12] His work had a critical impact on the discussion of prostitution and disease in Britain. Parent not only provided those in England who favoured regulation with an explicit language to express their concerns, but furnished them with an extensive working model of how this could be done. Parent saw prostitutes strictly in terms of a public health problem. He viewed the control of prostitutes in much the same way as the control of sewers.[13] Prostitutes were to be treated as sexual canals used to drain the seminal excess of male desire. The task of the public hygienist was to sanitize these sewers so as to promote their cleanliness and efficiency. Parent wrote:

Prostitutes are as inevitable in an agglomeration of men as sewers, cesspits, and garbage dumps; civil authority should conduct itself in the same manner in regard to one as to the other: its duty is to survey them, to attenuate by every possible means the detriments inherent to them, and for that purpose to hide them, to relegate them to obscure corners, in a word to render their presence as inconspicuous as possible.[14]

Parent had provided a methodical and scientific approach to prostitution that reinforced the idea that the sexed female body was a diseased body. The British medical establishment was quick to take up the imagery of prostitutes as sewers. In a review of *De la prostitution*, the editor of the *Edinburgh Medical and Surgical Journal* wrote of Parent's initial hesitation in broaching the subject:

> Upon reflection, however, he could not perceive the reasonableness of this excess of delicacy. He remembered that he had already penetrated the public drains, handled putrid matters, spent part of his time in the filth and impurities of the laystalls and knackeries, and lived in some manner amidst every thing abject and disgusting; and why should he be ashamed . . . to approach a drain of a different sort, fouler perhaps than the others, so long as there was a hope of doing some good.[15]

Around 1838, the question of regulating prostitution in Britain appeared on the agenda of Lord Melbourne's government. This question of regulation was never raised in Parliament as it was considered improper to ask Queen Victoria, then a young unmarried woman, to sign an Act which effectively legalized prostitution.[16] The idea of regulating prostitution, as France had, appealed to a great number of social critics and was hailed as the obvious solution to the spread of venereal infection by many environmentalist doctors.

The work of Philippe Ricord too, did much to enhance the appeal of regulation. Ricord was American-born but of French parentage. He moved to France in the 1820s to study medicine and after some years as a country physician he went to Paris where he began to specialize in venereal diseases. Ricord began his researches at the *Hôpital du Midi* in 1831. Like many before him, Ricord was convinced that John Hunter's ideas about the 'unity of the virus' theory were incorrect. Ricord was, however, certain that he could prove by experiments in inoculation that syphilis and gonorrhoea were separate entities. His experiment with syphilis involved some 2,500 inoculations, mostly on inmates from asylums. He demonstrated experimentally that when pus was taken from the urethra in a case of gonorrhoea and inoculated upon the patient no result followed, whereas when pus was taken from a suppurating sore and inoculated subcutaneously, a suppurating chancre was always produced.[17] He thus traced the diseases through their various stages, demonstrating beyond a doubt that syphilis and gonorrhoea were distinct diseases.

The fame which Ricord achieved by disproving Hunter's theories was widespread. Ricord's work came to be treated with the same authority as Hunter's had previously. Not only were his ideas about the aetiology of the disease widely accepted but his theories on the control of prostitution were also well received. Like Parent-Duchatelet, Ricord believed that the regulation of prostitutes was an imperative duty of the state. Indeed, Ricord believed it was necessary for both doctors and the state to increase their control over prostitutes. He was particularly sceptical of the efficiency of the system of examination used by those doctors employed to examine *les filles publique*.

As early as 1833 Ricord had stressed the necessity of the speculum in the treatment of venereal disease in women.[18] The speculum is a gynaecological instrument that when inserted into the vagina allows doctors to view the vagina to the neck of the cervix. Ricord maintained that without the aid of the speculum it was impossible to verify whether or not women were suffering from a venereal infection. He attributed the failure of regulation to curb the increase in syphilis to the lack of adequate use of the speculum. Ricord asked of his colleagues 'which of them would blindfold himself to perform a genito-urinal examination on a male patient', likening such a procedure to viewing the vagina with 'the unaided eye'.[19] Such ideas were quickly disseminated through the British medical press. A review of Ricord's work in the *Medico-Chirurgical Journal* reported, 'He [Ricord] entertains no doubt that the usual inspections of the public women of Paris are perfectly illusory, and offer no security.'[20] The use of the speculum was generally considered as morally dubious in Great Britain.[21] Yet the impact of Ricord's research gave the implement a new credibility.

While Ricord's work clarified a number of questions regarding venereal disease, he did nevertheless make one crucial mistake. He failed to recognize the specific nature of gonorrhoea. He had proven that 'the clap' was not produced by the syphilitic virus. He argued that gonorrhoea was not a virus but a 'simple catarrh' which was due to a variety of irritants. Gonorrheal pus was the chief irritant that produced gonorrhoea but other secretions – menstrual, lochial and puerperal – he claimed could also produce the disease. Even sexual excesses in perfectly healthy individuals or merely prolonged sexual excitement and protracted erections without coitus, he argued were likely to produce a dose of 'the clap'.[22] Ricord's now proverbial prescription for catching gonorrhoea must be reviewed in this light. He told his medical students that to catch 'a clap' one must take

> a pale lymphatic woman, blond rather than brunette, and as leucorrhic as possible. Dine with her; begin with oysters and continue with asparagus, drink a good many dry white wines and champagne, coffee, liqueur. All this is well. Dance after your dinner and make your partner dance. Warm yourself up, and drink a good deal of beer during the evening. When night comes, conduct yourself bravely; two or three acts of intercourse are not too much, more still the better. On waking do not fail to take a long warm bath and make an injection. If this project is carried out and you do not get a clap, it is because God protects you.[23]

Ricord was suggesting that all women, but especially women with certain features, could cause men spontaneously to contract gonorrhoea. In effect, he was denying women the right not to have gonorrhoea. It was this misconception that allowed many medical men to blame women or, more precisely, pathological female sexuality for the spread of gonorrhoea. This was reinforced by Ricord's insistence on the use of the speculum. This emphasised the vagina as a pathological site by suggesting that it was a mysterious enigmatic organ, capable of producing secret and dangerous substances.

Parent's work on the vaginas of prostitutes heightened this gynaephobic anxiety by suggesting that it was often impossible to tell the difference between the vagina of a hardened prostitute and that of a virgin. Parent had recorded with a combination of surprise and disgust that there was nothing extraordinary about the clitoris, the labia minor, the vagina or the anus of prostitutes. The British medical press reported such observations with horror, claiming that it had a special significance to the field of medical jurisprudence.[24] At the same time, however, Parent noted that prostitutes were particularly prone to diseases of the vagina, such as tumours of the labia which he reported worsen with 'each menstrual period'. As Sander Gilman has pointed out, Parent's view that there is no adaptation of the sexual organ was overridden by his assertion that the prostitute was also prone to specific pathologies of the genitalia and 'the resultant image is of the prostitute's genitalia developing through disease, an altered appearance'.[25]

Ricord, for all his great medical expertise, was also a worldly cynic who was extremely sceptical of modern morality, especially the supposed virtue of women. Oliver Wendell Holmes commented that Ricord 'would have submitted Diana to treatment with his mineral specifics and ordered a course of blue pills for the Vestal Virgins.'[26] In his teachings he stressed the role of prostitutes as the main purveyors of venereal disease and replied caustically to those who begged to differ. Alexander Donné, a rival Parisian venereologist, had published some microscopic and chemical studies on venereal pus that contradicted some of Ricord's claims. Donné had discovered microscopic traces of *Triichonas vaginalis*. These organisms, he suggested, were the cause of gonorrhoea. When Donné indicated that one of the major problems in his research was the small amount of vaginal mucus he was able to obtain for study, Ricord observed, '[T]his last thought, on the lack of material, will undoubtedly come as a surprise to those who are familiar with the influence of Paris on vaginal hypersecretion'.[27]

Ricord's teachings widely influenced venereology in Great Britain. Most importantly, Ricord's ideas about gonorrhoea as a catarrh confirmed the interest British physicians had been taking in vaginal discharges. Earlier misogynistic assumptions now appeared to have the backing of experimental science and these ideas were easily assimilated into general notions about prostitution. It did not take long for the language and ideology underpinning the control of venereal disease to treat prostitution, female sexuality and disease synonymously. Such assumptions appealed to the reforming zeal of the medical profession and they treated the control of venereal disease in much the same manner as they treated the control of other contagious diseases. Prostitution was a source of contamination that must be in some way regulated.

One of the first texts on the venereal diseases produced in Britain following the publication of Ricord's findings was F.C. Skey's *A Practical Treatise on the Venereal Disease,* published in 1840. Skey at this time was consulting surgeon to Charterhouse and assistant surgeon at St Bartholomew's Hospital. He had been apprenticed to the eminent venereologist John Abernathy and went on to have an illustrious career in medicine. His *Practical Treatise* was an edited collection of lectures given to the medical students of St Bartholomew's during the period 1838–1839. Skey later became president of both the Royal Medical and Chirurgical Society and the Royal College of Surgeons. He chaired the 1867 Select Committee to Inquire into the Pathology and Treatment of the Venereal Disease. He received a CB for his services in this capacity. Due to the positions he held, Skey's ideas about the pathology of syphilis and gonorrhoea were very influential in forming the medical rationale in defence of regulation.

In many ways Skey simply reworked much of what had been written by venereal specialists since the end of the eighteenth century. He did, however, develop several significant theories which were germane to the discussions of prostitution and venereal disease. Skey maintained that the virus of syphilis did not necessarily develop as a contagious reaction passed

on from an infected person. He suggested that it could and did develop
as a type of allergic reaction when 'impure intercourse' occurred. Skey re-
examined the example of the inspection of prostitutes in France provided
in 1813 by Evans. Of the two hundred prostitutes inspected only two were
found to be diseased. At the same time, the men of the local regiment were
still presenting themselves with genital ulceration to the military hospital
at the usual rate. Evans had suggested that the inability to locate disease
in these prostitutes was not because they were not diseased, but because
the disease was located in their vaginal secretions. Skey went one step
further.

> Now either the disease in these women existed beyond the surface
> exposed – a supposition at variance with every day's experience – or the
> above facts are false; or the diseases under which these men were la-
> bouring, were spontaneous or at least self-generated. . . . The term self-
> generated . . . expresses something short of the idea I wish to convey. I
> mean that, in a certain condition of constitution, the elements of poison
> lie dormant, which may be developed by the action of a simple irritant,
> and that irritant may exist in the form of any apparently simple, but
> unhealthy exciting cause in the female, such as leuchorroea, menstrual
> fluid, or indeed any impure secretion of a puriform character; it may
> also be developed by mechanical irritation.[28]

Skey was not hinting at the notion of latent syphilis.[29] Rather, he was
suggesting that certain constitutions, especially female ones, harboured the
disease and during 'impure intercourse' infected the unsuspecting partner.
This disease did not necessarily result from past infection, but appeared
like an allergic reaction to 'impure' sex. 'Whence then arise these sores,
or forms of discharge from the urethra?' asked Skey:

> [T]hey are not strictly speaking spontaneous, but they certainly are not
> the product of a similar poison in the party contaminating, even if
> produced by a poison at all. May they not be reasonably referred to the
> presence of matter, irritating the surface applied, and co-operating with
> a constitution prone to the promotion of that peculiar form of local
> malady.[30]

Skey derived further substantiation for his theories from the earlier works
of Evans and Richard Carmichael. He argued that the reason that several
men might each acquire a different form of the disease after intercourse
with the same woman was because of the effect of such a reaction upon
a different constitution. In his view, venereal disease in men might develop 'without the presence of the disease in the female of any kind.'[31] He

illustrated this by reference to the case of a young patient who came to him labouring under a severe bout of gonorrhoea. The case not only shows the exceptional credulity of the doctor but illustrates most effectively the idea that no matter how pure a woman was, it was possible for her to transmit disease through 'impure' intercourse. 'One of the worst cases of gonorrhoea I ever prescribed for,' he insisted,

> occurred in the person of a youth who seduced a young lady, residing in the same house. There was not up to that event the slightest grounds of suspicion against her, but, on the contrary, every confirming circumstance of her previous purity; and as regards the youth himself, it was notorious in his social circles that he had *never sinned*.[32]

Skey went on to to suggest that the cause of the man's ailment was having intercourse during his partner's menstrual period. This he maintained was the only logical explanation for the severity of the disease in the man and its total absence in the woman. Following Ricord's teachings, he treated gonorrhoea as a 'catarrh' that developed as a response to a variety of different stimuli. He went further, however, suggesting this was also the case for syphilis and other ulcerative genital ailments. He added a further moral dimension by suggesting that such afflictions generally arose as the result of 'impure intercourse'. One of the main criticisms of Skey's theories was the argument that if gonorrhoea and syphilis were allergic responses, they should arise more often in monogamous couples. Skey's answer to this criticism was ambiguous. He recognized that those who distrusted his views asked why these diseases did not attack married men.

> Why should either sex be exempt from them? I believe that they are not exempt; that such diseases occur not unfrequently [sic], in the early period of married life. At least I am satisfied, that our sex by no means rarely pays the penalty of seduction, more especially of very young women, and even when the act is not completed. I can readily conceive reasons why it is not more frequent in married life; but on them I shall not now dwell. It is sufficient for my purpose, that gonorrhoea does occasionally occur between healthy persons having intercourse with none other.[33]

Skey was hesitant to admit the possibility that monogamous couples 'generate' venereal disease because ultimately his model of infection is a punitive one. Men who seduce women are the prime targets for infection. Indeed, the tale of the young man who had '*never sinned*' can be read as a classic narrative of divine retribution. There is however the suggestion that sex is in itself polluting. It is this idea that underscores Skey's conceptions. Moreover, he suggested constantly that it is men rather than women who become infected. Skey went to great pains to show that the women in his case studies were essentially 'pure' women who succumbed in a moment of weakness to their partner's desires. He tends to avoid giving examples of men who acquired the disease from prostitutes, as he gave their stories little credibility. But his ideas contributed much to pathologization of the sexualized female body. Skey's teachings helped to validate the widely held suspicion that the female body created disease within itself. Skey did not state this overtly, yet it is the unavoidable conclusion that must be drawn from his text. The idea that female bodies were in some sense polluting became an underlying theme in much of what was written about venereal disease until the end of the century.

Other venereal specialists continued this trend. Langston Parker, Surgeon to the Queen's Hospital, Birmingham, published his ideas on the treatment of syphilis in 1845. At this time he was widely referred to as 'Birmingham's answer to Philippe Ricord'. His ideas about gonorrhoea, however, followed a more Hunterian model. Like Hunter he maintained that there were three types of gonorrhoea: a simple gonorrhoea, which resulted from sex with a woman during her menstrual period or at the time of a vaginal infection – this type was not capable of propagation; an ordinary gonorrhoea which resulted 'from connexion with a woman labouring under the symptoms of gonorrhoea; and a gonorrhoea that was the result of a venereal sore in the urethra'. While Parker's idea essentially restated much eighteenth-century opinion on the transmission of gonorrhoea, he was not entirely adverse to the notion of gonorrhoea as a catarrh and suggested that not only sexual excess but the practice of what he considered immoral or immoderate pursuits could also cause gonorrhoea. He wrote:

> Gonorrhoea is also due to other causes apart from sexual intercourse, as [sic] masturbation, habitual cositiveness, inflammation of the prostrate gland, certain morbid conditions of the bladder or uterus, particularly the presence of calculi in these parts, piles, the excessive or immoderate use of wines or fermented liquors generally, the warmer spices, more particularly cayenne pepper.[34]

Parker was going beyond Ricord's model which suggested under what conditions gonorrhoea might be generated and was implying that excessive use of wine, hot spices, even constipation could cause gonorrhoea. Syphilis and gonorrhoea were diseases that had always had moral meanings, as they were always considered punishment for sexual misbehaviour; now however they were being linked to other forms of excess. Even masturbation was increasingly being treated as a cause of venereal disease.

In such a climate the prostitute became the obvious symbol of sexual excess and the easiest target for sexual regulation. Not surprisingly when one examines the texts dealing with prostitutes from this period one finds that, as well as being pathological in the sense that they were sexually active women, it is also often noted that prostitutes were vigorous masturbators, habitual exponents of 'tribadism', chronic alcoholics and addicted to immoderate foodstuffs. This model of behaviour established by Parent-Duchatelet was frequently expounded in England. While Parent did not claim that prostitutes were innately pathological, his work was often interpreted in this way. Many drew the inference from his categorization of prostitutes that they were inherently different from other women. No longer could prostitutes be solely viewed as frail women who fell into prostitution in a moment of moral weakness. They were abnormal women who not only transgressed the accepted code of female morality, but who threatened the social and political order by their excesses.

Prostitutes were made to appear not merely as fallen women, but something less than women. This of course created a gulf between the upright woman and the fallen woman. The prostitute's body became not only the representative sexualized female body, but a site of abnormal indulgence. The proverbial sterility of prostitutes was seen as a key to their pathology. In contrast, the body of the virtuous woman came to be desexualized, her sexual characteristics co-opted as maternal characteristics. In this way the body of the prostitute came to be synonymous with venereal disease. Prostitutes were not merely agents of transmission but somehow inherently diseased, if not the disease itself.

During the 1850s, the language and ideology underpinning the discussion of syphilis and gonorrhoea treated prostitutes and disease synonymously. The terms 'social disease' and 'social evil' were used interchangeably. Prostitutes came to be seen as both physically and metaphysically responsible for the spread of venereal disease. W.R. Greg, failed cotton merchant turned journalist and social critic, in one of the first major articles on the subject in the non-medical press, referred to prostitution as 'the hideous gangrene of English society.'[35] James Miller, Professor of Surgery at the University of Edinburgh, called prostitution 'a festering sore' on 'the body politic'.[36] In discussing the problem of prostitution, the *Medical Times and Gazette* referred to it as 'this large source of corruption'. Solutions to the problem were discussed as 'antidotes'. The author added, 'No remedy, it is certain, will act effectively upon this social malady which does not tell directly upon the causes which produce it. The roots of a poisonous tree must be destroyed if the vigour is to be arrested.'[37]

One of the greatest proponents of this idea was Dr William Acton. Acton was the author of several works dealing with urology, venereology and prostitution. A pupil of Ricord's during the 1830s, by the 1850s he was working at St Bartholomew's Hospital in London. It is generally agreed that Acton has earned a reputation far beyond his modest contribution to Victorian medicine. He has been taken up by many recent historians as a sexual radical with liberal ideas and a modern outlook. The view that Acton's work breaks with the representative Victorian perspective on prostitution is misguided. Far from being a novel approach to prostitution and venereal disease, Acton's work is rather like a museum devoted to all the mythologies of prostitution fostered during the nineteenth century. Acton claimed to be exploding certain misconceptions about prostitution by redressing the idea that the prostitute's course is necessarily downwards. But for all this, Acton effectively reinforced the notion that prostitution and disease were inseparable entities.

Judith Walkowitz is correct in describing Acton's work as part of a 'literary genre' rather than a piece of scientific or sociological observation.[39] His writings are a maverick collection of personal reminiscences, traditional wisdom, pseudo-medical opinion and folklore. His sources were various and his reliance on scientific method minimal. Much of his writing is informed by works such as Parent's: indeed, many of his key descriptions come directly from that source. In this respect Acton's work is typical of medical writings of the period. While it has been claimed that Acton sought to make the prostitute seem less alien to his respectable audience, his text does no such thing. Rather it makes her seem as much unlike his male reader's wife or daughter as possible. If he drew similarities between the prostitutes and respectable women, it is because he could not overcome the suggestion that female sexuality is in itself pathological. For Acton and for his contemporaries the prostitute was an aberration. He constantly referred to the dominant ideology of innate female purity and established his discussion of prostitution within that framework. It is due to this framework that most of the contradictions arise in his work.

If one looks at the body of Acton's work, it appears that venereal disease was used not only as a diagnosis but as a metaphor to disguise masculine loathing of female sexuality. The broader medical discussion of venereal disease in Great Britain had implicitly made this connection, but Acton drew it out explicitly. Acton voiced fears about prostitution and women's sexuality that had been developing since the eighteenth century. He may appear to be unique in his lack of concern about the class mobility of prostitutes, but Acton's almost obsessive insistence on differentiating between natural feminine sexual anaesthesia and the nymphomania of prostitutes belies this. Fear of venereal disease had become the way in which men articulated the anxieties caused by prostitution. It opened the debate on prostitution, by making it a health problem. It allowed an expression of the idea that prostitutes were a necessity. On one level it left the notion of women as innately pure and untainted, by making the prostitute pathological. But on another level it meant that all women were tainted because of the connection between venereal disease and femininity. Acton's work is a classic example of this misconception.

Acton's first book, *A Complete and Practical Treatise on the Venereal Diseases and Their Immediate and Remote Consequences*, was rooted firmly in his conviction that women were the main source of venereal 'poison'. In the short history of the diseases he gave in the first chapter, nearly every example of ancient wisdom he provided referred to the source of venereal disease as 'foul women', 'leprous women' or 'unclean wombs'. For Acton the vagina was the source of most venereal poisons. In the case of gonorrhoea for instance, Acton claimed that femininity was a 'predisposing cause' of the disease. 'It is an indisputable fact,' he recorded,

> that the female is more liable to discharges of a blennorrhagic character than the male. In Paris, says M. Ricord, women may be said to have habitually a discharge. . . . I should say that it is a hundred times greater in the little girl than in the little boy; a thousand times greater in the adult female than in the male.[40]

Acton cites as evidence of this an 'experiment' which is particularly curious, not only in its total lack of clinical precision, but also because of its blatant voyeurism and fetishism. The experiment was carried out by M. Lisfranc, a contemporary of Ricord who had been called away to the country to perform an operation on a washerwoman. While waiting for his attendants,

> he amused himself, *out of scientific curiosity* . . . examining the linen of the Parisian ladies, a load having arrived, (for his patient did washing on a large scale) he found that evident symptoms of blennorrhagic discharges were present upon nearly all. This may give the reader an idea of how common the disease must be in the French capital.[41]

Although Acton did not hold that women could spontaneously create syphilis, he maintained that the vagina was the principal medium through which the disease is transmitted. He explained this process in the same way Astruc had done a century earlier.

An individual suffering under chancres has connexion with a girl; a quantity of the virus is left in her vagina, but produces no action, as the mucous membrane is covered with a secretion. Should a second individual have connection with this female under these circumstance, the virus may affect him, and no local sore be discovered on her genital organs, even after the most minute examination. Such cases are not unfrequent. [*sic*] Here the penis has performed the part of a sponge, and completely cleaned the vagina, which was simply a passive agent of transmission.[42]

Acton stated that the penis too could passively transmit the disease but this was not something he followed up. It was the vagina of the prostitute that was his particular concern. While women who were not prostitutes, according to Acton could and did spread disease, it was the peculiar occupation of the prostitute and her supposed promiscuity and sexual responsiveness that enabled her to become a 'passive transmitter' of the disease.

Acton's next major text, *A Practical Treatise on the Diseases of the Urinary and Generative Organs (in both Sexes)*, was published in 1851. In this text Acton made even more explicit his belief in the link between femininity and disease. More than any other Victorian commentator, he stressed that sex during menstruation caused venereal disease in men. Acton wrote:

Menstruation has its influence in producing the affection in question. Of this fact no people were more aware than the Jews. We find it strictly forbidden in the Mosaic law to have connection with a woman about this period, and the command, no doubt, arose out of the fact that such intercourse was found to produce blennorrhagic affections.[43]

The idea that menstrual blood could cause gonorrhoea arose because doctors confused gonorrhoea with minor infections such as trichomoniasis. That is not to suggest that menstrual blood causes these infections, but low vaginal acidity during menstruation does exacerbate them. For Acton, however, the connection between menstruation and disease was the ancient Judaic taboo about feminine uncleanliness. In his view, menstruating women were unclean and therefore likely to produce disease. Such ideas were out of keeping with the gender-specific notions of cleanliness that developed during the nineteenth century. Cleanliness had come to be seen as a moral as well as a physical attribute. Women were considered to be more 'pure' than men so subsequently they were considered by nature more moral and more cleanly.[44] For Acton, however, uncleanliness was a specifically feminine vice. He wrote with great disgust about lack of feminine hygiene:

I have been accused of traducing . . . the character of my countrywomen. Considerable experience has, however, shewn [*sic*] that such has not been the case; and it is incredible how inattentive women, even those living in the greatest splendour, are to the necessary ablutions of these parts. I have been told that my observations apply only to prostitutes, and that class of women. Surgeons however, who are consulted on uterine affections, and on venereal diseases know that the women of the town are particularly careful, and employ plenty of water.[45]

In suggesting that prostitutes were more cleanly than virtuous women Acton was stepping outside the accepted ideas of his time. Acton's ideas meant that all women were seen to be responsible for the spread of venereal disease. Acton suggested that the typical gonorrhoea carrier was not a prostitute but a

delicate, fair, pale creature, who has been suffering in her general health for years, liable to indigestion, nervousness, and its attendant evils, complaining of pain in the back, shooting down the front of the thighs, able to undergo little exertion, and in consequence leading a most indolent life.[46]

Acton's depiction of the type of women most likely to cause gonorrhoea is directly attributable to Ricord. Acton's version however could also refer to many middle-class women invalids. Acton does not claim that such wives were impure: on the contrary, he indicated that in such women 'sexual desire . . . has been reduced to its lowest ebb, and infidelity is not one of their sins'.[47] Implicit in Acton's work is the notion that women are diseased by virtue of being female.

In 1857 Acton published *Prostitution, Considered in Its Moral, Social and Sanitary Aspects*, the text for which he is best remembered, and *Functions and Disorders of the Reproductive Organs*. *Prostitution* was written to sell the idea of regulation to the British medical establishment. As a pupil of Ricord's, Acton was impressed by the French system of dealing with prostitution and venereal disease. He was very keen to see a system of regulation introduced into Great Britain and, when it was implemented in garrison towns, he advocated its establishment throughout the country. His reasoning for this was that few women stayed in the 'state of prostitution' for any length of time. For too long, he maintained, those dealing with prostitutes had made 'three vulgar errors'. These he outlined were: once a harlot always a harlot; there is no possible advance, moral or physical, in the condition of the actual prostitute; and that the harlot's decline was short and rapid.[48] He argued that it was better for the women themselves and for the nation, that prostitution should be regulated, so the prostitute could pass through that stage of her life with as little injury as possible. This reinterpretation of the career of prostitutes was meant to serve his propagandist aim, which was to promote the implementation of the Contagious Diseases Acts.[49] If it bore any resemblance to the truth it was only by chance, as Acton's research can only be described as slipshod and haphazard, yet it was very influential. British medical journals responded favourably to *Prostitution*, several publishing reviews stressing the importance of acknowledging the 'three vulgar errors'.[50]

Prostitution has received considerable attention from historians who have generally welcomed it as the most important study of the subject during this period.[51] Acton did, however, come closer than his contemporaries to defining female sexuality as diseased. His description of 'the prostitute' contradicted his idea that women moved in and out of prostitution because by his definition once a woman became a prostitute she ceased to be a woman. He considered the prostitute bereft of femininity, if not humanity. He described the prostitute in these terms:

> She is a woman with half the woman gone, and that half containing all that elevates her nature, leaving her a mere instrument of impurity; degraded and fallen she extracts from the sin of others the means of living, corrupt and dependent on corruption, and therefore interested directly in the increase of immorality – a social pest, carrying contamination and foulness to every quarter to which she has access.[52]

At other points in the text he describes prostitutes in animalistic terms as 'brutes', 'stock-in-trade' or 'women farmers'. Like his contemporaries, Acton could only define the prostitute in the terminology of pestilence. He concluded his description with a quotation from Tennyson's *Idylls of the King*

> Like a . . . disease . . . .
> Creeps, no precaution used, among the crowd,
> Makes wicked lightenings of her eyes . . . .
> . . . . and stirs the pulse,
> With devil's leaps, and poisons half the young.[53]

Acton's defence of regulation was centred around the idea that prostitution and venereal diseases were intrinsically linked. He took this one step further. His essential argument was that these women were really only infectious while they were practising prostitution. This certainly went against all contemporary knowledge of the infectiousness of syphilis and was quite illogical in the face of other evidence he provided. The only explanation for his rationale was a deep-seated belief that prostitution itself was the source of venereal infection and that when a woman no longer practised prostitution she was no longer the source of infection. While Acton's ideas may be extreme, they were not unique. Many observers of prostitution maintained that the 'wages of sin', such as suicidal tendencies, alcoholism and sterility only existed while women practised prostitution. This notion was the linchpin around which he based his strategy for regulation.

It was, however, at odds with his discussion of the prostitute. Acton could not overcome these contradictions. Rather, he displaces these paradoxes by making all women suspect. For Acton 'the dirty intoxicated slattern in tawdry finery and an inch thick in paint' was not the real threat. It was those women who were not obviously 'corrupt' that posed the greatest danger. In an ominous tone he warned his readers:

> The Gorgon of the present day against whom we should arm our children should be a woman, who whether sound or diseased, is generally pretty or elegant – oftener painted by Nature than by art – whose predecessors cast away the custom of drunkenness when the gentleman of England did the same – and on whose backs, as if following the poet's direction, *in corpore vili*, the ministers of fashion exhibit the results of their most egregious experiments.[54]

The prostitutes who most resembled middle-class ladies were most frightening to Acton. It was their behaviour that he desperately desired to show was unwomanly and indeed unnatural. These women, he believed, were like sexual vampires sucking the lifeblood out of England's youth. In *Functions and Disorders of the Reproductive Organs*, he counselled nervous young men who were on the verge of matrimony that little would be expected of them. 'The majority of women (happily for society)' were 'not very much troubled by sexual feelings of any kind.' To those men who had had sexual experience with prostitutes he stated emphatically that this was entirely different from the joys of conjugal bliss. 'Such women,' he said, 'give a very false idea of the condition of female sexual feeling in general.' Such women he asserted, faked orgasms to impress their customers. This behaviour created the erroneous idea that marital duties would be beyond the strength of many men. He instructed that there was no need for men to dread marriage on this account as many women felt no sexual excitement 'whatever'. [55]

By maintaining the idea that pure women were only sexually responsive because of their maternal instincts, Acton was attempting to dispel the notion that sex necessarily tainted women. He could not however transcend the contradictions that his ideas created. For Acton the 'pure woman' became the most dangerous woman as her fall was the least expected.

> The woman, the castle of whose modesty offered the stoutest resistance to the storm of the seducer often becomes in time the most abiding stronghold of vice. Saturated with misery and drink, perhaps then crime and disease, dead long in heart, barely willing to live on in the flesh . . . she will passively drift down the stream into that listless state of moral insensibility in which so many pass from this world into the presence of their Judge.[56]

Underlying Acton's claims was the fear that sex, even marital sex, somehow created depravity in a woman. This was the defence often articulated by supporters of prostitution, who claimed it was better for men to channel their lust into prostitutes than to risk the sanctity of the home. Prostitutes were thus perceived by men such as Acton as both a social necessity and a constant reminder of the frailty of femininity.

At the root of all these contradictions was Acton's inability to represent how a system of regulation really worked. In France, regulation was not primarily meant to save women. The aim of the system was to either stigmatize prostitutes so much they could never re-enter 'society' or to inculcate them with as many bourgeois values as possible. Both these methods were supposed to reduce the threat prostitutes posed to 'decent' society. While this was effectively what happened in Britain under regulation, it would not have been popular to advertise the fact that far from reforming prostitutes regulation actually kept women 'on the town'. Acton, like his mentor Ricord, really held all women as sexually suspect and treated female sexuality as something inherently pathological. The discrepancies and incongruities that arise in his works are the result of his trying to accommodate this idea with what is at least superficially a humane version of regulation.

Few doctors were as extreme in their opinions as Acton. Much of the work on prostitution that was written in the 1850s emphasized the prostitute as abnormal and attempted to obscure her similarities to other women. Doctors expanded the idea that prostitutes 'naturally produced' venereal disease through their bodily discharges. This was to become the underpinning of regulation in Britain. It is not surprising then that we find military doctors at the forefront of such debate.

Holmes Coote, army surgeon and author of the work *A Report on Some of the More Important Points Connected with the Treatment of Syphilis*, published in 1857, did much to foster the view that women produced disease within themselves. He claimed that 'the poison' [syphilis] was 'engendered by the mode of life to which prostitutes are exposed'.[57] Many doctors had suggested that this was certainly the case for gonorrhoea, which they considered only a catarrh. Coote was amongst a select group of doctors who maintained the same was true of syphilis. Coote took umbrage at Acton's suggestion that 'all experiments made to produce it [syphilis] *de novo* have completely failed'. In an uncharacteristic flash of scientific logic Coote retorted that he knew of 'no series of experiments which any person had tried, or would like to try, even if he had the power, to ascertain this point'. Although he could claim no positive proof of this point he maintained that this was 'the only explanation of the ubiquity of syphilis throughout all nations'.[58] A comment in his introduction further illustrates this point:

> Let us consider for a moment the career of the female from whom a healthy man contracts a syphilitic sore. Originally virtuous, and perhaps the object of admiration, she receives as many men during the day as she can bear, for the purposes of maintenance. Many of the lower order of prostitutes have informed the sister of the ward under my care that they have admitted seven or eight men a day, and perhaps even more, for the period arrived when the combination of drink and excitement paralysed the action of the brain, and the state of half consciousness supervened, during which nothing is remembered. It is, I presume, under circumstances like these that the source of the syphilitic virus must be investigated.[59]

Apart from his somewhat prurient fascination with the sexual exploits of prostitutes, the rationale behind Holmes Coote's statement is that these women were morally polluted and therefore a source of syphilitic pollution. The more degraded the prostitutes the more likely they were to be contagious. Coote continued in this vein, likening the prostitute's body to a swamp from which poisonous miasma flowed:

> if . . . it can be shown that the poison acquires a positive virulence through the habits of excess in promiscuous intercourse by the woman, I see no difficulty in imagining that this is the source whence the poison may have originated in the beginning: that nature has established laws, the transgression of which is followed by vitiation of the natural secretions, producing poison capable of acting upon the human frame, in the same way as the decomposition of vegetable matter will produce the miasmata, the breathing of which will produce marsh fever.[60]

Miasma theory was the most popular form of disease theory during the nineteenth century, as it accommodated itself well to the scientific materialism of the day. Miasma was putrid matter believed to be given off by marshes, drains, sewers and cemeteries. The idea that miasma was responsible for many contagious diseases was very popular, as it was graspable at the level of public debate – effluvia could be pointed to and graphically illustrated.[61] It is not difficult to see why medical professionals would pick up the miasmic model of disease to explain the idea that prostitution was inevitably connected with venereal disease. The prostitute had been defined in terms reserved for other public health problems, such as drains and sewers. She was considered both a social necessity and a public health risk. By describing the bodily discharges of the prostitute as a form of miasma, doctors were merely extending an already over-used metaphor.

Coote's model of the disease was similar to both Skey's and Parker's. He believed that essentially syphilis was the result of 'impure intercourse' and that a regime of moderation would reduce the risk of contagion and prevent the likelihood of its generating spontaneously. For Coote, the sexualized female body was the source of the disease. He maintained that all the bodily discharges of the prostitute were poisonous. Increased secretion in a virtuous woman due to 'sexual excess' could also cause an outbreak of the disease. His writings seem fraught with sexual anxiety. His discussion of catching gonorrhoea is illustrative.

> Women of the town are rarely free from discharge, even when in what they consider health; and it is remarkable, that some men are exempt from contagion, while others are always unlucky. I have heard of a case, in which profuse discharge followed a first connexion on both sides, between two people; but I must confess to never having witnessed such an occurrence. In respectable married life, the class of disease of which we are speaking is uncommon.[62]

Coote's ideas reaffirmed the conception that not only was syphilis spread by illicit intercourse, it was created by 'impure' intercourse. The disease not only had a moral meaning but it came to be measured along a continuum of immorality; the more sexualized the female body was, the more diseased it was. This became a common assumption. Dr Gordon, surgeon of the 10th Regiment of Foot, produced a pamphlet *General Statistics of Local Venereal Ulcers* based on a similar premise. In this pamphlet, he suggested that the more depraved the prostitute was, the more poisonous was the disease she inflicted. He based this theory on the fact that not only did the relative prevalence of different forms of local ulcers vary according to the station of the regiment, but that in large garrison towns such as Chatham, Canterbury and Dublin the 'Hunterian chancre', a particularly malignant form of sore, was extraordinarily prevalent. He concluded that 'it may be presumed that the filthy habits of the prostitutes of such stations had something to do with the prevalence of this form'.[63]

Filth and squalor were not viewed as the result of poverty but of depravity. Poverty itself was considered morally contagious. The women who lived with soldiers or around garrisons were considered particularly loathsome. *The Lancet* referred to such women as 'infesting . . . military posts'.[64] Most commentators writing on 'soldiers' women' expressed disgust at their habits. The journalist Henry Mayhew, for example, wrote '[T]here is not much to be said about soldiers' women. They are low and cheap; often diseased.'[65] In the early 1870s, the *Pall Mall Gazette* ran a series of articles on the prostitutes who squatted amongst the furze of Curragh Common servicing the garrison there. The author of the articles claimed that these women were as savage as any 'Australian native'.[66] The disgust was due to the fact that they were very badly paid, which resulted in their having to sleep with a number of soldiers to earn a subsistence wage and consequently they had to live in abject squalor. Acton claimed that the usual honorarium granted by 'the generous and prodigal sons of Mars' was a shilling. 'To obtain a subsistence, a woman must take home with her eight or ten lovers a night.'[67]

The same principle was applied to prostitutes in naval ports. Such women, in the view of *The Lancet*, 'rendered these [naval] stations the very *foci* of the syphilitic virus . . . [prostitutes] in our great seaports are not only affected in a higher ratio than are others of the same class elsewhere, but that the more severe forms of venereal affections are commoner amongst them, and those whom they infect.'[68] Such reporting led many doctors to infer that syphilis was positively increased by the deplorable lives of prostitutes. While certainly such women were at a greater risk than other prostitutes as they had to solicit more custom, this is not the focus of concern. The fact that these women could engage in intercourse with many men seems to be the issue. It is their immorality that makes them more contagious. These concerns were to be more explicitly articulated in later Committees and Commissions on the Contagious Diseases Acts.

Bracebridge Hemyng, London journalist and colleague of Henry Mayhew, added a particularly racist dimension when he stated that the disease communicated by prostitutes who cohabit with 'the Malays, Lascars and Orientals' was the 'most frightful form of lues to be met with in Europe'.[69] Such ideas were derived from the racial sciences that sprang from Enlightenment theories such as the Great Chain of Being.[70] Historians of science and medicine such as Sander Gilman and Londa Schiebinger have shown that such theories were highly influential in creating notions of sexual difference that were imbedded along a racial hierarchy. Along the Great

Chain of Being, black men and women were marked as inherently different from white men and women.

These theories impacted on ideas around sexual morality. Recently, the legal theorist Carol Smart has extended this idea to show that sexual morality during this period was also constructed not only on gender lines but also on those of race. Indeed, she has argued that 'the concept of sexual morality is clearly white'.[71] Those who failed to meet the accepted standard of morality were seen as less than white, less than British. Venereal disease was therefore also 'raced'. Many argued that it was an 'imported' or 'foreign' disease. Hemyng's comments relate to a wider discourse of disease as a threat to Empire. The prostitute engaging in sexual intercourse with 'coloured men' is viewed as both unBritish and spreading a 'foreign disease'.[72]

From the 1850s onward, concern about the health risks involved in prostitution came to be raised in the non-medical press. W.R. Greg was amongst the first non-medical writers to affront the public with the question of the great 'social evil'. In his article in the *Westminster Review*, he advocated a system of regulation not unlike the French system. The basis of his concern was the belief that prostitution and venereal infection were one and the same. He placed prostitution along with other matters of public health as something to be controlled and regulated. He wrote:

> One of the most important practical points connected with this painful subject is the deplorable extent and virulence of the disease which prostitution is the means of spreading throughout the community. Sanitary matters occupy so large a share of public attention at the present moment, that so important a branch of them cannot be wholly overlooked. . . . Where there are 50,000 prostitutes scattered over the country spreading infection on every side of them, quarantines against the plague, and costly precautions against cholera, seem very like straining at gnats and swallowing camels.[73]

Because Greg assumed prostitutes to be the source of the disease, he could readily overlook the fact that the only people prostitutes spread infection to were their clients. It was in fact their clientele who were then responsible for its spread throughout the community. Like other Victorian male commentators, Greg took any reference to prostitution to refer only to the prostitute. The idea that prostitution involved a male component or a relationship was impossible for him to conceive. Greg, and those who preceded him, chose to obscure the fact that men might in some way be responsible for the spread of venereal disease, placing the blame solely onto prostitutes. Greg accepted the double standard of morality that made sexual desire natural in men but pathological in women and hence chose to deal with the problem of venereal disease and prostitution as a matter of public health. In a passionate defence of regulation he insisted that

> If public health is an affair which merits the attention of the government, or lies within proper functions, – if the late movement of popular feeling in favour of sanitary measures be not wholly a mistake, and a step in the wrong direction, – if compulsory vaccination of paupers, – if quarantine regulations against imported pestilence, – if enforced cleanliness in times of cholera visitation, – be justifiable and right, then the natural *a priori*, *a fortiori* conclusion unquestionably is, that it is an imperative duty on the administrative authorities to take all needful and feasible measures to check the spread of a malady more terrible than all epidemics.[74]

Others were not as 'moderate' as Greg and chose to view prostitutes not as a health problem but as criminals. Bracebridge Hemyng made this point most explicitly when he suggested not only that the prostitute was the source of contagion but that she was in effect a murderess.

> A woman was pointed out to me in a Music Hall in Knightsbridge, who had only yesterday had two buboes lanced; and yet she was present at that scene of apparent festivity, contaminating the very air, like a deadly upas, and poisoning the blood of the nation, with the most audacious recklessness. The woman was no better than a paid murderess, committing crime with impunity.[75]

The medical profession used all its newfound influence to sway public opinion on the question of the regulation of prostitution. Popular fears about the prostitute as contaminator were exploited. Both the medical and the non-medical press warned the public of the increasing visibility of prostitutes. Their riotous behaviour was said to be threatening the very moral fibre of society. Since the late 1840s the London *Times* had been demanding new legislation to deal with 'such very disgusting nuisances'.[76] The implication of these complaints was that not only were prostitutes physically contagious but that their presence tainted the environment. An article in *The Lancet* in 1857 illustrated such concerns, using imagery directly related to other sanitary issues.

> The typical Pater-Familias, living in a grand house near the park, sees his sons allured into debauchery, dares not walk his daughters through the streets after nightfall, and is disturbed from his night slumbers by the drunken screams and foul oaths of prostitutes reeling home with the

daylight. . . . Yet he refuses to sanction any practical means for remedying the evil, or to lend his aid to reform. He not only allows dirt to accumulate, because it is dirt, but scrupulously carries out the social code under which prostitution has so notably increased of late years.[77]

Regulation was not the only solution posited by medical and social commentators. The medical press demanded a greater availability of Lock Hospitals. There were calls for a government inquiry into the subject of prostitution. Other more rigorous observers looked to patterns in prostitution in order to establish ways of overcoming the problems it was seen to entail. A Dr Thomas Holland sent a letter and survey 'in connexion with prostitution and syphilis' to the secretary of every medical society, to the head constable of every town with a population over 5,000 and to the master of every union, workhouse, refuge and prison. 'By these means,' he hoped, 'to obtain . . . statistics and trustworthy facts regarding prostitution, and its resultant diseases.'[78] One of the most popular suggestions proffered in the medical press was the establishment of a Board of Moral Health. It was argued Rescue Homes had failed to stem the tide of the disease and a more serious approach was called for. A Board of Moral Health should be established in each of the major towns. Like local boards of public health they would be funded and run by local 'honest and well-paid' citizens. Their role would not only be the care of the diseased prostitute but the 'control of all evils which are injurious to society either by their existence or by the excesses to which they are carried'.[79] While there was some contention over the success or failure of Rescue Homes, the idea of a Board of Moral Health was very well received.

Some commentators looked to flaws within society to blame for the growth of prostitution and the subsequent 'epidemic' of venereal infection. They argued that the demands of society such as late marriages necessitated prostitution and enhanced the course of venereal diseases. While occasionally men were held to blame for their part in maintaining such a state of society, these commentators never reached the obvious conclusion that men were responsible for prostitution itself and therefore largely responsible for the diseases associated with it. This was because much of the writing was based around the assumption that male sexual privilege was a biological necessity that forced the existence of prostitution.

Even when prostitution was held to be a necessary evil, few really considered men responsible for its continuation except in indirect ways such as seduction. Men might be responsible for the initial fall, but few considered them responsible for women's continuation in a 'downward path'. Women solicited men and were therefore responsible. A comment from *The Lancet* is illustrative of this idea: 'At present their [prostitutes'] wretched condition makes them objects of pity, whilst they continue also centres of danger. They purchase existence by spreading widely the infection from which they themselves suffer.'[80]

Those who did not believe prostitution to be an inevitable factor of modern society still saw it as responsible for the spread of venereal disease. James Miller, Professor of Surgery at the University of Edinburgh, though firm in his conviction that prostitution was an 'unnatural' product of society, still maintained that prostitution was responsible for syphilis. Prostitutes, or rather, 'the multitudinous Amazonian army the devil keeps in field service' tainted the 'very atmosphere'.[81] Miller offered a wide range of solutions to the problems of prostitution that in many ways resembled other sanitary reforms. Amongst his suggestions were better education in cleanliness and better and less crowded housing. He also believed that an elevated tone of society would vastly improve the situation. He called for more Lock facilities, although he does not specifically refer to prostitutes, they were primarily meant for their benefit '[L]et our hospitals receive the more sorely stricken victims, till they are healed. . . . By kindness, judgment and patient care many a one might be thus reclaimed from their vicious course, and restored to their friends and to society.'[82]

As the medical disasters that the British army endured during the Crimean War became known to the general public, the government was forced to hold a Royal Commission into the health of the armed forces. The high incidence of syphilis amongst the troops sent to the Crimea became a national scandal. It was estimated that the inefficiency arising from the loss of services of men afflicted with the disease was equal to the loss of three regiments for the whole year.[83] This was not news to the War Office who had known since the 1850s that the treatment of venereal disease in the armed forces cost around £4,000 per annum.[84] These statistics were used by the medical establishment to push the question of regulation. In 1862 Florence Nightingale convened a Sanitary Commission to look into the problem of venereal disease and the army. The report of this committee was tabled in late 1862 and recommended the establishment of voluntary Lock Hospitals, improved sanitary and recreational facilities for soldiers and a policy of punishing soldiers for concealing, not contracting venereal disease. Nightingale recommended strongly that the regulation of prostitution not be considered as a means to control the disease.[85] Several of the committee members dissented on this issue. Increasingly, both civil and military authorities came to favour a system of regulation.

There was little protest against this trend. Harriet Martineau published a series of letters in the *Daily News* in 1863 but they were largely ignored.

The Lancet and *The Times* maintained a crusade supporting the institution of regulation, placing considerable pressure upon the War Office. The hastily drafted and ill-considered Contagious Diseases Prevention Bill was introduced into Parliament in mid-1864. The Bill was suffixed with the parenthesis 'not dealing with animals'. The language and legal connotations of the Bill were borrowed directly from those Acts dealing with cattle.[86] This pointed to the very rationale behind the Acts. Prostitutes were considered the source of the disease and, like cattle or drainage, they were to be carefully monitored to check the spread of the infection. Prostitutes would no longer have the same rights as 'virtuous women', they would no longer have legal personalities. They would merely be considered a source of disease to be contained.

PART II
Regulation

I look upon a prostitute, diseased or undiseased as a public nuisance, and I think if legislation recognises nuisances of various kinds, and crimes of various kinds, so legislation should recognize such a nuisance as that.

Rev. C.T. Wilkinson
Vicar of St Andrews, Plymouth
Royal Commission upon the Contagious Diseases Acts 1871

In fact, you will in vain multiply the number of your examinations and redouble your care in practising them.... Make your examinations then, use your injections, your ointments, your suppositories; cauterize the poor girls, impregnate them with mercury; examine them once more, cauterize them afresh, mercurialize them yet again; impose upon them humiliation after humiliation, suffering upon suffering; nay, more, as in Belgium, organize around them and even between themselves a hideous espionage; finally, compel them to descend from degradation, even to the point that they are no longer women; and yet the virus, latent and unseizable, but obstinate, will still be there, ready to perpetuate its actions and its influence.

Dr Turenne
Congrès Médical International, Paris, 1867

3 Implementing the System

On 20 June 1864, the Bill that was to enforce a system of regulated prostitution in naval ports and garrison towns throughout Great Britain was introduced to the Parliament by Sir Clarence Paget, Secretary to the Admiralty. It aroused no debate. On 19 July the Bill went to Committee for amendments and on 21 July at two o'clock in the morning with only fifty men in the House the Bill was adopted. It received royal assent on 29 July 1864. The Act provided for the compulsory hospitalization of any woman who was suspected of being a prostitute with a venereal disease, on the evidence of one policeman before a magistrate, in any of the eleven nominated districts.[1] If the woman was found to be diseased, the magistrate could order her detention for a maximum of three months. In order to escape this interrogatory process a woman could voluntarily submit to examination.[2] If a woman refused to submit to examination she could be imprisoned for up to two months.

In 1866, Sir Clarence Paget introduced a second Contagious Diseases Bill. The life span of the original Act was three years and this Bill was meant as a renewal measure. It was passed again with little opposition and received royal assent on 11 June 1866. The 1864 Act had made little impact as it was only implemented in four districts but the 1866 Act instituted a full scale system of regulation. Under the new Act, a magistrate could order a woman to a fortnightly medical inspection for up to a year and the period that a woman could be detained in a Lock Hospital was extended to six months. A clause calling for adequate provision for the moral and religious instruction of women detained in hospitals was added.[3]

Again, the new Act received little criticism and shortly after its implementation demand increased to have the Acts extended. In 1867 an Extensionist Association was formed. Its primary aim was to see the Acts extended to the civil population of London and other large towns. This Committee was quite effective in gaining support for this proposal and in 1868 Viscount Lifford, a member of the Extensionist Association, called for the House of Lords to form a Select Committee to consider the whole subject of extending the Acts.

The Committee first met in May 1868. All but one of the eighteen witnesses called before the Committee were in favour of extension. The Report of the Committee was published on 2 July 1868. The report stated that it was outside the realms of the Committee to consider the application of the Act to the civil population. Committee members agreed however that the 1864 and 1866 Acts had been successful from a 'moral and sanitary' point of view. They nonetheless suggested several ways in which the workings of the Act could be made more effective. The Committee recommended that the five-mile limit for subjected districts be increased to fifteen miles as it was believed that many prostitutes had simply moved five miles out of town to avoid detention. They also wanted to make it possible for visiting surgeons to be able to issue warrants for the police to apprehend women refusing to appear on their appointed day. It was further proposed that the limitation of detention be extended from six months to nine months. The Committee found that the Acts were ineffective in the treatment of diseased children and pregnant women. They suggested that children found diseased should be sent to some form of industrial school at the expense of their parents and advised that diseased pregnant women should be allowed to spend their confinement in the government Lock Hospitals rather than receive no treatment. It was also suggested that the periodical inspection of troops be reinstituted.

The government acted quickly on the report and another Act was passed in August 1869. This Act did little but remedy certain defects highlighted by the 1868 Select Committee. It extended the maximum period of detention to nine months and added a further six to the existing twelve subjected districts. It also made it possible for women to be detained for up to five days if they were 'unfit for examination'. This Act marked the completion of the systematic regulation of prostitution in Great Britain. It also marked the beginning of the campaign to see the Acts repealed.

The implementation of the CD Acts, the struggle to have them repealed and the impression that they made on the women and the districts affected have been of considerable interest to historians of prostitution in Victorian Britain. In a recent reconsideration of the Acts, F.B. Smith has contended that the historiography of the campaign has been deeply influenced by the Repealers' 'attractive and voluminous' attacks on the Acts and has consequently misrepresented the intentions of those who sought to regulate prostitution and the actual impact of the system upon the prostitutes themselves.[4] While there is much that is controversial in Smith's article, he is correct in stating that much of the analysis of the CD Acts has focussed on the rhetoric of those involved in the campaign, while scant attention has been paid to their medical rationale. Moreover, because historians have tended to concentrate on the struggle between Extensionists and Repealers, the entire struggle has been represented as a crusade of the forces of good against the forces of evil.

Such an approach is too simplistic as it treats the opinions of Repealers and Extensionists as if they were entirely oppositional. It is necessary to examine the medical evidence that was put forward both in favour of and against the Acts. A detailed textual analysis of the evidence presented at the Select Committees and Royal Commissions into the workings of the CD Acts allows the Acts to be read as more than an 'authoritarian technological advancement' and shows the ways in which medical discourse attempted to construct the prostitute's body as 'contaminated' in and of itself.

Before the Act was properly implemented, a Committee of medical men chaired by F.C. Skey FRCS, was established to enquire into the pathology and treatment of venereal disease. It began taking evidence in December 1864. The Committee was prompted into activity by the publication of a pamphlet entitled 'Proofs of the Non-existence of a Specific Enthetic Disease' by Dr David Macloughlin. In this pamphlet, Macloughlin claimed that the constitutional disease syphilis did not exist: the symptoms usually attributed to constitutional syphilis were, he suggested, due to the excessive use of mercury to treat the primary symptoms of the disease. He was extremely critical of the role of army and naval surgeons and their excessive use of mercury to treat every venereal symptom. 'The War Office,' he wrote, 'has an army of upwards of 400,000 men and a staff of about 1,500 medical officers'. He suggested these officers were:

> directed to the study of the pathology, the etiology [*sic*], and the medical treatment of this so-called syphilitic disease, and if the researches of these 1,500 medical officers were carefully and scientifically recorded, in a few months there would be an amelioration as to this so-called syphilitic disease in the army – the army medical officers would not go on as they are now going on to consider every ulcer on the genitals as syphilitic, and to be treated only by mercury, and consequently injure their patients.[5]

Since the early nineteenth century, some medical authorities had begun to question the wisdom of using mercury to treat venereal diseases, but by the mid-century the claim of excessive use of mercury by military medical officers clearly troubled the government. This concern and disagreement about treatment and diagnosis was indicative of the general lack of understanding regarding the aetiology and pathology of the disease syphilis. The tasks of the Committee included: defining the disease syphilis, distinguishing it from other venereal diseases, differentiating between the soft and the hard sore, determining whether or not constitutional syphilis was contagious and establishing the best mode of treatment.

The Committee was made up of eminent medical men, such as Skey and James Donnet, an expert on tropical diseases. Witnesses called before the Committee represented the elite of the civil and military medical profession including the Queen's physician, William Jenner, and her surgeon, James Paget. The Committee, however, did little to improve medical knowledge regarding the venereal diseases and continued to reinforce many misconceptions about the diseases. Macloughlin's ideas were totally dismissed. Syphilis was found to be a disease 'universally recognised by the medical profession'.[6] But what constituted the disease was still a matter of much contention. Several doctors remained confused as to the question of the 'duality of the virus' theory. Since the 1850s this term had been used to designate the problem of determining whether or not chancroid was a symptom of syphilis or a separate disease. Certain witnesses, however, still confused this with Hunter's ideas about gonorrhoea being a symptom of syphilis.[7] Although many witnesses were questioned about constitutional syphilis and hereditary syphilis, little was resolved.

While most of the witnesses examined before the Committee stated that they believed that syphilis was derived through transmission and absorption of a virus or poison into the blood, some six witnesses believed that it could be generated spontaneously. The idea that syphilis could be created *de novo* related to the idea of the female body as the source of venereal poison. Mr James Symes, Professor of Clinical Surgery at the University of Edinburgh, told the Committee that he believed syphilis to be the 'poisonous influences of an unhealthy female'.[8] Holmes Coote concurred, stating that he understood 'that syphilis may be produced and will be produced as long as the world exists'. He claimed 'whenever one woman receives a number of men there we find syphilis, and no law can prevent its recurrence. I believe it is generated under those circumstances.'[9]

The Committee also found that women spontaneously generated gonorrhoea and 'soft' sores. It was generally agreed that 'impure intercourse' was the principal cause of gonorrhoea. The Committee upheld Ricord's ideas that gonorrhoea was a non-specific infection and could be generated under many circumstances. This was also held true of other non-specific or soft sores. These afflictions, the Committee found, were generally the 'morbid product of merely contagious secretions'. Such 'secretions' were 'comparatively innocuous in the female' but became 'a poison to the recipient'.[10] All women, not merely prostitutes, were thus held responsible for its spread.

The findings of the Committee reinforced the idea that the female body was an infectious site. Hence, they argued that the body of the prostitute should be policed in the same way drains and sewers were policed. Army and naval medical officers stationed in the colonies continued the discourse started by commentators such as Acton, Mayhew and Coote relating to the continuum of pollution. As we have seen in Britain, authorities had claimed that it was the oldest and poorest prostitutes, most particularly Irish women, who were the source of the worst cases of syphilis. Those medical officers stationed in Hong Kong and India claimed that cases of syphilis were far worse in these colonies, using the same rationale but relating it to a racial (racist) hierarchy.

Mr George Busk, Surgeon to Dreadnought Seaman's Hospital, claimed that the worst sores were to be found in Asia. 'There are classes of sores which I have frequently seen in men who have come from China or India,' he reported to the Committee, that he termed 'phagendic sores'. Such sores, he stated, were impossible to check 'for they were as intractable as cancer, destroying the whole penis, and sometimes the scrotum, and eating under the arch of the pubis'.[11] In part, the virulence of these sores was put down to uncleanliness. David Deas, Inspector-General of Hospitals and Fleets, told the Committee that the Chinese had a greater problem with venereal diseases than any other race because of their uncleanliness. 'The Chinese,' he stated, 'have a great disinclination to use water, of which they have a great dread, seldom using anything but a damp cloth . . . for the purpose of cleansing their person.'[12] He suggested the problem was as great in the seaport towns of England. It was also considered that the general health of the troops was worse in the Asian colonies and it was believed that this meant their immunity to such diseases was reduced. That colonial doctors took these ideas and transferred them onto the indigenous people under their care indicates how widespread and accepted such notions were. Such comments also relate to ideas of moral superiority being linked to racial superiority. Throughout the nineteenth century, sexual immorality was being characterised as unBritish. Continental Europeans, especially the Belgians and French, the Irish and 'coloured' colonials were perceived not only as immoral but steeped in disease. Syphilis was not only constructed as a feminized disease but as a disease that was, to use Carol Smart's term, 'raced'.[13]

Central to this discussion was the suggestion that the symptoms of syphilis were worse in Asia because the prostitutes were considered more degraded and promiscuous. Dr A.E. Mackay, Deputy Inspector-General of Hospitals and Fleets, stated that it had occurred to him that 'considering the wretched and miserable character of the . . . common prostitutes of Hong Kong . . . it is possible that a more aggravated and more virulent species of the same poison may be found'.[14] Such discussion reaffirmed the belief that syphilis was a disease that could be measured along a continuum of morality and pollution: the more depraved the female was, the more poisonous the disease she inflicted.

The Committee was not only concerned with the type of female constitution most likely to create an infection in a man: they were also
concerned about what sort of masculine constitutions were most likely to
submit to the disease. All authorities agreed that the virus could manifest
itself differently upon different constitutions. Men of delicate health were
said to be most vulnerable to the disease. Mr William Stuart, Surgeon-
Major to the Bombay Army, reported that amongst European men it was
'the nervous type' rather than the 'phlegmatic' man who was more susceptible to the disease.[15] Dr Dickson, Medical Inspector of Customs to the
Royal Navy, reported that in his experience 'men with light hair and very
delicate complexions, and some fine white skins, seem to be more liable
than others, both to indurated sores and to the more obstinate squamous
eruptions'.[16] Men of scrofulous appearance were considered both more
susceptible to the disease and more greatly affected by it. Young recruits
were said to be especially prone to the disease. Mr Stuart stated that 'the
young lads who come out as recruits are those who fill the hospital the
quickest with disease'.[17]

Men with large members were held to be at great risk. Largeness of the
penis, and other 'deformities' of that organ were said to result in injury
and excoriation during intercourse that allowed the virus to be easily transmitted. Circumcised men were said to be at a distinct advantage from the
point of view of both cleanliness and reduced risk of injury to the prepuce.
In India it was said that gonorrhoea and other venereal diseases prepon-
derated in the Hindoo (*sic*) over the Mohammedan. Moslem men were
circumcised. Hindu men, however, would lose their caste if circumcised
and the doctors questioned stated that the Hindu mother 'rather encourages
in the infant the growth of the long prepuce' rendering him more prone to
such diseases.[18] Jewish men were also said to be at little risk. When asked
about this Samuel Solly, Senior Surgeon to St Thomas' Hospital, claimed
this was due to 'cleanliness, from want of a foreskin' and to the fact that
their skin was 'harder' and 'less absorbent'.[19] Recently, Sander Gilman
has discussed the question of Jewish men and syphilis in the nineteenth
century, pointing out that the sexuality of the Jew was also considered
polluting. For centuries, Gilman argues, the Jew and the prostitute were
believed to have a special relationship: 'Both the Jew and the prostitute
have but one interest, the conversion of sex into money or money into
sex.' During the late nineteenth century, this special relationship took on
an added dimension and syphilis was linked to Jewishness through the
agency of the prostitute. Medical authorities put down the perception that
Jewish men were immune to the ravages of the disease, to 'centuries of
exposure'. He writes, '[J]ust as Jewishness was an inherited tendency', so

too was the nature of Jewish sexuality, 'a sexuality so markedly different that it was claimed that some Jewish male infants were born circumcised'.[20]

These ideas related to a more general notion of the syphilitic being pathological: just as it was believed the least feminine of women were the most susceptible to disease, so the 'unnatural', feeble, unmanly man was also seen as a high risk. These ideas related to a growing anxiety, around the development of the medicalized category of the homosexual.[21] Homosexuality was no longer constituted as a set of practices, but a condition, a way of being. The homosexual came to represent an opposition to all that was idealized as 'manly'. This feminization of homosexuality reinforced its medical construction as an affliction. Like the prostitute, the homosexual was morbidified. His sexual practices were constructed as pathological and his constitution (mental, moral and physical) was defined as diseased.

Such contradictions passed through the Committee without comment. Moreover, there was no discussion of what such delicate men were doing in the armed services. This reversal of assumptions was continued on a moral level when it came to the question of examination. While there was no discussion of how prostitutes responded to enforced examination, much sensitivity was shown on the question of reintroducing the compulsory inspection of troops. The traditional 'dangle parade' had been abolished in 1859, as it was considered that the mass inspection of troops was degrading for the men and went against the attempts to improve the moral tone of the standing army instituted by Florence Nightingale and her followers. After this it was left to the discretion of the Commanding Officer of a regiment whether men should be examined on a regular basis.[22] Few of the military medical officers questioned favoured its reintroduction while some evinced a positive loathing of the idea.

Despite being given such an array of information the Committee went on to recommend the maintenance and extension of the Contagious Diseases Acts. As the historian Sandra Holton has pointed out, detention of prostitutes was practically useless in light of the fact that the Committee believed that women could spontaneously generate gonorrhoea, simple sores and possibly even syphilis, and that they could transmit the disease without themselves being prior victims to the disease.[23] Nor could these medical authorities claim with any certainty that once they had detained a syphilitic woman they could cure her. The presumed universality of gonorrhoea amongst women led to its trivialization and meant that the concern with the prostitute was specifically targeted at her as the spreader of syphilis. The Skey Committee merely reinforced the notion that the prostitute's body was a site of infection and as such should be treated like any other health risk. This notion was most clearly illustrated by Mr Longmore, Professor of Military Surgery at the Army Medical School. He told the Committee that prostitution should be treated as a dangerous trade.

> I do not understand why a woman who plies a trade which is dangerous to others, should not be as much restrained as what attention has lately attracted to [*sic*], namely the carrying of gunpowder down to the river. It seems to me that one is plying a dangerous trade as much as the other, and should be equally subjected to what restrictions are considered necessary.[24]

Nearly all the witnesses questioned supported some form of regulation and most were in favour of the extension of the existing Act. Only three of the sixty-three men called before the inquiry posed strong objections to regulation. There was little scientific logic used to defend the support of regulation and ideas about prevention were entirely structured around notions of morality and immorality, cleanliness and pollution. The expression of ideas about prostitution and disease made little sense outside this framework. For instance, Mr Hutchinson, Surgeon to the London and Metropolitan Hospitals, stated before the Committee that he believed that 'prostitutes who . . . suffered from syphilis at some former period' were very much more safe than young prostitutes who have never had it.[25] Hutchinson's comment referred to the belief that the more promiscuous the woman was the more likely she was to transmit infection. He reasoned that women who had already had a dose of syphilis were more likely to take care with cleanliness. He considered young prostitutes to be both uncleanly and more promiscuous and subsequently more infectious. The same logic was demonstrated by Mr Byrne, Surgeon to Westmoreland Lock Hospital, but to a completely different end. Byrne claimed that it was easier to cure young prostitutes as there was 'not the same extent of body surface as there is in old prostitutes, or those who have borne children'.[26]

The underlying principle fostered by the Committee was that the most important feature of regulation was removing the visible signs of the disease. This meant not only removing the prostitute from the streets as the most visible purveyor of disease, but removing from the prostitute's body all signs of the disease. This did not mean cure for prostitutes. Most doctors examined before the inquiry stated that they were generally opposed to the use of the more 'heroic' style treatments of syphilis, such as salivation and escharotics. Salivation was one of the earliest treatments of syphilis and in its worst form involved submitting the patient to high doses of mercury, both externally and internally. At the same time, the patient was wrapped in blankets and forced to maintain an extremely high temperature in order to sweat the disease out. Not suprisingly, some of the worst symptoms of syphilis were later attributed to mercury poisoning. Escharotics involved the application of any substances in order to burn off sores or growths. The report of the Committee stated that in the case of the 'hard sore', the most commonly recognized symptom of syphilis, 'the application of local agents' to destroy the sore was 'useless'.[27] But in the case of prostitutes some doctors still urged such harsh treatments. When Mr Samuel Lane, Surgeon to St Mary's Hospital, was asked by the Committee how he would treat prostitutes in order to diminish the disease, he answered that he would 'at once destroy every poisonous or supposed poisonous sore, by escharotics.' He was at pains to state that he would only do this in the case of prostitutes as he considered them 'exceptional beings' that should be 'treated exceptionally'.[28]

Such comments not only betray the sadistic intention of certain medical authorities who supported the regulation, but also reveal the generally punitive nature of the system. Amid all the discussion about the effective cure of prostitutes and the protection of the armed forces, it was the control of the prostitute's body that was the primary focus of regulation. Such control meant not only compulsory examinations and enforced detention, but also brutal, painful and punitive treatment. In this light, regulation cannot be viewed as a system that benefited prostitutes in any way, but rather as a form of punishment. F.B. Smith's argument that prostitutes benefited from the system and 'built up a relationship with their surgeons, policemen and hospital matrons that helped their self-esteem' should be relegated to the realms of fantasy.[29] Not only does he unproblematically accept uncorroborated evidence provided by the police about their treatment of prostitutes but he ignores evidence provided by the Extensionists themselves, that force was necessary to maintain the system. The police were certainly not beyond lying, whoring and corruption. As Frances Finnegan's study of prostitution in York in the mid-nineteenth century indicates, one in every six identified clients was a policemen. Finnegan's study shows that many police were involved in petty corruption such as demanding protection money from prostitutes and bribery.[30] More importantly, Extensionists blatantly accepted the need to brutalize women in order to gain their co-operation. As the Liberal politician John Morley said in defence of the Acts,

[They] affect the very dregs of the population – the lowest kind of prostitutes on the one hand, and on the other the most vicious of the common soldiers. . . . [These are] masses of men and women, who are virtually in the condition of barbarians and whose practices can only be repressed by the same widely coercive methods which have always been essential to raise a barbarous community into a civilized state.[31]

Those in favour of the Acts maintained that repressive and coercive methods were needed if venereal disease was to be suppressed. During the final Select Committee into the workings of the Acts, the medical press in Britain were scathing in their criticism of the suggestion of voluntary Lock Hospitals. Quoting Extensionist witness James Lane, before the 1881 Select Committee, the *British Medical Journal* accepted that

> in his opinion, nothing would be of material service in suppressing venereal diseases which stopped short of frequent examination, and early seclusion, with compulsory detention in hospital until cured. . . . From a long experience of this class, [he] knew that they would not willingly seclude themselves until they had become seriously diseased.[32]

Many doctors remained adamant that compulsory detention was necessary if venereal disease was to be prevented.

Fear of the harsh tactics of the police and the poor treatment women received in Lock facilities was etched into the popular imagination of the urban working class. As late as the 1913 Royal Commission on Venereal Disease, doctors were reporting difficulties in getting women treated voluntarily as the spectre of compulsory detention still loomed. Dr Wilson Still told the Commission that there was a 'traditional fear' amongst the 'poorest kind' of prostitute that if they went into a Lock Hospital they would be smothered. 'The belief is that when a woman is thoroughly rotten, she goes into a Lock ward, and they smother her. So naturally, they do not go until they are really tired of life.'[33]

4 Resisting the Acts

Since the 1970s, the implementation of the Contagious Diseases Acts and the struggle to have them repealed has attracted a considerable amount of historical attention. The Acts have become something of a watershed for historians of the mid-nineteenth century and have been used to demonstrate the emergence of feminism and social purity in Britain, developments in public health, radical reform in the army and struggles within the Liberal Party. In examining the feminization of venereal disease in relation to the Acts, it is important to focus away from a more general analysis and concentrate specifically on the medical debate between Extensionists and Repealers. A close reading of the Select Committees and Royal Commissions into the Contagious Diseases Acts, as well as the more general medical literature dealing with the Acts, shows that the defence of the Acts depended on an idea of the innate pathology of the prostitute. Historians writing on the CD Acts have not placed enough importance on the medical opposition to them. Many of those doctors who opposed the Acts were amongst the British medical elite. Not only did they question the notion that prostitutes were necessarily diseased but they challenged a rather complaisant medical establishment with new ideas about the diagnosis and treatment of venereal disease. It is also necessary to challenge the idea that the repeal of the Acts was an inevitable result of scientific progress. By looking closer at medical debates around regulation it can be shown that medical advances were never perceived as ways to end regulation but rather as ways to make regulation more effective. In view of this, it could be argued that as more became known about venereal disease, medical attempts to control female sexuality became less rational and less scientific.

Opposition to the Contagious Diseases Acts began in earnest in late 1869. In October of that year the National Anti-Contagious Diseases Acts Association (NA) was formed and shortly after this a Ladies National Association (LNA) was established. John Chapman, editor of the *Westminster Review*, published a series of articles condemning the Acts in late 1869 and early 1870. Harriet Martineau wrote another series of letters to the *Daily News* protesting against the Acts. Josephine Butler, one of the founders of the LNA, began to lobby the support of working men and women in northern England. On New Year's Day 1870, the *Daily News* published a protest against the Acts written by Harriet Martineau and signed by 124 women, including Florence Nightingale, Josephine Butler and

Mary Carpenter. The sensation caused by the publication of the Ladies' Manifesto aroused further interest in the Acts and protest committees were formed in London, Edinburgh and Glasgow. In March 1870, a repeal journal called *The Shield* was launched. By the end of the parliamentary session of 1870 some 600,000 signatures had been collected to protest against the Acts.

Those involved in the repeal campaign attacked the Acts on a variety of counts. The principal complaint was that they appeared to legalize prostitution. It was also charged that the Acts were unconstitutional as they interfered with the liberty of the subject. In addition to this, it was claimed that the system did not effectively diminish disease. The LNA also made some specifically feminist attacks, claiming that the Acts unjustly punished the sex who were the victims of vice and placed poor working-class women at the mercy of the police. They also maintained that the process of examination was both degrading and gruelling.

Ostensibly, those engaged in the campaign to repeal the Acts saw prostitutes as victims of male lust, yet in rejecting regulations they positively fostered an image of the prostitute not unlike those in favour of extension. Both parties treated prostitution and syphilis as if they were synonymous. The reforming journalist John Chapman's articles on regulation in the *Westminster Review* were particularly striking in this way. Chapman began his attack on the Report of the 1866 Select Committee on the CD Acts by stating that he intended to examine a disease that was at once 'social, moral and physical'. This disease he said was prostitution. 'Of all the maladies with which humanity is afflicted,' he wrote,

> prostitution is . . . the worst: its causes are the most persistent, its physical effects are the most terrible, its social and moral complications are the most numerous and inextricable, its whole aspect is the most saddening and its cure is the most difficult.[1]

Of course, Chapman was talking of the symptoms of syphilis but like those who favoured regulation he used the terms prostitution and disease interchangably. Chapman's articles are curious in that they use much of the evidence put forward to defend the CD Acts in order to attack them. He agreed with Acton that prostitution was often a transitory state for many women. However, instead of using this argument as a basis for regulation, Chapman used it to show the futility of such a system. He offered quite telling documentation of the longterm effects of syphilis and claimed that, regardless of compulsory detention, doctors had little real proof that they could cure syphilis.

While the Repealers exposed the double standard of morality implicit in the Acts it was not to their advantage to reduce the risk posed by prostitutes. The most effective argument against the Acts was that they were unsuccessful in stemming the flood of infection passed on by prostitutes. Indeed, opponents of the Acts argued that venereal diseases positively flourished under them. Given this was the cornerstone of their campaign, it was impossible for the groups such as the NA and the LNA to challenge the dominant discourse that inseparably connected syphilis with prostitution. In her 'Appeal to the People of England' written in 1870, Josephine Butler explained that,

> while contagion on the one hand may be to a *certain extent* diminished by the surveillance exercised upon fallen women, on the other hand so many more men are induced, by fancied security from the danger, to indulge in illicit intercourse with these women, that risks run by the community at large are in the one case as great as the other nay – they are greater.[2]

Annie Besant, the Neo-Malthusian sex reformer, was also a fervent advocate of repeal. In a pamphlet on the subject of regulation, she asked,

> Does prostitution promote the nation's health? If so, why this necessity for legislation to check the spread of contagious diseases? Those diseases spring from sexual irregularities and are an outraged Nature's protest against the assertion that prostitution is the right method of providing for the sexual necessities of man. As surely as typhoid results from filth and neglect, so does the scourge of syphilis follow in the wake of prostitution. These unfortunate women who are offered up as victims of man's pleasures . . . become their own avengers, repaying the degradation inflicted on them, and spreading ruin and disease among those who want them to exist as a class.[3]

The protests of Butler and Besant illustrate the way in which reformers, while wanting men to accept their responsibility for the spread of venereal disease, failed to challenge the pathological image of the prostitute.

The *Westminster Review* did the Repeal movement a great service when it published the Eleventh Report of the Medical Officer to the Privy Council, as it showed up the lack of unity amongst government medical authorities regarding the Acts. The report, written by Sir John Simon, Medical Officer to the Privy Council, was extremely critical of the findings of the Skey Committee and strongly opposed the extension of the Acts to the civil population. Simon had presented these findings as part of his evidence to the 1868 Select Committee, where he made his position explicit: 'at present I very decidedly refrain from recommending any change in that neutral position which English law has hitherto held in regard of the venereal diseases of the civil population'.[4] Simon believed that the government should endorse the policy of *caveat emptor* where civilians and prostitutes were concerned. Far from promoting it as an extension of a more general public health policy, Simon warned that enforcing the CD Acts upon the civil population would be seen as both 'odious and immoral'. 'In most municipal constituencies' he informed the government,

> there are swarms of persons who already find it no easy matter to satisfy the collectors of rates and taxes; they would see the prostitute kept in hospital at their expense for weeks or months, not necessarily from the exigencies of severe illness of her own, but essentially that she might be made clean for hire, lest any of her users should catch disease from her; they would remember in contrast, that for themselves wonderfully little is done by authority to protect them against adulterations of food, or against false weights and measures; and they might regard it as a strange caprice of law which should oblige them to contribute to the cost of giving an artificial security to their neighbour's looseness of life.[5]

While Simon did not dismiss the Acts entirely it is evident from the terms he used, such as 'artificial security', that he felt any benefits from the Acts were illusory. It has been suggested that Simon privately felt that it was quite reasonable to extend the Acts to other military and naval centres, but that he violently objected to the broad terms of the Bill drafted by the War Office and Admiralty.[6] Recently, however, the medical historians Dorothy Porter and Roy Porter have convincingly argued that Simon had considerable reservations about regulation as he did not want to embroil the medical profession in 'the disreputable business of acting as moral jailers'.[7]

Whatever his personal opinions, his public criticisms appear to have been ahead of their time. Simon maintained that both the severity and extent of syphilis were experiencing a natural decline. He complained that there was much confusion caused by the inability to distinguish between pseudo-syphilis and syphilis, and suggested that this led to grave overestimates of the extent of the disease. These arguments were in fact to become crucial to the case for repeal, yet they were not immediately taken up. Repealers tended until the end of the 1870s to focus upon moral outrage rather than medical evidence when it came to challenging the Acts.

By the end of 1870, the governing Liberal Party had been embarrassed into creating a Royal Commission to examine the Acts. The Commission started hearing evidence in January 1871. The principal concern of the Commission was to look into the workings of the Acts, to determine whether or not venereal disease had diminished in the subjected districts and to investigate the veracity of the Repealers' complaints about the treatment of women under regulation. All in all, the Commission achieved very little. The evidence provided about prostitution was generally ambiguous and often contradictory. As Paul McHugh has stated, the Report of the Commission was 'so anodyne' that both Repealers and Extensionists 'could use it to support their contentions'.[8] What is of interest here is the evidence regarding the body of the prostitute provided by those doctors who worked in government Lock Hospitals. The evidence they gave shows that medical opinion continued to perceive the prostitute as a pathological creature and that the workings of the Acts reinforced this notion. The doctors questioned by the Commission assumed that these women were diseased by virtue of being prostitutes. Their evidence highlighted the idea that prostitutes were inherently different from virtuous women and thus should be treated only as a site of disease to be contained.

Much of the evidence provided by the visiting surgeons focused on the question of what discharges or sores they considered to be 'contagious'. This was of considerable importance as the Acts only provided for the detention of women when they were suspected of being contagious. This was very problematic in the case of gonorrhoea as a discharge from the vagina was the primary symptom of the disease and some doctors claimed that it was impossible to verify whether or not certain discharges were contagious. There had been a suggestion that women should not be detained if they only had symptoms of gonorrhoea. Indeed, the Inspector of Hospitals under the CD Acts, William Sloggett, had been publicly criticized by Devonport doctors for sending in cases of gonorrhoea 'of a very trivial character'.[9] In a letter to the government defending his position, Sloggett set out the types of sores and discharges he felt were contagious. These included ulcerations on the genitals, on the vaginal mucous membrane, on the os and cervix uteri; symptoms of constitutional syphilis including all forms of syphilitic eruptions; purulent and muco-purulent discharges from the vagina, os or cervix uteri and vaginal warts. While he maintained that conditions such as vaginal warts could be found in virtuous women, in practice such afflictions rendered prostitutes infectious.[10] Sloggett later told the Commission that 'all discharges' found in prostitutes should be considered infecting because 'all discharges of that kind in prostitutes will clearly give gonorrhoea'.[11]

The government surgeons interviewed upheld this position. Like Sloggett they agreed that it was difficult to tell if certain discharges in women were contagious, yet they simultaneously insisted that prostitutes were different from other women and were therefore more likely to be diseased. Mr Milner

Montgomery Moore, Surgeon to the Royal Albert Hospital Devonport, argued that all cases of uterine discharge brought in by the CD Acts should be treated as contagious, as prostitutes were accustomed to certain discharges 'seldom found in modest women'.[12] He went on to claim that he would consider any abnormality in the vaginas of prostitutes, such as uterine discharges, abrasions, or ulceration of the cervix to be contagious. He reasoned

> looking at these things alone and not knowing any history of secondary syphilis, I should say I think that they are contagious, *because they are prostitutes*. I believe the diseases are contagious and the ulceration of the *os* is contagious because the women are prostitutes, and are out plying their trade.[13]

Sloggett also presented evidence to the Commission that suggested that the contagiousness of prostitutes was dependent on their behaviour. He instructed the Commission that certain discharges could alter their character, depending on the behaviour of the patient. '[I]n older prostitutes,' he stated, 'these discharges very rapidly subside, or rather the character of the discharge becomes rapidly altered, and from being muco-purulent becomes white and apparently innocuous'. That is, the discharge becomes as harmless as a discharge from a modest woman. What is interesting here is that what alters the nature of the discharge is not the treatment that prostitutes receive in hospital but the enforced modification of their behaviour. In Sloggett's view 'the absence from drink, the absence from sexual excitement alone, with the rest and cleanliness which they get in hospital . . . will entirely alter the character of these discharges'. Moreover, he suggested that the longer this modified behaviour is enforced the less infectious the discharge becomes.[14]

In effect, the witness was suggesting that it was the pathological behaviour of prostitutes that made them infectious. The notion that sexual excitement caused ordinary discharges to become morbid relates to the discussion of the natural sexual anaesthesia of 'pure' women espoused with hysterical commitment by doctors such as Acton. Mr Berkeley Hill, Assistant-Surgeon to University College and an ardent Extensionist, expressed a similar sentiment later in the inquiry when he stated that he thought it very likely that women who were in the habit of 'prostituting their bodies' were more susceptible to disease 'because they must have more constant excitement of those organs, they are in an *unnatural state*'.[15] Such comments reflect the idea that it is not constant exposure to men possibly infected with such ailments that increases the susceptibility of prostitutes to the disease but their supposed state of constant sexual excitement.

Clearly, the concern about unnatural discharges here relates to the fear and loathing those medical authorities felt about natural female sexual secretions.

It was not only the discharges of prostitutes but any abnormality in the vagina of the prostitute which these doctors treated with suspicion. For instance, Mr Pickthorn, Visiting Surgeon to the Devonport District, when questioned about distinguishing between ulcers of the cervix, uterine discharges and discharges consequent on venereal disease, answered that he looked on 'all ulcerations of the genitals in prostitutes, [and] women having indiscriminate intercourse, as dangerous . . . whether they are virulent or not'. He qualified this statement, claiming that in modest women there were ulcerations and discharges that were not dangerous, but he stated, 'no man will dare to say that any ulceration in a prostitute is safe, or that those who consort with her would be safe'. He concluded, '*I want to separate prostitutes from other women.*'[16] Mr Christopher Bulteel, Surgeon to the Royal Albert Hospital Devonport, dismissed the suggestion that confusion over whether a sore was infecting or non-infecting would affect the detention or non-detention of prostitutes. He replied with alarming candour that such would not be the case 'because we regard them all as contagious'.[17]

While these surgeons put forward very strident opinions regarding their knowledge of the infectiousness of prostitutes, it is almost certain that they spent very little time actually examining the bodies of the women in their care. In his letter to the Admiralty, Sloggett admitted that Visiting Surgeons were rather lax in their use of the speculum and from other evidence it appears that women received little more than cursory attention from the medical staff. This is in keeping with other reports on the medical inspection of prostitutes throughout Europe. In his mammoth study of European prostitution, the reformer Abraham Flexner reported that the medical inspection of prostitutes was so haphazard that it had 'less effect in reducing disease than a rainy night or a spurt of police activity'.[18]

Of all the government surgeons questioned before the Commission only one, Mr Sedley Wolverstan, ex-Surgeon to the Royal Albert Hospital Devonport, objected to this reasoning. He complained that the 'fact of a woman being a prostitute' was being taken as evidence that her disease was 'contagious'.[19] This statement was in keeping with evidence given by doctors who were not in the service of the government. Mr James Lane, FRCS and Senior Surgeon to the London Lock Hospital, contradicted much of the evidence provided by the government surgeons by stating that he could not tell 'from a woman's discharges whether she [was] a respectable woman or a prostitute'.[20] Dr Routh, a physician in private practice in London, claimed that it was very likely that confusion between gonorrhoea and vaginitis could lead to the false detention of prostitutes. He told the Commissioners

> where there is a slight excoriation or vaginitis present you might have the most virtuous woman, one's own wife, for instance affected with a disease that would be capable of producing disease. As a medical man seeing her although diseased, would know she was perfectly pure, but a prostitute might be similarly affected, and unfairly sent to hospital.[21]

These doctors questioned the belief that formed the basic premise of the CD Acts – the belief that the body of a prostitute was substantively different from that of a modest woman. Most doctors working with prostitutes under the Acts accepted this without question and it supported their righteous belief that they could and should detain prostitutes. It was not only vaginal abnormalities that made prostitutes pathological. Other sexually related functions such as menstruation and pregnancy were said to occur differently in prostitutes. Dr John Coleman Barr, Surgeon to the Lock Hospital at Aldershot, defended the practice of detaining menstruating women because prostitutes menstruated for a longer period than virtuous women.[22] Mr W. Square, Surgeon at Plymouth, claimed that very few children were born to prostitutes as 'continual prostitution caused abortion about the third month'.[23]

Syphilis could, of course, be held responsible for this. Square, however, made the distinction between prostitutes and other women with syphilis, claiming that prostitutes miscarry only in the second or third month. Maternity was considered the supreme role of women and prostitutes who were often sterile and generally characterized as lacking in maternal feeling placed themselves outside the only truly acceptable role for women. In the 1840s it had been claimed that only one in fifty prostitutes bore children and then they were usually small and puny.[24] This sterility was of course generally caused by venereal infections, a fact not unknown to the medical profession of the time; however, medical authorities found it was easier to explain women's recourse to prostitution as a desire to eschew maternity than to acknowledge the real cause of their infertility. The idea that prostitutes were infertile also related to the notion that commercial sex was necessarily 'unproductive'. In Thomas Laqueur's terms, the barren prostitute represented 'a confusion between the dangerously asocial world of commercial exchange and the healthy social world of married love'.[25]

While those who defended regulation were intent on showing how physically different prostitutes were from 'normal women' they were, at the same time, very keen to display how the Acts lessened this distinction by changing the external appearance of these women. One of the most praised features of the Acts was the marked change in the appearance of prostitutes in the streets. All those witnesses in favour of the Acts stressed that regulation had caused prostitutes to appear in the streets clean, free from vermin and in respectable garb. William Wakeford, the Superintendent of Metropolitan Police, instructed the Commission that before the Acts prostitutes in his district 'were in the most miserable and abandoned condition. They herded together in miserable apartments in large numbers; they were without food, and they were covered with dirt and vermin.' Following the implementation of the Acts the same women appeared 'relatively well clothed, and well fed, and live in decent places, and are certainly now as a rule . . . in their persons, cleaner than the class of honest people from which they come'.[26] Mr Miller, an undertaker from Portsmouth, told a similar tale. Before the Acts he said

> you could see the women walking about like ghosts, one bloated out with dropsy, and another you could look through, with her nose gone and her features blotched all over in a way to make you shudder to look at them.

With the beginning of regulation he described these women as 'strong healthy looking girls'. He continued

> The women use soap and water now and wash themselves and keep decent in their dress. They have bonnets and shawls and I notice when they go to hospital they are always dressed decently as the wives of working men would be, and a casual stranger would not observe the difference. Of course, I know them.[27]

Some attributed this reversal to the fact that these prostitutes had to go through the streets in daylight to be examined. Others suggested that the process of examination instilled in these prostitutes a sense of self-respect and a desire to be clean. Often this change was expressed in terms of a cure. Dr F. Row, surgeon in charge of the Lock wards in the Royal Albert Hospital, stated that before the Acts prostitution was rampant. But under the Acts he claimed 'that is now cured; it [prostitution] does not present itself in its loathsome and degrading form as it did before'.[28]

Inculcating prostitutes with the bourgeois values of cleanliness and respectable dress was seen by those in favour of the Acts as a way of reducing the threat posed by prostitution. Medical authorities claimed that the new clean, well fed and healthy prostitutes were less likely to spread disease and less likely to suffer from the worse forms of syphilis. Implicit in the desire to see prostitutes become cleanly and respectable was the belief that the conditions engendered by poverty were in some sense morally contagious. Syphilis was considered a disease that positively festered under certain conditions. The most decrepit and destitute prostitutes had always been considered to be the most potent carriers of disease. Rather than suggesting that the disease was exacerbated by poor nutrition, poor working conditions and bad housing, it was implied that poverty necessarily meant immorality and the greater the poverty the greater the immorality and the greater the subsequent disease. By this logic, if the visible symptoms of poverty were reduced, the disease itself was reduced.

Witnesses before the Commission were at pains to assert that the improved appearance of the women did not mean improved business conditions. For instance, when Dr John Coleman Barr was quizzed on this point he stated that 'whenever the vice has increased the adjuncts to it increase; I believe if a woman has more men visit her and more money to spend, dirty habits will follow, some of the old habits will come on again'.[29] This rather dubious response was due to the fact that it was not the purpose of the Acts to be seen to increase immorality and facilitate the business of vice. The logic underpinning the statement, however, highlights the fact that morality and immorality were judged along a continuum of cleanliness and pollution; that is, the more depraved the woman is the more 'polluted' and 'polluting' she will be perceived to be.

For the Repealers the notion that regulation actually improved the prostitute was particularly galling. Rather than maintaining that this was an advantage of the system, those in favour of repeal argued that it heightened the degradation of these women. Far from lauding the alleged improvements in the conditions of prostitutes brought by regulation, Repealers claimed that inspection totally shattered any remnant of femininity. In their view, only the most degraded of women could go along with inspection. The prostitutes of France were often used as an example of the depths of degradation to which regulation allowed woman to sink. Daniel Cooper, Secretary of the London Rescue Society, claimed that even those English fallen women who frequented the Haymarket, spoke with 'utmost abhorrence of the greater degradation of the foreign women' who worked the same area. The Parisian *filles de joie* became merely animals after being subjected to inspection. Nor were Repealers impressed by the attempts of Extensionists to inculcate prostitutes with bourgeois values. Josephine Butler wrote with contempt of the French prostitutes who treat their 'fall' as a 'regular trade' and save money to retire in comfort. 'The English fallen woman,' she comforted her readers, 'rarely, if ever saves but rids herself as soon as possible of the ill-gotten gain as if it were contaminating, or its possession a curse.'[30]

Such statements were an interesting inversion of the logic of Extensionists. For Repealers, the salvation of prostitutes was seen to be dependent on their apparent hopelessness. For Extensionists, however, the Acts succeeded by embourgeoisifying the prostitute. That is not to say that these views were necessarily oppositional, as each was dependent on the idea of the prostitute as a pathological entity. The Report of the Royal Commission reflected these ambiguities. Both Repealers and Extensionists believed that they had successfully argued their case, but in effect they had only served to confuse the Commissioners. In addition to the main report, seven minority reports with dissents and provisos were appended.[31] The government was loath to act upon the Report. The radical MP, A.J. Mundella, who served on the Royal Commission, failed three times in attempts to introduce a Repeal Bill during the Summer of 1871. In August of that year William Fowler, another commissioner, moved to remove the sum for the maintenance of the CD Police from the army estimates, arguing that as sixteen of the commissioners were opposed to regulation there were no grounds for continuing to maintain the police. This attempt proved to be unsuccessful.

In 1872 H.A. Bruce, the Home Secretary, introduced a Bill that was intended to supersede the CD Acts, by prohibiting solicitation, and then examining all women prisoners. Any female prisoner found to be diseased was to be detained in the prison infirmary for up to nine months. The Bill also sought to raise the age of consent to fourteen, provide harsher penalties for harbouring girls under fifteen for the purposes of prostitution and summary convictions for brothelkeepers. Those involved in the Abolition movement were deeply divided over the Bill. Josephine Butler particularly objected to the Bill because despite its abolitionist intent the principle upon which the Act was based was still rooted in the double standard of morality. 'It was impossible,' she said, 'for us to accept a measure which had at the heart of it the very principle which we had determined to get rid of.'[32] So despite much opposition the LNA stood firm against the Bill. The Bill, however, was never passed.

The primary thrust of the Repeal movement had up until this point been to attack the immoral principle upon which the Acts were based. Little attention was paid to the practical workings of the Acts in terms of their ability to prevent the spread of venereal disease. Josephine Butler expressed the sentiments of many Repealers when she told the Royal Commission,

I know scarcely anything of the garrison towns . . . of the operations of the Acts I neither can nor will speak, and I must decline to do so because I have no interest in the operation of the Acts. It is nothing to me whether they operate well or ill, but I will tell you what you wish to know as to my view of the principle of the Acts.[33]

This was not the case for the opposition, who were quick to pick up on the weaknesses in the Repeal movement. During 1872, H.A. Bruce was bombarded with petitions from doctors in favour of the Acts. Extensionists, however, saw that it was necessary to present an argument to the government that stressed both the sanitary and moral advantages they believed were produced by the Acts. One petition to the Home Secretary was signed by some 2,500 doctors, including the illustrious names of William Jenner, Sir James Paget and Erasmus Wilson. In this letter they reminded the Secretary of State of the supposed benefits attributed to the Acts and defended themselves against charges of immorality:

> [I]f then Sir, we are warranted by recorded facts in our belief that the temporary seclusion of these diseased women in a more healthy, moral atmosphere has been found to contribute in no unimportant proportion to them to their restitution to the paths of virtue; if both physically and morally, they have been raised in the scale of humanity, we trust you will not listen to a factitious opposition founded on a most imperfect knowledge of the character and altered nature of these women and the extent of the evils to be remedied.[34]

At this stage Repealers chose not to enter into that debate, preferring to induce the Liberal Party into reform by bringing pressure to bear on MPs and candidates. The failure of the Liberal Party to win government in early 1874, however, was also a sound defeat for Repealers. During the period of Conservative government the Repealers did not become inactive, but considerable effort was diverted into the campaign to end regulation abroad.

5 The New Campaign

Following the failure of the Royal Commission to recommend the repeal of the Contagious Diseases Acts there were some within the Repeal movement who believed that the campaign should be put on a more scientific footing. In late 1874 the National Medical Association for the Repeal of the Contagious Diseases Acts (NMA) was instituted under the leadership of the Liverpool consultant, John Birkbeck Nevins. The NMA published its own journal, the *Medical Enquirer*, in an attempt to redress the medical press's regulationist bias. Historians of the CD Acts have tended to dismiss the significance of the NMA. Recent studies of the Acts have tended to concentrate on the influence of social puritanism on the campaign for Repeal. This has meant that the Repeal campaign is conflated with other social purity campaigns, such as the raising of the age of consent. As a result, opponents of the Acts have been characterized as narrow-minded and prudish and their actions have been seen as restricting the liberty of the working-class woman. The scandalous impact of other social purity campaigns has meant that the discussion of the medical campaign for repeal is generally ignored.[1]

Yet the evidence collected by Nevins and his colleagues was to become perhaps the most effective defence against the Acts that the Repeal movement put forward. Those doctors who opposed the Acts cannot be categorized merely as social puritans. As Sandra Holton has argued, medical Repealers advocated personal rights as key to government and social progress. They opposed the Acts on the grounds that such legislation infringed the liberty of the subject and were greatly concerned with the extension of state powers in medical matters.[2]

In 1879 the Conservative Government created a Select Committee to examine the operations of the Acts. James Stansfeld and Harcourt Johnstone, two of the Repeal movement's most enlightened members, were appointed to the Committee which began to meet in July 1879. The official medical evidence supporting the Acts was first to be heard before the Committee. The case put before the Committee was weak. The first witness, Sir William Mure Muir, Director-General of the Army Medical Department, said much that contradicted the official line which insisted that venereal rates in the army had declined since the implementation of the Acts. The most damage was done by Muir's claim that there had been no significant decline in the rates of secondary syphilis and that gonorrhoea had only begun to decline since 1873 – the year of Lord Cardwell's Order regarding the stoppage of pay for soldiers sick with venereal disease.

The question of pay stoppage for venereal disease had vexed the army since 1862. In that year, the Report of the Committee upon Venereal Disease in the Army and Navy, had agreed that it was unfair to punish a soldier or sailor for contracting the disease, but suggested that they should be punished for concealing it. In 1867, another Committee recommended that the hospital stoppage should be reduced from 10 shillings to 7 shillings. At the same time it examined the possibility of retaining the higher stoppage as a maximum to be applied in the case of soldiers in hospital 'for diseases directly traceable to their own vice'.[3] This suggestion was, however, rejected. In 1873, Lord Cardwell reduced the hospital pay stoppage from 10 shillings to 8 shillings. For men with venereal disease, however, he insisted, '[W]here it is reported upon medical authority that the soldier is in hospital from causes for which his own conduct is responsible, we intend to stop his whole pay, not merely a portion of it'.[4]

This Order was the subject of much controversy. Many argued that it would simply lead to concealment of the disease. In effect, its underlying intention was in direct opposition to the workings of the Acts. That it could and did lead to concealment and subsequent lack of treatment was only one factor of concern. The Acts were based upon the assumption that sexual activity was essential for the well-being of the soldier; it was the role of the State therefore to make such activity as safe as possible. Lord Cardwell's Order, however, suggested that abstinence was the best prophylactic. This was at odds with the widely held idea that the State should be responsible for providing disease-free prostitutes for the armed forces.

Muir believed that the 1873 Order had led to a substantial amount of concealment of the disease, which in turn increased both the extent and severity of the secondary symptoms of the disease. He believed that to attribute the decline in primary sores and gonorrhoea after 1873 to the Acts was illusory. He maintained that any decline could be put down to concealment. The lack of decline in the rate of secondary syphilis he believed confirmed this. Unlike his colleagues at the 1871 Royal Commission, Muir claimed that it was difficult to distinguish between infecting sores (syphilitic sores) and non-infecting sores (non-specific sores without constitutional symptoms).[5] This meant that he assumed that doctors who diagnosed troops with syphilis often diagnosed incorrectly. This made a difference before the stoppage of payment as there was no penalty to the troops if the disease was incorrectly diagnosed. Following the 1873 Order, however, men with the disease would be loath to come forward unless it was absolutely necessary. Thus those afflicted with non-infecting sores or mild gonorrhoea would not appear on the sick-lists as they would recover naturally or at least become asymptomatic, whereas men with syphilis would continue to show up in the lists for constitutional syphilis.

Generally, Muir's testimony was muddled due to the fact that if he really believed in the negative effect of Lord Cardwell's Order it was impossible to provide a cogent argument for why the Acts should continue. The evidence of the Surgeon-General Mr Lawson was also very contradictory; he was, however, more adamant about the benefits of the Acts than Sir William Muir. Although Lawson claimed to have no practical experience of the effect of Lord Cardwell's Order, like Muir he believed that it led to concealment which in turn increased the rates of constitutional syphilis. In the subjected district of Aldershot, for instance, in the six years succeeding the Order, the rates of constitutional syphilis remained exactly the same amongst enlisted troops.

In effect, this was suggesting that the CD Acts were futile when it came to preventing the spread of real syphilis. Constitutional syphilis was the only true sign of syphilitic infection. Repealers alleged that decline in primary syphilis and gonorrhoea should be attributed to a variety of factors apart from the Acts, especially the much vaunted improvements in cleanliness of both troops and prostitutes. While it was always accepted that primary sores were no real indication of syphilis, supporters of regulation had generally assumed that all signs of disease in prostitutes meant that they were contagious. This was also true of doctors in military hospitals, where both types of sores were treated under the heading of 'primary sores'. The practice of the Acts would have probably caused the decline in non-infecting sores but it was very unlikely that true syphilis would 'cure' itself.[6] This would mean that the rates of constitutional syphilis in the armed forces would remain steady. This hinted at the most profound argument against regulation which was that, despite all these prophylactic measures, medical authorities could not really guarantee either protection or cure.

It was this line of questioning that was stressed by James Stansfeld and Sir Harcourt Johnstone, the Repealers on the Committee. The lack of interest in the medical side of the Act that the Repeal movement had shown in the early days of the campaign had meant that this Committee was the first real opportunity for Repealers to challenge the medical authority upon which the Acts were premised. By forcing government officials to examine their own statistics, Repealers were shifting the argument away from the idea that the prostitute was necessarily a pathological creature and forcing those in favour of the Acts to defend their rather dubious medical conclusions.[7] Once the argument moved away from the idea that prostitution and disease were synonymous, it became impossible for the Acts to be maintained on the grounds that they prevented the spread of disease.

This became most conspicuous in the evidence put forward by Dr John Coleman Barr. As Surgeon to the Lock Hospital at Aldershot, Barr had testified in favour of the Acts before the 1871 Royal Commission and in 1878 he remained a staunch supporter. Barr's evidence not only showed up the questionable wisdom by which the Acts were justified but his testimony suggested that it was impossible for the Acts to function effectively if all that was said in their defence was true. Like other Government witnesses, Barr conceded that the 1873 Order had affected the workings of the Acts but, unlike Sir William Muir, he failed to acknowledge that there was any difficulty in discovering the disease in women. He rejected any suggestion that surgeons in the government Lock Hospitals would either fail to detect infection or would wrongly diagnose the disease when it was non-existent.[8]

Barr upheld many of the conclusions of the Skey Committee, most especially the idea that a woman might pass on the disease without in fact having it herself.[9] This notion had existed since men began to speculate on the spread of syphilis. Originally it related to the idea that if a woman had intercourse with two men in quick succession, the first man would deposit the infection into the woman and the second man could withdraw it from her. The second man would become infected while the woman remained free of disease. Later authorities tended to dismiss this notion and favoured the idea that women actually created disease within themselves. The Skey Committee reported that women could spontaneously generate both gonorrhoea, simple sores and possibly even syphilis, and that they could transmit the disease without themselves being prior victims to the disease. Opinions proffered at the 1871 Royal Commission did not challenge these conclusions.

Barr did not entirely reject the idea that women could pass on venereal disease without having it themselves: he related it back to the older idea of 'mediate contagion'. He told the committee that gonorrhoea, syphilis and soft sores could 'all be propagated' while the 'woman herself remain[ed] free'. He claimed this phenomenon to be the result of 'contagious matter that she retains within her as the result of intercourse with a diseased man'.[10] Barr complained that this problem of 'mediate contagion' corresponded to the success of the Acts in diminishing the number of women practising prostitution. This, he said, meant that the same number of men were forced to use an ever-declining number of prostitutes. While he was keen to suggest that he was not in favour of increasing the number of prostitutes in order to stem the spread of the disease, he confessed that from a sanitary perspective the danger of infection was decreased if more prostitutes were available. While Barr was appearing to move away from the idea that women created the disease within themselves, his theories of 'mediate contagion' were not in fact very different from the ideas expressed in the 1860s by authorities such as Holmes Coote and Dr Gordon. Both argued that gonorrhoea and syphilis were 'coexistent with promiscuous sexual intercourse . . . *i.e.*, where one woman receives several men'.[11] While Barr was implying that the disease was simply transferred from the woman to the man without her becoming diseased, the suggestion of inherent disease within the female remained.

Barr revealed to the Committee that the number of diseased women admitted to the Aldershot Lock Hospital had increased since 1870, while the number of women practising prostitution in the area had decreased. This was the paradox of the Acts. If it was true that the Acts were successful in reducing the number of prostitutes in subjected areas, it must also be true that they were unsuccessful because this created more disease. Barr acknowledged that part of the problem was the influx of diseased troops to the subjected districts but he would not concede that, without similar restrictions placed on diseased troops, it was impossible by this means to reduce the spread of venereal disease.[12] When questioned about the futility of only examining women, his answer obscured the issue by merely restating the rationale of the Acts:

> There is no analogy between the two [sexes]. A woman gets her living by it. She is bound, if she adopts prostitution as a living, to keep her person clean, and submit to proper inspection, for if she is diseased, more mischief is propagated by one woman than could be by 100 different men.[13]

As Barr continued with his evidence, his attempts to conceal this paradox became more desperate. For instance, when asked whether he believed that the Acts, by making prostitutes 'more attractive', tended to increase the amount of sexual intercourse, his reply has the tone of a man grasping at straws:

> I do not believe that the more attractive condition of the woman makes her more sought after by the soldiers. I do not for one moment believe it. Another point is, that often these men are drunk when they are with prostitutes, and there is a certain class of soldiers who, instead of picking out such women as you refer to, would select the very dirtiest tramp that comes along the road.[14]

It is difficult to conceive how Barr thought this was a recommendation of the Acts. If soldiers were inclined to solicit the 'dirtiest tramp[s] that came along the road' surely this attested to the pointlessness of regulation. Yet Barr continued claiming that if the Acts were repealed and the women were rendered less attractive that intercourse would, in fact, increase. 'I should think', he said, 'that it would decidedly increase'. He went on, oblivious to any contradictions in his statements:

> The women having been freed from legal control, taken away from the influence of the hospital, and those connected with the carrying out of the Acts, would simply return to the old state of affairs; the old want of shame, the old filthy conditions, and the wholesale prostitution, and the state of things would be as bad or worse than ever.[15]

Far from confirming the success of the Acts, Barr's evidence was a testament to their failure. His answer to James Stansfeld on the question of the declining number of prostitutes can be read as an admission of this failure. He told Stansfeld that while he did not want to see an increase in prostitution he advised that 'the people who take an interest in the soldier should do all that they possibly can to lessen the amount of unrestrained sexual feeling in them. Let them know that by yielding to amorous propensities among a few, they are likely to be diseased.'[16]

The other witnesses before this sitting of the Committee did little to alleviate any of the damage Barr had done. Surgeon-Major Frederick Robinson of the Scots Fusilier Guards and Arthur B. Myers, Surgeon to the Coldstream Guards, spoke only of their experiences within their own regiments and offered little that could defend regulation.

Not surprisingly, those in Repeal circles were delighted with the course of the Committee. In March 1880 the Repeal Campaign's chief medical witness, John Birbeck Nevins, was called before the Committee. During the course of the campaign Nevins had become invaluable to Repealers. As President of the NMA Nevins had busied himself issuing cost analyses of the Acts and refuting the statistical reports of the government. He had published a book in 1874, *Statement upon which the CD Acts are Opposed*, laying down his medical arguments against the system. Although his journal the *Medical Enquirer* was not a financially successful venture, the evidence that he had collected in his years as editor would seriously help to damage the case for regulation.[17]

Nevins claimed that the supposed success of the Acts in reducing the levels of venereal disease in the armed forces was based on false statistics. He had two major complaints against the regulation. First, he did not accept that the Acts were responsible for the diminution of syphilis. But, more importantly, he challenged the validity of army statistics that showed this decline because they made no differentiation between non-infecting and infecting sores. Nevins believed that the decline in syphilis attributed to the successful working of the Acts had begun as a natural decline in the disease before the Acts were implemented.

The decline in syphilis amongst troops had begun to show up in army returns from 1860, some four years before the first Act was passed, and there was evidence to suggest that it had been declining in both the military and civil population since the 1850s. Moreover, between 1870 and 1877 the proportion of men constantly in hospital with primary sores was reduced in greater proportion at the unsubjected rather than at the subjected stations.[18] A natural decline in syphilis continued until after the Second World War, only punctuated by transitory increases of almost epidemic proportions during times of war, political unrest and movements of population.[19] In retrospect it is easy to see why at this time there appeared to be a reduction in the rates of syphilis. Part of this decline can be directly attributed to improvements in the treatment of syphilis, especially the decreasing importance of 'heroic treatments'. The drop in the status of mercury as a cure, for instance, almost certainly aided this apparent reduction. By the 1860s doctors were more restrained in their use of mercury for all types of venereal sores and so subsequently minor sores would not necessarily develop into worse ailments that could be confused with syphilis. Syphilization, which became quite popular in certain European countries in the 1850s, was also lapsing into disuse. Syphilization was based on the idea that soft sores were indicative of a mild dose of syphilis. Treatment by syphilization involved injecting healthy subjects with pus from a soft chancre in order that they might become immune to the disease. Dr Auzias-Turenne was its main advocate in France and it was widely practised in Piedmont under Dr Sperino and in Christiania (Norway) under Dr Boeck. Didot, a Belgian physician, claimed before the Belgian Academy of Medicine that he had used syphilization to arrest chancre in early 1852.[20] In that same year it was condemned as dangerous by the Imperial Academy of Medicine in France. The Skey Committee heard evidence from Dr Boeck on his experiences in Norway and Dr Patrick Heron Watson, Surgeon to the Royal Infirmary, spoke glowingly of his experiences of the practice in England. Other doctors such as William Acton claimed that they had used inoculation as a practice but had gone on to other things.[21] The Committee Report decided that it was 'repugnant to the habits and feelings of the profession' in Great Britain, but not before suggesting that it should be tested on men in the army.[22] Fortunately, this was not taken up and by the 1870s such practices were dying out in Great

Britain. It is worth noting, however, that Christiania was reported by Nevins to have the highest rate of patients in hospital beds (24.9 per cent) with syphilis among all the areas he surveyed.[23]

The medical press in Great Britain reacted to Nevins' testimony with great hostility. Both the *British Medical Journal* and *The Lancet* were clearly in favour of the maintenance of the Acts and unblushingly supported all that was said by pro-CD Acts witnesses. The *British Medical Journal* claimed that the evidence presented by Sir William Muir, Inspector General Lawson and Barr 'showed conclusively that the Acts had brought in immense improvements to the health and efficiency of soldiers in protected areas'.[24] In February 1880, *The Lancet* reported that the 'evidence in support of the advantages of the Acts . . . is so sufficient, and the statistics are so convincing, that their repeal seems to us an impossibility.'[25] Clearly, Nevins' testimony came as a shock. Nevins' evidence was dismissed and his medical authority was called into question. The *British Medical Journal* wrote, 'This term "pseudo-syphilis" used by Dr Nevins, we do not remember to have seen in any standard work on venereal diseases; and indeed, Dr Nevins' interpretation of the term is by no means clear, for he included in it what he called "dirt sores", whatever they may be.'[26] Ironically, they were also very sceptical about his claims of a general decline in the rates of syphilis.

Yet it would seem that Nevins was almost certainly correct. Moreover, the most significant cause of this decline was no doubt the fact that doctors had become more skilled in actual diagnosis. It was becoming apparent to many doctors since the eighteenth century that certain sores on the genitals were not syphilitic. By the 1850s, doctors had divided these sores into three main categories: local sores, soft sores and hard sores. Most doctors agreed that local sores were not syphilitic but there was considerable confusion as to whether both soft sores and hard sores were syphilitic. Again this confusion was referred to as the 'unity or duality of the virus theory'. The terms unity and duality alluded to the supposed identity or otherwise of the poison or virus causing them. Significantly, the only proof doctors had that any of these sores were not syphilitic was that they did not develop further syphilitic symptoms. Consequently, many doctors still considered any sore on the genitals as definitely contagious and more than probably syphilitic.

Philippe Ricord had long asserted that both types of sores were syphilitic. By the 1850s several medical practitioners in France had questioned this wisdom. In 1852 Leon Bassereau produced evidence that the soft chancre was different from the hard sore. Julius Bettinger and Rollet of Lyons followed suit in 1855 and 1858 respectively.[27] In 1858 Joseph Rollet also described a mixed chancre (*chancre mixe*) which he claimed to be made up of both viruses. The British medical profession however was unmoved by revelations in France and in the 1860s many doctors still clung to the idea of the unity of the virus theory.

The Skey Committee in 1867 attempted to clarify, with little success, what sores should actually be classified as syphilitic. The Report of the Committee stated that it was found that the local sore had 'nothing in common with the local products of syphilitic poison beyond its ulcerative action'.[28] It was generally agreed that the characteristics, form, progress and duration of the local sore were distinctly different from the syphilitic sore and therefore the Committee dismissed the notion that the local sore was derived from the same poison as the syphilitic sore. The Report recognized, however, that while the local sore might be innocuous in the female, any secretions it might give off 'could become a poison to the recipient', not however a syphilitic poison.[29]

The Committee rejected the possibility that the soft and hard sore were the results of two types of poison and opted for the unity of the virus theory. This meant little more than, regardless of how the sore was originally classified, if it resulted in secondary syphilis, it would be considered a syphilitic sore. At least, that was the general conclusion of the Committee. Several witnesses stated their belief that all venereal sores were produced by the one poison, referring to an absence of constitutional symptoms rather than absence of syphilitic poison.[30] One venereal specialist still confused the discussion of unity and duality of the virus with the old belief that gonorrhoea and syphilis were one and the same.[31]

While the Committee failed to offer any plausible diagnostic signs to distinguish between a local sore, a soft sore and a hard sore, its Report indicated an attempt by the medical profession to reduce the number of false diagnoses. The idea that local sores were not syphilitic would, of course, decrease the rates of syphilis. In practice, the way the Acts functioned went against the advice of the Skey Committee. All forms of sores on both soldiers and prostitutes were categorized under the heading primary sores. The government statistics showed a positive decline in men brought in with primary sores. Nevins maintained that this led to a false sense of security because their statistics included both infecting and non-infecting sores. He considered the decline in the number of primary sores to really be a decline in the rates of non-infecting sores. Rates of secondary syphilis had remained the same. Effectively, Nevins was claiming that doctors could only reduce the rates of local sores, while rates of the constitutional disease remained constant. The Acts therefore had made no impact on the spread of true syphilis.

A general election and a change in government put an end to Dr Nevins' testimony and the Committee did not begin hearing evidence again until 1881. The evidence of the pro-Repeal witnesses, Dr Routh, Dr Drysdale and Professor Lee, heard before the new Committee, was to make explicit Nevins' case against the Acts. Dr Routh took up where Nevins had left off. Like Nevins he showed that there had been a natural decline in the rate of syphilis before the Acts had been established. Moreover, he showed that there had been no decline in gonorrhoea until Lord Cardwell's Order in 1873. In fact, until 1873 the average rates of admission for gonorrhoea in subjected districts was higher than the rates in unprotected districts. Any decline in the rates of gonorrhoea after 1873, he claimed, could thus only be attributed to concealment.[32]

Routh also turned the government's evidence against itself. He took up Barr's point that the reduction in the number of prostitutes in any one district must necessarily result in an increase of disease.[33] Unlike Barr, however, he stated that he thought the improved conditions for the prostitutes fostered by the system meant that they had a more extensive clientele and this increased the hygienic risk they posed. Routh was the first Repeal witness to publicly oppose the Acts on the grounds that 'increased sexual indulgence' was in and of itself dangerous to the state of the army. Repealers had long complained that the Acts endangered the moral health of the soldier and argued that the protection against venereal disease by the Acts was perfectly illusory. Routh, however, was arguing that promiscuous sexual intercourse weakened the physique of the soldier, leaving him debilitated and enervated. He told the Committee:

> [T]he more nations are allowed to indulge in sexual debauch the worse soldiers they become, and therefore I look upon it as an intense calamity to this country that we are encouraging soldiers to debauch themselves more and more. . . . We know in private practice that a man who is a rake has no physical power, and these Acts, I think, have a tendency to pervert our soldiers in that direction.[34]

The need for sexual intercourse amongst unmarried men had often been used to justify the idea that prostitution was an inevitable factor of modern society. Yet such an idea did not go entirely unquestioned. It was also argued that non-procreative sexual activity could be physically harmful to men. Supporters of regulation argued that measures such as the CD Acts were necessary to ensure the health of the army. They claimed that the unvaried diet, the monotony of barracks life and the tedium of garrison duty drove soldiers into 'intemperance and debauchery'.[35] They reasoned that the soldier must be protected from the consequences of this artificial lifestyle. Attempts to improve the morality of the standing army were treated with disdain by regulationists. Indeed, most regulationists and many army officers held that it was not possible or desirable to make the soldier 'moral'.[36]

Nor did those in favour of the Acts see such measures as immoral. *The Lancet* stated bluntly that 'We have no more belief that men are made moral by the fostering of dirt and diseases.'[37] Ignoring the claim that regulation involved the state sanction of vice, supporters of the Acts relied on the belief that the 'curative functions of medicine provided their own *moral* guarantee'.[38] By the 1880s, however, many of those men sympathetic to regulation were more cautious in their declarations about the morality of the soldier. In part this related to the fact that the compulsory inspection of prostitutes had not reduced the likelihood of catching venereal disease, as Barr's evidence had shown. But it also related to changing perceptions of masculinity and militarism. In the 1850s British soldiers were understood to be 'helplessly subjected to their irrepressible licentious natures'.[39] The army's demand for celibacy and middle-class notions of pre-marital continence were seen as at odds with the prevalent ideas on working men's sexuality, which equated sexual promiscuity with manliness.[40] Yet, by the end of the nineteenth century, the traditional belief that profligacy was fundamental to the military lifestyle was being called into question. Contesting discourses of masculinity were developing. Manliness was increasingly being equated with self-control, freedom from sexual passion and the sublimation of sensuality into leadership of society and nation.[41] These competing discourses of masculinity came into direct conflict over the CD Acts. Routh's statements about nationalism and sexuality clearly illustrate the growing importance of the healthy male body to the nation.

Perhaps Routh's most important contribution to the Repeal argument was his evidence about the inability of doctors to correctly diagnose syphilis. Using information gleaned from the most recent studies on syphilis at the time, as well as evidence put forward at the government enquiries into the Acts, Routh showed that doctors both in favour and against the Acts experienced considerable difficulty in diagnosing primary syphilis. Routh maintained that in women the first signs of syphilis were often too minute, painless and ill-defined for doctors to observe and so, consequently, such cases were ignored while women with non-infecting sores which were frequently large and painful were detained.[42] This of course defeated the purpose of the Acts because it meant that women with syphilis could continue to infect men until the secondary symptoms of the disease developed while women without syphilis were wrongfully interned. It also meant that doctors at government Lock Hospitals experienced a false sense of their own ability to cure syphilis. This was not a point taken up by Routh, who maintained that if primary syphilis was properly cured no secondary syphilis would come. But it was taken up by subsequent Repeal witnesses.

Dr Drysdale, Senior Physician at the Metropolitan Free Hospital, continued Routh's line of attack when called before the Committee. Like his colleagues, Drysdale challenged the Army Medical Report's classification of the venereal diseases. He claimed that they should be divided into four groups; gonorrhoea, true primary syphilis, soft sore and a mixed sore. Drysdale insisted that primary syphilis was always followed by constitutional syphilis and that there was no such thing as syphilis without the 'constitutional derangement'.[43] Such revelations were not new, but Drysdale continued, arguing that many doctors remained puzzled over the question of 'pseudo-primary syphilis' or chancroid. The Skey Committee had denied that the 'soft sore' or chancroid was different from syphilis. In France, however, medical authorities had gradually come to recognize this distinction, especially after Ricord recanted his original position as a unicist in the late 1850s. In Britain too, many doctors had become convinced that there was a duality of the viruses. Drysdale went one step further than Routh by claiming that it was the soft sores that doctors could cure, not syphilis. He stated that regardless of treatment it was impossible that a hard sore should not be followed by constitutional syphilis. Drysdale was not at all convinced of his profession's ability to 'cure' syphilis. He told the Committee that he 'would not be in the least surprised to see' any patient that he had treated for syphilis 'ten years afterwards with paralysis. . . . Syphilis is so uncertain that if you have the slightest attack of it, it may kill you in the long run. If a person has had syphilis at the age of 18, they may die of it when they are 60.'[44]

Drysdale was suggesting that what doctors at government Lock Hospitals were successful at treating were non-infecting local sores and chancroid. Both these diseases could be said to have declined during the course of the Acts. Syphilis, he claimed, could not be cured and this was indicated by the fact that rates of secondary syphilis remained steady throughout the period.[45] He was, of course, correct. Not until the advent of penicillin in the 1940s did doctors have a safe and reliable cure for syphilis. Local sores and chancroid could and did respond to treatment.[46] Moreover, local sores were often avoided by simple practices such as washing with soap and water or wearing clean clothes and thus declined as a result of the improved facilities offered to soldiers and prostitutes under the Acts.[47]

Professor Henry Lee, the Repealers' next witness, told the Committee that he thought that such improvements could be attributed to the fact that the people were 'less filthy' and that the lower class of women was 'more civilized'. 'Civilization,' he claimed, 'was making inroads in all directions, even amongst the poorest, and the consequence is, you have not the amount of soft sores you used to have; they are caused by great want of care and by living pell-mell.'[48] Lee's evidence added further substance to Drysdale's argument by claiming that true syphilis did not often manifest itself by a repetition of primary and secondary sores. The patient could remain contagious but his symptoms would be latent. Non-syphilitic sores on the other hand, he argued, may be constantly reproduced. This led him to surmise that most of the women treated in government Lock Hospitals were suffering from non-syphilitic sores. Drysdale had contended that in the early stages of syphilis the hard sore would not in any way impede a prostitute in her trade, whereas a soft sore was extremely painful and would necessitate treatment. This meant that when a woman was most highly contagious her condition was most easily overlooked.

The evidence of the pro-Repeal doctors caught the government unawares. If their arguments were to be believed, there was little point in continuing the system. From the onset of the Committee the government's medical officials had made a very poor showing. When Mr James Lane took the stand this tradition was continued. Mr Lane was the Senior Surgeon at the London Lock Hospital and he had given evidence before the Skey Committee and the 1868 Select Committee. Lane's job was to refute the evidence of the Repeal doctors and he did so even at the cost of ignoring much of what had been shown to be standard medical opinion at the time. Lane was steadfast in his belief that syphilis could be cured and maintained that if it was picked up early enough no secondary symptoms would develop. He denied that soft sores never developed into secondary syphilis and he entirely discounted the possibility of a mixed chancre. He attempted to undermine the evidence of Repeal doctors by claiming that their emphasis on the difference between soft and hard sores was entirely incorrect. He asserted that 'medical opinion in favour of the unity of the venereal poison was on the whole increasing'.[49] He also attempted to salvage the damage done by Dr Barr with his theories of 'mediate contagion'. While he conceded that in areas where there was a decline in prostitution some prostitutes would have intercourse with up to a dozen men a night, he insisted that 'mediate contagion' was very unlikely. He told the committee that

a woman does not have connection with one man, and with another man five minutes afterwards. There is almost always an interval of time elapsing, and during that time she will in all probability either wash

herself or wipe herself, and wipe this contagious matter away, because
as I have said before, it is almost always wiped off and left about the
external parts of the female.[50]

Again it is difficult to see how Lane thought this might lower the incidence of contagion. It is interesting to note, however, the shift in the image
of the prostitute over time. In the 1850s the lack of hygiene amongst
prostitutes was being used in order to create legislation to prevent the
spread of syphilis; in the 1880s the cleanliness of prostitutes was being
used to defend it.

The medical press continued its tirade against the Repeal witnesses and
the evidence of Dr Routh, Dr Drysdale and Mr Lee was completely rejected. The evidence of James Lane, however, was taken as conclusive
proof that the CD Acts were a success. Clearly, however, there was concern that Extensionist witnesses had put on a bad showing. Reports in the
medical press began to stress the reformative qualities of the Acts, stating
explicitly that many prostitutes were saved as a direct result of the Acts.
The incidence of vice was said to be greatly reduced, as were the rates of
juvenile prostitution.[51] Arthur Cooper, a staunch supporter of the Acts, in
a review critical of the work done by the French reformer Yves Guyot,
wrote:

> For example, in his abstract of the CD Acts, M. Guyot omits altogether
> one of the most important and distinguishing provisions – namely that
> (Act of 1866, Sect. 12) 'A Hospital shall not be certified under the Act
> unless at the time of the granting of the certificate adequate provision
> is made for the religious instruction of the women therein detained
> under the Act.'[52]

Ironically, all such moral aspects of the Acts were implemented due to
pressure from Repealers.

The Majority Report of the Committee was written by Richard
O'Shaughnessy, who had replaced the Hon W.N. Massey, who had died,
as chairman in late 1881. The Report was a complete endorsement of the
Acts or, to use Paul McHugh's terms, 'a eulogy' to the Acts. The Report
totally discounted all the medical evidence provided by Repeal doctors
and ignored any statistical evidence that suggested that the Acts did not
diminish syphilis. It recommended that:

> The hygienic and other benefits conferred by the Acts in their present
> narrow application appear to your Committee to warrant the belief that
> if extended to the United Kingdom generally they would become still

more effective for the diminution of venereal disease and other beneficial purposes.[53]

A Minority Report drafted by Stansfeld and signed by six members of the
Committee condemned the Acts and 'found them deficient on every conceivable ground'.[54] For Repealers this was not considered a stalemate.
Schisms were developing in the Repeal camp. The question of whether to
treat the Liberal Party as friend or foe had vexed Repealers since the loss
of the general election in 1872. Many in the National Anti-Contagious
Diseases Association (also known as the National Association, or NA)
saw the Majority Report as a declaration of war and felt it was quite
appropriate to attack the government. Other campaigners, especially those
in the north, believed that if Repeal was to become a reality it was necessary to forge links with the Liberal Party and pressure MPs from within.
There was much discussion amongst provincial Repealers of developing a
Parliamentary Committee to enable them to work with the Liberal Party.
The National Association however were far from keen about this idea.
Eventually, a compromise was reached and the NA agreed to sponsor the
new body as its Parliamentary Committee. While provincial Repealers at
first accepted this proposal, they quickly regretted it. Led by Henry J.
Wilson, the Sheffield radical, another Committee was established and called
the Political Committee in order to distinguish it from the National Association's Parliamentary Committee. Wilson's Committee marked a change in
direction for the Repeal movement and it united Liberal Repealers in a
whole-hearted effort to swing the party organization against the Acts.[55]

Ultimately, this approach proved successful for Repealers. In April 1883,
the National Liberal Federation voted to support the Repeal of the Act;
later that month the government suspended the compulsory examination
clauses of the Acts. With compulsory examination abolished, it was generally conceded that the Acts were ineffective.[56] While this decision was
greeted warmly by Repealers, many doctors believed the results would be
disastrous. The *British Medical Journal* bemoaned the decision, claiming
'[the] over-eagerness to promote virtue by resolution of Parliament has
directly and scientifically spread contagion'.[57] In another article the *British
Medical Journal* stated that never 'was the inherent weakness of our party
system more lamentably perceptible than in this sacrifice of innocents to
the ignorant sentimentality of the friends of free trade in disease'.[58]

Following the suspension of the Acts, it was reported that the average
number of men in hospital had risen from around 100 to over 200. It was
also claimed that 'the type of disease' had 'a more obstinate nature than
before'.[59] Dr Alfred Cooper lamented the fact that the disease was again

becoming increasingly prevalent 'in consequence of the free license given to prostitutes to ply their trade in any public places they may select'.

> England deservedly has the credit of preserving syphilis and pheasants better than in any other country. The practical repeal of the Contagious Diseases Act recently, effected by a vote of the House of Commons in servile obedience to the demands of an ignorant and fanatical section of the populace, will no doubt further aid the spread of syphilis.[60]

The Daily Telegraph complained that 'it is not often that the mischievous consequences of the unregulated zeal on the part of would-be-reformers are so quickly and disastrously demonstrated.'[61]

Many doctors continued to lobby the government to reintroduce some system of compulsory regulation. Compulsion was seen as absolutely necessary to prevent both vice and disease. The *British Medical Journal* reported:

> without compulsory examination the Acts have no *raison d'être* . . . without compulsory examination the Acts are worse than useless. This has been abundantly proved by the results of the utterly absurd combination of voluntary admission with compulsory detention of women in hospital that is now in force.[62]

The Acts were finally repealed in 1886, but many within the medical profession and the armed services continued to demand their re-enactment. In British colonies such as Malta, India and Hong Kong a system of regulation and compulsory examination remained intact until the end of the century. The discovery that the gonococcus was the causative agent for gonorrhoea in 1879 had made little impact on the regulation debate. The discovery in 1906 that syphilis was caused by *Treponema pallidum* and the subsequent breakthroughs in treatment with the Wasserman Test and salvarsan (606) also failed to stop the demand for some form of regulation to be reimplemented. Major H.C. French, the War Office Specialist on Venereal Diseases, was at the forefront of this discussion. He wrote in 1907:

> [I]f we recognise the cardinal fact that prostitution has always existed and unfortunately must continue to do so for all time, since it is primarily dependent on poverty, it is then self-evident that to control disease which is the direct outcome of prostitution, it becomes necessary to more effectually control all *irreclaimable* persons, and to place restraint on the secret spread of disease by women who are known as *clandestines*.[63]

Yet the government was loath to reopen the issue of regulation. Another Royal Commission on Venereal Disease was appointed in 1913. While part of the function of this Commission was to examine the possibility of renewed state intervention, the government made efforts to distance the Commission from the question of regulation. The terms of reference of the Commission excluded any reconsideration of the Contagious Diseases Acts. It was appointed to

> inquire into the prevalence of Venereal Diseases in the United Kingdom, their effects upon the health of the community, and the means by which those effects can be alleviated or prevented, it being understood that no return of the policy or provisions of the Contagious Diseases Acts of 1864, 1866, or 1869 is to be regarded as falling within the scope of the inquiry.[64]

Many of the doctors interviewed before the Commission claimed that it was imperative that some form of compulsion be used to hospitalize prostitutes. Prostitution was said to be a most 'prolific source of syphilis'.[65] It was said to outweigh all other forms of immorality in its danger.[66] Compulsory examination of prostitutes was considered by many witnesses as the only viable solution to halt the spread of disease.

Historians such as Judith Walkowitz and Barry Smith have suggested that with the breakthroughs in medical science, such as the isolation of *Spirochaeta pallida* and the discovery of salvarsan or 606, the end of medical examination was inevitable.[67] Yet it would seem more accurate to say that the medical profession viewed such improvements in microbiology and pathology as ways of making regulation more successful. Medical men clung tenaciously to the idea of the prostitute's body as an infectious site and attempted to maintain control of this body, in spite of their increased knowledge regarding the aetiology of the disease and their growing power to cure it. It is necessary to view the Contagious Diseases Acts not as an aberration within medical and legal discourse, but rather as part of a continuum of oppressive legislation against women, that equated control of venereal disease with control of women.

PART III
The Question of Child Prostitution

6 Pathologizing Children

The question of child rape or 'seduction' was considered a crucial factor in the creation of prostitutes. Rescue workers claimed that most prostitutes had been seduced by the time they were sixteen. Josephine Butler maintained that if girls were prevented from 'falling' at such an early age, it was quite likely that they would not enter into prostitution. Without a recognition of the effects of the 'vice of men', Butler asserted that a 'permanent harlot class' would always be sustained.[1] It was argued that if the age of consent was raised to an age when girls could understand the implications of sexual activity, this would go a long way towards the prevention of prostitution.

This was, however, not the case. Legislators facilitated a system whereby the claims of reformers such as Butler were not only acknowledged to be true but defended as part of an acceptable sexual economy. A close examination of the debates regarding the raising of the age of consent in the 1880s indicates that men in Parliament were acting to protect what they considered were their sexual rights within this economy. The demands made by feminists and reformers regarding the protection of young girls were seen as a direct threat to male sexual privilege. The most common claim was that made by the Earl of Wemyss who asserted that if they raised the age of consent, they would drive professional prostitution from the streets, the consequence being that 'seduction would increase; and the evil when driven from the streets would find its way into private life'.[2] Implicit in such statements is the confirmation of reformers' claims that the supply of prostitutes was kept up by the seduction of young girls. Men such as the Earl of Wemyss considered that it was necessary to sacrifice the children of the working class to protect the virtue of middle-class homes. Some speakers were more blatant in their attempts to protect what they considered were their natural sexual rights. Indeed, Lord Oranmore begged the House of Lords to prevent the passing of such legislation so that these privileges could be handed down to future generations. He stated that he believed 'that there were very few of their lordships who had not, when young men, been guilty of immorality'. He hoped they would pause before passing a clause within the range of which their sons might come.[3]

The reluctance of Parliament to act to change the laws relating to child prostitution and age of consent coincided with a similar hesitancy to deal with such issues on the part of the medical and legal profession. A reading of the medical discourse on child rape demonstrates the disinclination of

the medical profession to accept the existence of child rape and consequently a failure to act to protect young girls. This lack of interest can be
attributed to ideas about venereal disease, particularly ideas about the
pathological female body. Cases of child rape reported in medical jurisprudence are particularly useful in revealing Victorian attitudes to child
sexuality. On one level, the suggestion of child rape created moral outrage
and great emphasis was placed on childhood purity and innocence. Yet,
when faced with the reality of child rape or prostitution, the moral outrage
was often directed onto the child victim. Any suggestion of corruption or
knowingness in the child made her suspect. This was particularly true in
the case of the child prostitute, who came to be seen as the demonic
antithesis of pre-pubescent innocence. The image of the naturally depraved
child fostered within the medico-legal literature pervaded all discussion of
child prostitution and hampered reform.

The failure of the medical and legal establishment to deal with the rape
and prostitution of children amply illustrates the implications of the
pathologization of female sexuality in these discourses. The fact that many
authorities held such children responsible for their own fall demonstrates
the widespread acceptance of the conflation of female sexuality, disease
and deviance. Moreover, the treatment of child prostitutes vividly shows
how the pathologization of female sexuality obfuscated any discussion of
pathological male sexuality and maintained dearly-held beliefs in male
sexual privilege.

The question of child prostitution in Great Britain during the nineteenth
century has been clouded by the figure of W.T. Stead and the scandalous
'Maiden Tribute' incident. The story of the radical journalist's dramatic
campaign to force a reluctant Parliament to pass the 1885 Criminal Law
Amendment Bill, in order to raise the age of consent from thirteen years
to sixteen, and the notoriety that followed the revelations of his rather
questionable investigative methods, has captured the imagination of historians writing on prostitution. Stead was indeed a colourful personality:
writer, social critic, philosopher and self-confessed prophet.[4] Stead first
came to prominence over his support for Gladstone in the agitation against
Turkey for the Bulgarian atrocities. In 1880 he began to write for the *Pall
Mall Gazette* and as editor of that journal he revolutionized newspaper
writing in London. Stead believed in 'journalism with a mission'.[5] He
popularized the techniques of the 'New Journalism', such as illustrations,
interviews and signed articles. His fall from grace following the publication of the 'Maiden Tribute' series only enhanced his growing legend.
Bramwell Booth called him a 'Modern Galahad'.[6] Millicent Garrett Fawcett
wrote to Stead in prison, claiming that he was 'the hero saint who in every

age of world history has been picked out for misrepresentation'.[7] His mythical status was enhanced in death when he went down with the *Titanic*.

The *Pall Mall Gazette* began running 'The Maiden Tribute of Modern Babylon' on 6 July 1885. The central theme of these articles came from Ovid's tales of Theseus. In Stead's version, however, the Cretan labyrinth became the 'maze of London brothels', the Minotaur represented the 'insatiable lust' of English gentleman and Theseus was Stead himself.[8] Stead argued that if the Athenians who were pagans finally rebelled against this horrendous 'tribute', why would not the men who governed 'Christian England'?[9] With a surge of sensationalism Stead began revealing the findings of the secret commission under intriguing sub-headings such as 'Virgins Willing and Unwilling', 'Confessions of a Brothel-Keeper' and 'How Girls are Bought and Ruined', each title more scandalous than the preceding one.

Stead claimed that these revelations were the results of the investigations made by a small group of social purity workers such as Benjamin Scott, Chamberlain of the City of London and tireless worker for the National Society for the Protection and Care of Children, the Salvation Army leader William Booth and Josephine Butler. Yet the Eliza Armstrong scandal tends to suggest that much of the work was done by Stead alone. Indeed, most historians have tended to focus on the infamous newspaperman's contribution to the debate on child prostitution and ignored any other discussion of the problem or its relationship to other issues such as venereal disease. The whole incident is treated with considerable scepticism and this has tended to colour all discussion of child prostitution for this period. Such scepticism is indeed warranted and it is not my intention to present Stead as a misunderstood hero. I do, however, want to examine how this concentration on the scandalous 'Maiden Tribute' has deflected and obscured a more serious analysis of the issues raised by child prostitution throughout the nineteenth century.

The obsession with the passing of the 1885 Act has meant that peripheral issues, such as Henry Labouchere's attempt to thwart the Act and the question of Stead's hidden intentions, have clouded many of the other social, medical, economic and sexual issues involved in an analysis of child prostitution.[10] Historians have tended to dismiss the existence of child prostitution simply because Stead appears a less than reliable source. Michael Pearson wrote of Stead and his companions, '[T]he sex revolutionaries often cheated – sometimes without realising they were doing so. Obsessed as they were with their cause, they regularly distorted facts – some of which were horrific enough without any promotional treatment.

Zealously they operated on the assumption that the end justified any means they chose to employ.'[11] The most damning comments however come from Ron Pearsall who insinuated that the whole series of articles was a grubby publicity stunt:

> Stead's new journalism was inner conviction wrapped around a small kernel of fact. He did not need to drink champagne with questionable characters to find out the facts; he only had to sit down with a pen and let his mind dwell on the subject. He was a happy accident. It was further fortunate that he had allies, men and women who were equally impressionable.[12]

Such comments could be dismissed as attempts to equal Stead in sensationalism.[13] Yet the passing of the Criminal Law Amendment Act is also treated as central to an understanding of child prostitution in more scholarly work on prostitution such as that done by feminist historians, particularly Judith Walkowitz, Ellen Dubois, Linda Gordon and Deborah Gorham.[14] These historians too have rejected Stead's position in the mythology of the social purity movement as a combination of St Paul, Sir Galahad and Lord Byron and portray him instead as obsessive and neurotic, but most fundamentally an opportunist.

This concentration on Stead has greatly affected the scholarly treatment of child prostitution. It has meant that historians have rejected the idea that child prostitution existed to any great extent during this period. The movement to create protective legislation for children has been dismissed as little more than a misguided and ill-conceived plot to impose middle-class attitudes of respectability and sexual purity onto the women and girls of the working classes. Judith Walkowitz dismissed Stead's findings, claiming that the lurid tales found in the 'Maiden Tribute' had more in common with the Music Hall than with investigative journalism.[15] She maintains that 'the throngs of child prostitutes so highly advertised during the white slavery campaign of 1885 must be dismissed as the imaginary product of sensational journalism intended to capture the attention of a prurient Victorian public'.[16] Such a characterization of Stead would be of little importance, except that his excessive character and his personal foibles have been used to characterize any discussion of child prostitution both before and after the 'Maiden Tribute' series. Deborah Gorham, for instance, argues that the raising of the age of consent 'was specifically designed to deny the working-class girl the right to make decisions about her sexuality'.[17] Ellen Dubois and Linda Gordon contend that the emphasis on child prostitution allowed feminists and social puritans to see themselves as 'rescuers of slaves', when in fact the raising of the female age of consent fostered hostility towards the sexual activity of working-class girls and created a new class of female offenders: the teenage sex delinquents.[18]

These historians have come to such conclusions because they have chosen to contextualize the debates surrounding child prostitution solely within the confines of the 'Maiden Tribute' affair. On the simplest level, this credits Stead with far too much influence in the workings of state. It is possible that, given the political circumstances of the period, the Act may have passed without any impetus from the gutter press. To suggest that the sheer weight of public opinion forced the government's hand ignores the fact that the Act had gone to Committee before the 343,000 signatures were sent to the House, and that the Act was passed before the glorious protest rally in Hyde Park. In the midst of the 'Maiden Tribute' scandal there had been a change of government. The Gladstone government, which had been indifferent to this cause when the Bill was first enacted, had fallen. A conservative government led by Lord Salisbury had taken office in the interim. With the new government, parliamentary sessions were being well attended and it is likely that there was a renewal of interest in the Bill.[19] Moreover it has been suggested that Gladstone had not previously taken up the delicate issue of the age of consent because he did not want to shatter the fragile consensus the party had reached on the question of Home Rule for Ireland. As the opposition, however, Liberal MPs did not necessarily have to toe the party line and those who supported the Bill could vote with their conscience.[20]

Nor was the Act particularly effective in dealing with the prevention of child prostitution and child sexual abuse. While the Act of 1885 raised the age of consent to sixteen and made it a misdemeanour to take away a girl under eighteen against her will out of the possession of her parents and with the intent that she should be carnally known, it was made ineffective by the 'reasonable cause to believe' proviso. This clause in the Act made it possible to use the belief that a girl was sixteen as a defence. The 'reasonable cause to believe' defence was very popular with defendants. Judges often pointedly asked defendants if they believed the plaintiff to be sixteen.[21] Feminists continued to lobby the government to improve the legislation regarding the sexual abuse of children until the mid-1920s.

Child rape was depicted in Victorian medical and legal discourse as a heinous crime and, when both medical and legal experts were satisfied of its occurrence, the most dire consequences greeted the perpetrator. Yet proving that such a crime had occurred became a greater problem as the century progressed. Concern was tempered by several factors. The desire to help the child was always overshadowed by a fear of wrongful hanging.

F.W. Lowndes, Surgeon to the Liverpool Lock Hospital, expressed this fear most succinctly:

> Of all the cases in which medical evidence is required few, if any, are less inviting than those in which men are charged with criminal assaults on females of tender age. To a conscientious medical witness . . . the responsibility appears to be very great; for any remissness on our part to state every circumstance which may be favourable to the accused on the one hand or to strengthen the case for the crown on the other, may be productive of serious consequences. In the former case it may lead to the conviction of a man who is perfectly innocent of the crime with which he is charged, and his sentence to penal servitude for a considerable portion of his future life; with the latter it may assist in the acquittal of a guilty man, guilty of as vile an offence as man can be guilty of.[22]

During the course of the century medical practitioners became the most important witnesses in trials of child rape, and their findings had a profound impact on those attempting to rescue child prostitutes. The question of what a medical witness should look for in the case of a suspected assault was much considered by the Victorian medical and legal professions. Venereal disease came to be the determining factor.

It is not surprising that concern about child rape sprang from the discussion of venereal disease, as it would seem that syphilis was one reason why child rape existed to such an extent. As Antony E. Simpson has suggested, an explanation for child rape in the great cities of Britain derives directly from its relation to venereal disease.[23] He contends that the 'defloration mania' that others had noted is better explained by the fear of catching syphilis than by 'the secret desires of [the] inhabitants' of the metropolis.[24] Sex with a virgin was seen as a way to avoid venereal disease, but there also was a commonly held belief that sex with a virgin cured venereal disease. J.L. Caspar, Professor of Forensic Medicine in Berlin, whose work was highly influential throughout Europe, wrote of the frequency of rapes on children that 'among the lower classes there prevails an absurd and horrible opinion that a venereal complaint is most certainly and quickly cured by coitus with a pure virgin, and most indubitably with a child'.[25]

Alfred Swaine Taylor, the most revered of English medical jurists, concurred claiming that the frequency of child rape in Britain was directly attributable to the belief that sex with a virgin cured gonorrhoea.[26] While there was no medical basis for this belief, it was often used as a defence in rape trials.[27] While such acts were viewed with horror, it was far more acceptable to believe that such men were attempting to cure or avoid syphilis than that men could and did sexually abuse, torture and even murder small children for sexual pleasure. For the most part, discussion of these practices suggested that they were only carried out amongst the working class, especially the rural poor. This suggestion does not tally with the evidence from rape trials however, which show that widespread child rape and prostitution was a metropolitan phenomenon and not restricted to any class of men.[28]

While medical authorities were aware that the desire to be cured of syphilis was often the cause of child rape, this did not necessarily mean that the evidence of violence and disease upon a child was taken as conclusive proof that a rape had occurred. Indeed, the presence or absence of disease upon the child was extremely problematic from the medico-legal point of view. The absence of such an infection was often used as evidence to prove that the child had not been violated, while the existence of the disease was often used as a sign that the child was a prostitute and therefore responsible for her own fall. Sometimes, if doctors believed it to be gonorrhoea or syphilis, it was enough to bring a man to trial. At other times, if the child appeared to be infected with these diseases it was enough to cast aspersions on her veracity as a witness. Moreover, if the doctors were unsure of the specific nature of the infection there was a general tendency to err on the side of caution, so often cases were dismissed.

This was increasingly the case in the nineteenth century. Until the late eighteenth century, any purulent discharges in children were widely considered to be signs of a violent attack. The case of Jane Hampson, recorded by Dr Thomas Percival in 1791, was to become a lesson in caution for all doctors on the issue of child rape.[29] Jane Hampson, aged four, was admitted as an out-patient to Manchester Infirmary, her genitals highly inflamed and painful. The child had slept for several nights with a boy of fourteen and complained that she had been 'very much hurt by him'. Leeches and internal remedies were applied, but after several days the child died of 'mortification of the vagina'. The coroner was of the opinion that the child's death was due to external violence and a verdict of murder was returned against the boy with whom she had slept. Within weeks of the trial, however, several girls came down with similar symptoms where there was no reason to suspect external violence. The coroner decided he was mistaken, and informed the judge presiding over the boy's case. The boy was acquitted due to lack of evidence. Jane Hampson was said to have died from a disorder known to accompany typhus fever, known as *noma pudenda*.[30] This case was widely cited in medical journals and legal textbooks. It was argued that doctors could no longer treat any discharges

from or injuries to the vagina as signs of a violent attack. As more became
known about the specificity of these diseases, doctors were urged to be
more cautious in their presumptions.

Much discussion of the subject of venereal and non-venereal infections
in children appeared in the medical press. During the early part of the
century, rapes upon children were said to occur only rarely. Many doctors
maintained that certain purulent discharges in children had often wrongly
been assumed to be the result of rape. Thomas Weedon Cooke, Medical
Officer, Diseases of Children, Royal Free Hospital wrote in *The Lancet*,
that '[I]n approaching the consideration of discharges from the vagina' he
could 'not remember how large an attention this subject had received from
some of the most distinguished members of [his] profession.'[31] He added
that he had heard many stories of 'the sad consequences of attributing this
very common and innocent affectation to causes which are happily a rare
occurrence in this country'.[32] The 'purulent discharges' that doctors found
present in children were usually dismissed as innocent. Mr Pettigrew Jnr
cited a case where he thought the discharge was caused by 'the little
patient having walked a considerable distance'.[33] Cooke stated that 'the
muco-purulent discharges to which little girls are obnoxious' were frequently traced to the exhaustion produced by 'fevers' such as measles.[34]
Others were more ambiguous. *The Edinburgh Medical and Surgical Journal* commented:

> [T]he possibility of this disease being considered as evidence of vene-
> real infection and violence offered to an infant is not to be overlooked . . .
> but we must take care of running into the opposite error of ascribing
> inflammation, ulceration, in cases when violence has been alleged, to
> this disease, without sufficient grounds; for it is extremely improbable,
> that a disease, which occurs so rarely, should happen to appear in a
> child to whom violence was offered, unless the violence had some
> effect in producing it.[35]

The article concluded with the fact that 'attempts to deflower female children have been frequently known to produce a purulent discharge from the
vagina, independent of any gonorrhoeal taint in the offending party'.[36]

Some specialists chose to cast doubts on the capacity of most practitioners to properly recognize specific infections. In so doing, they cast doubt
on all such evidence. While this was no doubt true, it is difficult to distinguish whether it was genuine concern that prompted such comment, or
whether it was merely used as a way to protect men against such charges.
A comment from Sir Astley Cooper to his medical students is illustrative
of this ambivalence.

It now and then happens, to a nervous woman, to be alarmed at such an appearance, and she suspects her child of having acted in an improper manner; and perhaps, not quite clear herself, she is more ready to suspect others, and says, 'Dear me (if she confesses), it is something like what I have had myself!' She goes to a medical man, who may unfortunately not be aware of the nature of the complaint I am speaking of, and he says, 'Good God! your child has got a clap.' (A laugh.) A mistake of this kind gentlemen, is no laughing matter; and, though I am glad to make you smile sometimes, and like to join in your smiles, I cannot do it on the present occasion, for it is too serious a matter. I can assure you a multitude of persons have been hung [*sic*] by such a mistake.[37]

The hilarity with which this discussion was treated suggests the lack of concern for the child victim of such crimes was shared by Cooper and his colleagues. His levity in dealing with the subject suggests that his main concern was to protect the perpetrator of such a crime, for he not only casts aspersions on the surgeon's ability but on the morality of the mother of the unfortunate child. It is impossible to ignore such obvious misogyny without suggesting that his aim was to protect the defendant and trivialize the instances of such crimes.

It would seem that the children of the lower classes were distinctly discriminated against in this way. Doctors were constantly being warned that such children were dirty and hence more likely to carry infections that resembled venereal diseases. David Ferrier and William Guy, experts on medical jurisprudence claimed, '[I]t is not uncommon to find among the ill-fed and dirty children of the poor, a slight inflammation of the vulva, with a purulent discharge'.[38] They attributed this mainly to worms. Francis Ogston, a lecturer in Medical Jurisprudence at the University of Aberdeen, noted several cases 'of a purulent discharge from the genitals closely resembling gonorrhoea of the adult'. He argued that it was 'not infrequently encountered in females of scrofulous parents, especially amongst the poor and uncleanly'.[39] There was no way these doctors could determine what was 'real' gonorrhoea and what was not. Ogston admits this himself when he states, '[I]t should be borne in mind besides, that we have no diagnostic marks sufficiently certain for our guidance in arriving at a decision which shall be beyond challenge on all occasions.'[40] So if the child who came before them was poor and uncleanly it was very likely that they would treat it as a case of vaginitis and dismiss any suggestion of rape.

Poverty also implied immorality. For instance, the immorality of the mother, in the case presented by Sir Astley Cooper, immediately made the

child suspect. While Cooper was stating that the child did not have gonorrhoea, the basis for this assumption seems to be his low opinion of the
mother. Cases of child rapes or attempts to procure working-class children
were treated sceptically by the medical profession as it was assumed that
such claims were part of an extortion plot.

Even when doctors were certain of the presence of gonorrhoea or syphilis in children there was a general tendency to downplay the possibility of
rape. In children it was argued that such discharges were usually innocent.
Certain doctors argued that many factors apart from sexual intercourse
could create 'simple' gonorrhoea in children. On this subject Michael
Ryan maintained that

> I [have] afforded abundant evidence of the liability of female infants,
> and of girls until the age of puberty, to purulent discharges from the
> vagina. We know that equitation, injury on the perineum, calculus in the
> bladder, stricture of the urethra, haemorrhoids, gout, rheumatism, cer-
> tain cutaneous diseases, as herpes, impetigo, serpigo, leper, &c.; in the
> terebinthinate medicines, lytta, spices, diuretics, sexual intercourse dur-
> ing the catamenial or lochial evacuations, the introduction and long
> retention of a bougie in the urethra, irritations in different parts of the
> alimentary canal, constipation, certain ailments and medicines, as new
> beer, asparagus, &c.; in a word, diseases of organs, which strongly sym-
> pathize with the genito-urinary system may cause simple gonorrhoea.[41]

Ryan's statement illustrates the flexibility of the medical profession in
analysing symptoms and determining cause. While it was acknowledged
that sometimes such factors may have caused a simple gonorrhoea in adult
women, doctors tended to interpret this in terms of the women being
inherently diseased, or spontaneously generating infection. It was also
generally considered to be due to her sexual immorality. In the case of the
child with such symptoms, the vast catalogue of contributing factors was
used as a way to dismiss any suggestion of sexual immorality. While an
understanding of the infection in both women and girls was constructed
within a model of pathological femininity, in the case of women this was
attributed to sexual misconduct but in the case of girls it was not. This no
doubt reflects the underlying fear of female sexuality that informed much
medical observation. Such fluidity of interpretation did not relate to ideas
about childhood innocence, but rather served to protect men. Adult women
were represented as agents in the spread of the disease; at the same time
doctors minimized the possibilities of children acquiring gonorrhoea. In
each case, male responsibility for both the sexual exploitation of women
and children and the spread of the disease was obscured.

The same was true of syphilis. While there is little suggestion of innocently acquired syphilis in adult women until the end of the century, in the case of children doctors attempted to explain its existence avoiding the possibility that sexual intercourse had taken place. In 1860 one doctor wrote to *The Lancet* stating,

> [W]hen a young child, the subject of primary syphilis, is brought before a surgeon, the disease is usually found to depend, in some way or other upon the accidental contact of the poisons by means of the clothes of an adult person, possibly a near relative of the child. This occurrence is by no means so rare, amongst the children of the poorest and most abandoned of our population.[42]

That such a statement could be made in view of the evidence that had come to light regarding incest in the 1850s, is indicative of the general reluctance of doctors to accept the reality of child rape. Incest was believed to have been quite common amongst the working classes in England.[43] It was, however, rarely referred to specifically with euphemisms such as 'promiscuous herding' and 'overcrowding' being used to signify its existence. In the Poor Law Commission of 1843, several witnesses made direct reference to its dangers in rural England. Mr Vaughan, a bourgeois farmer, spoke of his experiences in the counties of Kent, Surrey and Sussex. He claimed that due often to poverty and lack of room poor families would crowd together in their sleeping apartments. This he considered seriously infringed 'on the decencies that guarded female morals'.[44] Mr Rammell, a farmer from Surrey, concurred stating that 'additional problems could arise if a lodger was taken in. It is common to let off a room to a stranger. The benefit of an airy abode is thus lost; and other evils follow from the intimacy between a stranger and the grown up daughter.'[45] While this did not refer to incest, the idea of moral pollution is directly connected with problems of overcrowding and hygiene. Such findings were not peculiar to rural areas. In his report to the City of London, John Simon, Medical Officer of Health, emphasized that throughout the metropolis it was possible to find men, women and children 'styed together . . . in the promiscuous intimacy of cattle'. He claimed it was 'really superfluous to observe that in all offices of nature they are gregarious and public; that every instinct of personal and sexual decency is stifled; that every nakedness of life is uncovered there.' '[D]aily relationships,' he reported, were 'ruffianly and incestuous'.[46]

As more evidence of incest was produced it came to be considered as one of the chief causes of child prostitution and venereal disease in children. Yet, despite all this discussion of incest, both medical and legal authorities were loath to do anything but observe. Indeed, many authorities saw incest not as something to be prevented but as proof of the depravity of working-class children. It was argued that exposure to such licentiousness at an early age tainted the child irreparably and thus hastened her fall. Sometimes it was maintained that girls would enter prostitution to support the bastard offspring of an incestuous union. Incest, like prostitution, was treated synonymously with disease. The animal imagery used to describe the subject clearly expresses a notion of diseased sexuality. Comments in the *Morning Chronicle* on this subject illustrate the connection between incest, infection and prostitution. Referring to a case where some twelve people occupied the same bedroom, the author wrote:

> This is a frightful position for [the inhabitants] to be in when an infectious or epidemic disease enters their abode. But this, important though it be, is the least important consideration connected with their circumstances. That which is most so is the effect on their habits and morals. In the illicit intercourse to which such a position frequently gives rise, it is not always that the tie of blood is respected. Certain it is that, when the relationship is even one degree away from brother and sister, that tie is frequently overlooked. And when circumstances do not lead to such horrible consequences, the mind, particularly of the female, is wholly divested of that sense of delicacy and shame, which so long as they are preserved, are the chief safeguards of her chastity. She therefore falls an early and an easy prey to the temptations which beset her beyond her immediate family.[47]

In other cases, it was possible to ignore the evidence of child sexual abuse by throwing doubts on the veracity of the story given by the child or her parents. Alfred Swaine Taylor believed that it was not likely that false accusations be made, but warned the medical witness to always look for signs of external violence. He stated:

> [T]he absence of marks of violence on the genitals when an early examination has been made, furnishes a strong presumption that the rape was *not* committed on these young persons. It is obvious that a false charge might easily be made and sustained, if medical opinions were hastily given on the statements of a mother and child, when there was no physical appearance to corroborate.[48]

Taylor believed that most cases of false accusation arose from the fact that the child was affected by purulent discharges from the vagina and the parents could not explain it in any other terms.[49] Many doctors concurred that parental ignorance and fear may cause the child to concoct a tale to explain the symptoms. Many examples of this were brought forward, the most significant case of this type was that of Amos Greenwood. Here, it was not only the parents who were confused as to the cause of the disease; it seems to have bemused the great medical minds of the period.

Amos Greenwood, 22 years of age, was charged with the manslaughter of Mary Johnson, by rape in November 1857. Mary Johnson, an eleven-year-old child, died a terrible death several days after the alleged event took place. There was much confusion as to what had occurred. Mary Johnson was said to be the daughter of 'ignorant costermongers'. She was travelling as a servant with friends of her family, the Handcocks, and Amos Greenwood to the Wigan Fair. In late October 1857, she was placed in the same bed with Greenwood in a small room shared by the Handcocks. The next day the child appeared to be normal, but after two days it was noticed that she walked with a limp. When questioned she complained of a smarting between the thighs. She was examined by Mrs Handcock, who found her genitals to be sore and her thighs inflamed. All that night the child complained of great pain and was taken to the surgeon in Wigan the following morning. The surgeon diagnosed vaginitis, prescribed an astringent medicine and informed her mistress she was very ill. No suspicion was yet aroused, although her mistress asked if swallowing a sixpence might have caused this condition. The girl began to rapidly deteriorate. She was pressed by her friends to confess to the true cause of the ailment. After some time the girl asserted that on the night that she had slept with Amos Greenwood he had 'had connection with her and had produced this violence to her person'. She was then put on mercury, she worsened and after several days 'mortification of the vagina' set in. She died on 5 November 1857. Mr Jameson who attended her at Heywood swore she died of 'mortification of the genitals brought on by laceration, inflammation and venereal poison'.[50]

The trial of Greenwood took place at the Liverpool Assizes in December 1857. The prisoner was found to have genital warts and possibly syphilis. This was taken to be further proof of his guilt. The court found the child to have died of the injuries inflicted on her by forced connection and the subsequent outbreak of venereal poisons. The accused was sentenced to life imprisonment.

The case came to the notice of Mr W.R. Wilde of Dublin, a self-styled expert on infantile diseases of this nature. In 1853 he had published a pamphlet entitled, *Medico-Legal Observations upon Infantile Leucorrhoea.* Wilde believed Greenwood to be innocent, arguing that the evidence of the case was not fairly put before the jury. He maintained that Mary Johnson had died from *noma pudenda.* He wrote to the judge who presided over Greenwood's case suggesting that a grave error of justice had been made. The judge however disagreed. Wilde then petitioned twelve medico-legal experts with a view to eliciting their opinions as to the cause of death. He published these results in the *Dublin Quarterly of Medical Science*.[51] Much debate ensued.

The Greenwood case is of particular value to this study because Wilde collected the opinions from twelve of the most experienced medical jurists of the period on the subject of sexual assault on children. This is important to the historian as there was much disagreement as to the cause of her death, indicative of the rudimentary state of medical diagnosis at the time. They also offered many thoughts on child rape, working-class morality and on the reliability of the evidence of children. Most importantly, however, they show how the image of the depraved child allowed doctors the possibility of ignoring the evidence of child sexual abuse. If the child or the parents seemed to the doctor to be immoral, doubts were often raised. Poverty and ignorance in this case seem to have been equated with immorality in the minds of the doctors that were questioned.

The variety of opinions offered as to the cause of death in this case suggests that much of the diagnosis was purely guesswork. Although nineteenth-century doctors prided themselves on their diagnostic skills, it was impossible for these men to say how Mary Johnson died. This did not prevent them from passing unequivocal judgments on the case. Thomas Geoghegan, Professor of Medical Jurisprudence to the Royal College of Surgeons in Ireland, wrote:

> There is a peculiar and long recognised disease which attacks the genitals of young females, apparently a form of *pemphigus gangrenus* commencing in unhealthy inflammation, and proceeding to ulceration and gangrene, and frequently compromising life. Whether the deceased girl was the subject of a criminal assault or otherwise, I am of the opinion that the character of the local symptoms, and the progress and termination of the case are in conformity with those of the disease mentioned above [*noma pudenda*].[52]

William Acton, the expert on prostitution, was not so certain. He suggested 'phagedena or sloughing phagedena' may have produced some of the symptoms, but added 'whether this was superadded on simple ulcers, or syphilis, warts and purulent discharge, the evidence gave me no clue'.[53] Alfred Swaine Taylor disagreed with both these statements claiming, '[U]nder all circumstances, I am inclined to attribute death to inflammation from violence alone to the genital organs. I can perceive no adequate cause for the inflammation and death but this.' W.B. Kevesten, who later

1. Much used illustration of a vaginal examination from a French medical textbook of the 1820s. While less modesty would have been shown to prostitutes, it is not difficult to imagine why such examinations were less than successful in discovering venereal infections.

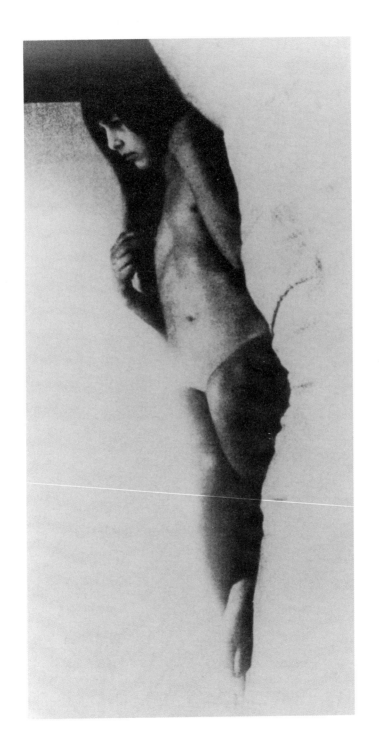

2. Photograph of a child prostitute, c. 1841, photographer unknown.

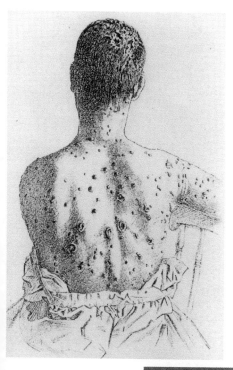

3. Head of a syphilitic prostitute, from the *Edinburgh Medical and Surgical Journal*, 1860.

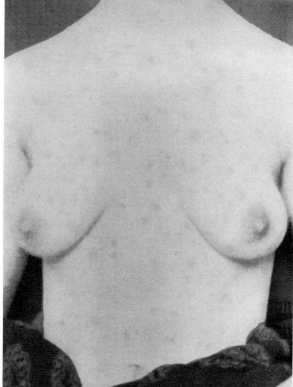

Body of a syphilitic prostitite c.1900. From D'arcy Power and J. Keogh Murphy, *A System of Syphilis*, Volume I.

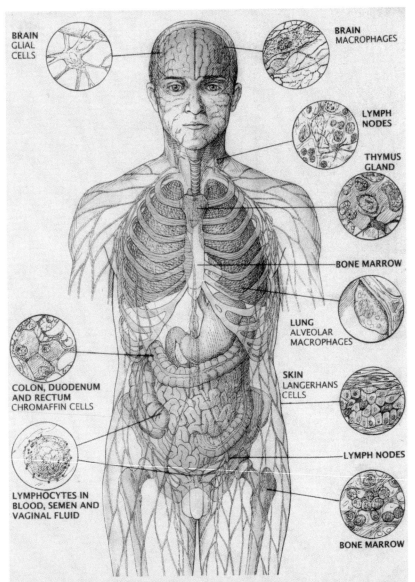

BRAIN GLIAL CELLS

BRAIN MACROPHAGES

LYMPH NODES

THYMUS GLAND

BONE MARROW

LUNG ALVEOLAR MACROPHAGES

COLON, DUODENUM AND RECTUM CHROMAFFIN CELLS

SKIN LANGERHANS CELLS

LYMPH NODES

LYMPHOCYTES IN BLOOD, SEMEN AND VAGINAL FLUID

BONE MARROW

DISTRIBUTION OF TISSUES in the body that can be infected with HIV is closely linked to the distribution of cells bearing the CD4 molecule. With the possible exceptions of glial cells in the brain and chromaffin cells in the colon, duodenum and rectum, every cell that can be infected with HIV carries the CD4 molecule on its surface.

5.   HIV – The Cellular Picture, *Scientific American*, October 1988.

wrote an article critical of Wilde's findings, differed from all parties by claiming that the death of Mary Johnson was caused by 'sloughing pha-gedena following an allowed sexual intercourse with some man afflicted with syphilis'. He believed the prisoner to be the most likely candidate as he was 'stated to have syphilis'. But he saw 'no evidence whatever to bear out the opinion that the lesions in question were the result of forced connection'.[54]

The case shows ample evidence of the way in which medical opinion could drastically differ on this subject. The doctors who were questioned were not unaware of this and, in order to obscure their lack of knowledge, they used subjective moral judgments of the victim and her parents to decide the guilt or innocence of the accused. The answers given by these experts provide considerable insight into how child rape and child sexu-ality was perceived by the medical and legal profession at the time and point to the real role of the medical witness – as arbiter of the victim's morals rather than medical expert.

This is clearly shown in their response to Wilde's question, '[W]hat amount of credence is to be attached to the evidence of children with respect to connection?' The answers given vary only slightly and were based on individual judgments regarding 'interfering mothers', the vera-city of the child victim and working-class mores. Fleetwood Churchill, Professor of Midwifery and the Diseases of Women and Children at the King and Queen's College of Physicians in Ireland answered, 'Little or no weight, unless the disclosure is voluntary, and made within a very short period. None at all, if the mother had catechized the child, for she is sure to put leading questions which indicate to the child what she is to say.'[55] William Acton, who began with the statement, 'I have much pleasure in answering your queries, as I think we should aid all in solving these odd cases in young girls, and rescue the man . . .' replied to the query, 'I should remark that the credence given to children should not be great, nor to the statements of the "immediate surroundings".'[56] Thomas Beatty, former Professor of Medical Jurisprudence at the Royal College of Surgeons in Ireland and author of the article 'Rape' in the *Cyclopaedia of Practical Medicine*, responded simply, 'None whatever.'[57] In a similar vein, W.B. Kevesten wrote:

[N]one whatever. Such delay afforded the strongest presumption that the child was a consenting party to the act. The social conditions of people living together in the manner of these persons must have ren-dered the child subject of the grossest desires, and must have been most unfavourable to the development of a regard for truthfulness.[58]

In these statements such experts betray a definite suspicion of anyone who chooses to become involved in a case of child rape, most particularly the child victim and her mother. If the mother had in any way dealt with the child before taking her to the doctors it was argued that the child had been interfered with and so their evidence lacked credibility. In the case of Mary Johnson, the child's peculiar situation – being alone in the company of strangers and having been allowed to share a bed with a young man – suggested to these medical experts her guilt rather than his innocence. The child was considered the product of a depraved lifestyle and the guilt or innocence of her assailant was of little importance.

Doctors who accepted the evidence of children were often forced to defend their opinions. A Dr Hudson wrote to the *Medical Times and Gazette* in 1861 to set the record straight, after a series of letters questioned his judgment in such a case. In the letter he tells of a case of a young child of eight years old who was brought to him by her aunt, who stated that 'the child had a running from her privates'.[59] The doctor treated the child for vaginitis. The following day the aunt brought the child back to the doctor. The aunt told the doctor that the child had said that while the aunt was shopping, Hodges, a vagrant, had taken the child onto his lap, opened her legs 'and hurt her very much with something'. The doctor stated, '[S]uch was the artless tale of the child told to me, not in the presence of any person, and without any threats or inducements'.[60] The child was suffering from gonorrhoea as was the prisoner, who was well known to the police. The child's vagina showed signs of forced connection and the prisoner's shirt was found to be covered in substances resembling semen and blood. Although the child had quite obviously been raped, her story was doubted by others. One doctor went so far as to produce a pamphlet to cast doubts on the child's story and the doctor's capabilities.[61]

It could equally be argued that a medical witness might coerce the child into a false confession. Ambroise Tardieu, a French forensic expert, unconsciously revealed his part in such a confession to a meeting of the Academy of Medicine in Paris in 1880. In his lecture *Simulation d'attentats vénériens sur des jeunes enfants*, Tardieu spoke on the subject of how to unmask the pretences of a child. He related the story of a child of eight who came to his office 'literally bathed in yellow pus oozing from her vagina'. Tardieu was suspicious of her story of a man who molested her, so he decided to win the truth from the child with money, candy, sweet words and finally 'a doll whose eyes moved'.[62] This, Tardieu stated 'decided my triumph'. After he had given her the doll, the child told him with great difficulty and much fear and hesitation that 'it was not a man who touched her, but that her mother, three times brushed her sexual parts with a waxing brush, forbidding her to tell any one about it'.[63] Here Tardieu used exactly the technique so criticized by his peers for gaining 'the truth' from an abused child. If doctors could claim that the child only stated what the mother wanted to hear, is it not possible that the child would, after such blatant coercion, say only what the doctor wanted to hear?

Tardieu's main concern was with the welfare of the accused man.[64] He believed that most cases of child sexual abuse were hoaxes for the purpose of extortion. Indeed, this became a constant theme throughout the literature on the subject. Case after case of the blackmail of an innocent man by a scheming child or her parents was revealed. Ogston wrote:

> It behoves the medical witness therefore, that in examining children under puberty to take special care that he does not become a party to the prosecution of a male person charged with this crime on insufficient ground, as it is known to be attempted for the most nefarious purpose, sometimes without any known object, and sometimes for the purpose of gratifying revenge.[65]

W.B. Kevesten also condemned this fiendish trend but not without passing racial slurs as well as moral judgments.

> It must not be hastily assumed that rape has been committed because the proofs of mechanical violence are present. Such injuries may have been inflicted with a view to false charges for the purpose of extorting money. Such occurrences do not often become subjects for Medical investigation in England; but in India such cases are not infrequent. . . . Hence our Indian possessions have afforded a more profitable field for observations upon this crime – crimes of all kinds and of the deepest dye, are revealed as common practices; practices so fiendlike and atrocious are recorded that one rather wonders at the mildness of the cruelties inflicted upon Europeans during the late rebellion, as compared with the diabolical cruelties which they have been wont to practise toward one another.[66]

In many such cases, the child had been sexually abused but not necessarily by the person accused. The object of the case was to determine who had abused the child, yet if there was a suggestion of the child being used for blackmailing purposes, the child was no longer perceived as a victim but as an agent in her own downfall, regardless of the circumstances. The emphasis in the medical evidence seems to be on maintaining innocence, rather than determining guilt. A case provided by Ogston shows this most clearly.

A tradesman of irreproachable character was accused by a woman of having violated her daughter of 11 years and having communicated a gonorrhoea to her. The child was scrofulous, the clitoris unusually developed, the entrance to the vagina inflamed and painful to touch, the hymen obviously stretched, and there was a copious urethral discharge. On examination, the defender was found to be free of the disease, and the cross examination brought out the fact that the mother, after having fruitlessly endeavoured to extort money from the tradesman, had delivered the child to her own paramour, who she knew to be affected with gonorrhoea.[67]

These cases also demonstrate the scepticism with which the legal and medical profession dealt with child rape. Even in cases where there was obvious external violence and the presence of a venereal infection, many doctors maintained that a charge of rape could not be brought. Sometimes this was due to their only rudimentary skills as diagnosticians. Michael Ryan's advice to doctors regarding the signs of defloration illustrates this most clearly:

> Are there certain signs of defloration? To determine this question we must decide whether there are any certain signs of virginity. In virgins, the external labia are thick, firm, elastic, and internally of a vermilion or rosaceous color, their edges in apposition, so as to close completely the orifice of the vulva. They are soft, pale and separated in women accustomed to venereal enjoyment, or subject to leucorrhoea, or who have practised masturbation. But these characters are not to be depended on, as women of strong constitutions may have the signs of virginity; and virgins the latter signs from leucorrhoea, or fluor albus. In fact, no positive conclusion can be deduced from the state of the internal or external labia.[68]

Ryan continued, stating 'that a great variety of causes besides coition' may destroy the hymen and that in fact sometimes the hymen did not exist. In other instances, women in labour were found to have their hymen perfectly intact. In concluding, he claimed that the hymen was 'no infallible sign of virginity, nor was its absence alone a positive proof of defloration'.[69] Others disagreed. As late as 1888, Ferrier and Guy maintained that 'a perfect hymen, with parts of generation and breasts conforming to the virgin type' afforded a 'strong presumption of chastity'.[70]

While Parent-Duchatelet's work on the physiognomy of the prostitute had indicated that there was no apparent difference between the vagina of a prostitute and that of a virtuous woman, medical witnesses in the case of child rape sometimes used what they considered vaginal 'abnormalities' to show that no rape had occurred. A case presented by Ogston is illustrative not only of this tendency, but of the way in which ideas of physical abnormality were absorbed into a model of pathological female sexuality. Ogston recorded that in October 1859, a girl of thirteen, unemployed and 'of wretched appearance and ill dressed', lodged a charge of rape against a man between fifty and sixty. She alleged the man had drawn her aside into a wood and had 'thrice forcible connection'. They then returned to town where he had treated her to a cup of coffee. Ogston reported:

> On examining this girl, some blood was found at the vulva, which she herself stated was menstrual. The hymen was entire, the vulvar cavity had considerable depth and the nymphae projected for about an inch beyond the labia. The girl admitted that she was not a stranger to sexual intercourse, which she commenced with a boy two years previously. Of course in such a case no charge of rape would lie, and the man was set at liberty.[71]

What is unclear here is why exactly Ogston believed no rape had occurred. It would seem that it was the combination of the girl's previous sexual experience with the 'over-development' of her vagina that signalled to Ogston the innocence of the accused. This is evidence that the medical profession were incorporating signs of hyper-sexuality in black women into their descriptions of 'depraved' white women and women bringing false accusations of rape. The description of the 'over-developed vagina' is clearly reminiscent of quasi-anthropological accounts of vaginal anomalies such as the Hottentot apron.[72] That such anomalies were now to be found in white women marks a shift from the physical anthropology of the late eighteenth century to the criminal physiognomy of the late nineteenth century.[73] Quite clearly, this is no reflection on the facts of the case but merely a subjective judgment on the part of the doctor. Ogston believed that the girl was a child prostitute who had tried to bring charges against an 'innocent' client. Indeed, Ogston warned other medical jurists that this was a common occurrence and instructed them on how to distinguish between the vagina of a child prostitute and a 'normal' vagina.

> The first thing that strikes the general observer in these young females is the contrast betwixt [sic] their general development and that of their genitals. While the former preserves its infantile character, the labia are enlarged and parted below, the nymphae elongated and projecting beyond the labia, the clitoris very bulky, exposed, often red and readily erectile.[74]

This related to the idea that all prostitutes, even children, were prone to specific pathologies of the genitalia. Not only did this work in favour of the defendant in cases of child rape, but it reinforced the idea that children who were raped were pathological.

Many doctors avoided the question of child rape entirely by claiming that sex with a child was not possible. Some doctors merely expressed bewilderment at the possibility that children could engage in sex, both from a physical and moral perspective. For instance, one doctor in a letter to *The Lancet* expressed his amazement at the case of a young girl of ten who came to see him with the symptoms of acquired primary syphilis.[75] He wrote:

> Her case is a very instructive one in a medico-legal point of view, for here we find that efforts of connection had voluntarily been made by a mere child, without any success beyond penetration of the vulva, yet it is followed by the communication of primary syphilis from a lad of fourteen.[76]

Others believed that it was a physical impossibility. Due to the difference in size between a young girl's vagina and an adult penis, it was held that connection was impossible. Often, despite copious injuries frequently ending in death, it was maintained that actual penetration could not take place.

One notorious case in 1840 serves to illustrate this quite vividly. During the march of a regiment through Ireland, a soldier offered to carry an eleven-month-old baby for its mother who was travelling with the sick car. The child was quite well when he took her; he walked on quickly and was out of the mother's sight for about half an hour. When she found him, he had the child standing on the grass facing him and was bent over her; with one hand he held the child's petticoats up, his other hand was covered in blood. He told the mother that the child was ill and passing blood. The mother rolled her in the shawl and carried her to an apothecary. No examination was immediately made but the following morning the mother noticed marks of violence when washing the baby. A surgeon examined the child some twenty hours after the alleged outrage, the baby was in a grave state and died several hours later. Taylor records that the child was severely injured, '[A]ll external parts of generation were torn nearly through; the nymphae . . . the labia and the clitoris were likewise lacerated, so that the whole presented the appearance of a large lacerated wound in a high state of inflammation.'[77] The post-mortem revealed other horrific injuries. '[T]he vagina was found greatly dilated and torn from its attachment to the neck of the womb posteriorly, making a large opening cavity of the abdomen, in which a quantity of bloody serum was effused'.[78] The soldier was found guilty of rape and was sentenced to be hanged. Yet the judge's decision was questioned by several independent witnesses who claimed that the damage to the child was produced by the man's fingers. The judge demurred and the prisoner was transported for life.

As Taylor has argued, the legal point involved was whether or not the soldier had produced such injuries to the child, not with what appendage this was done. He writes:

> This can scarcely be regarded as exculpatory; for if a female child is destroyed by culpable violence to the genital organs, it can create no difference, on a charge of manslaughter, whether the injuries were produced by the fingers or by the male organ.[79]

Yet this was considered enough to reduce his sentence. Curiously, the death of the child could be said to prove both that sex with a child was and was not a physical possibility. It was possible in the sense that penetration could be achieved, yet impossible in the sense that it resulted in the death of the child. Not surprisingly, W.R. Wilde was one of the soldier's chief defenders, claiming that 'there was no proof of the actual perpetration of rape'.[80]

What is absent in all such discussions is any question of male sexual pathology. The pathologization of the child victim meant that any question of male responsibility was ignored. This problem was exacerbated by the rhetoric of 'biological necessity' that characterized any discussion of male sexuality during this period. The rape of children could be dismissed as men succumbing to the temptations of 'depraved child prostitutes'.

Certain doctors maintained that the physical possibility of sex with a child was dependent on the environment which the child inhabited. Often the example of Indian child brides was used to demonstrate that young girls could and did have sexual intercourse with adult men. Dr Chever, a noted authority on this subject, cited many examples of young women who successfully cohabited with much older partners. Often his only experience of this came from post-mortems he had performed on girls who had died during childbirth.[81] It was frequently asserted that girls from tropical climates, such as India and Australia, physically matured at an earlier age. Others believed that it was the moral rather than the physical environment that was most influential. Dr Robertson of Manchester argued that 'the climate alone does not produce premature maturity. It is to the moral condition of the people that such precocity is to be traced.' He maintained that there were 'as frequent instances of precocious sexual development amongst the inhabitants of cold countries and the children engaged in Manchester factories' as there were in tropical climates.[82]

These ideas related not only to the physical maturity of such children, but conflated such maturity with sexual precocity. This connection reflects the underlying assumption of much medical and legal discourse during this period regarding child rape: that is, that working-class girls had an innate potential for youthful sexuality and hence prostitution. Displays of this innate propensity to prostitution were most often the result of poverty, rather than depravity. But, in these instances, poverty became equated with immorality. The reluctance shown by Parliament to raise the age of consent and the failure of doctors and lawyers to act in cases of child sexual abuse indicates that both medicine and the law assumed a potential sexual pathology in the female that could even manifest itself in the child.[83] By demonstrating that the child was physically different from other children it was possible to show that this was the cause of her fall, thus protecting the male offender from any share in the blame.

The most obvious and successful way to avoid the reality of child rape was to cast doubts on the morality of the victim herself. Caroline Conley, in her study of Victorian attitudes to rape and rape victims, has argued that the fundamental consideration in rape trials was the perceived character of the victim as opposed to the character of the accused.[84] Although her study deals predominantly with the rape of adult women, the conclusions she draws are also true of child rape cases. Francis Ogston cited several cases that clearly demonstrate this propensity. One case was of an infant with syphilitic sores who claimed to have been abused by a local clergyman of 'unimpeachable character'. The clergyman was found to be free of the disease and so released. Establishing the guilt or innocence of the clergyman was the only role of the medical witness in the case, yet Ogston felt it necessary to comment that 'the child herself' was 'an infant of mendacious habits and of low connection' who appeared to 'have been instructed how to play her part in the prosecution'.[85]

The image of the sexually knowing child enabled the medical and legal profession to ignore to a great extent the existence of child rape. The working-class girl was most often seen by such authorities merely as a potential prostitute. By representing girls in such a way, men were absolved of their part in the process of sexual exploitation. A girl's 'seduction' and her decline into prostitution were viewed as part of a process that was inevitable, due to her innate depravity. The presence of disease in such children merely reinforced this sense of their depravity. These ideas were to hinder reformers who sought to protect working-class girls from this cycle of sexual exploitation. Many reformers were greatly influenced by the image of the sexually knowing child and, despite their good intentions, considered fallen girls far worse than fallen women. By the end of the century, this image would shift away from the working-class girl as potential prostitute, to an idea that certain women were 'born prostitutes'.

7 Child Prostitution

Concern about child prostitution spread directly out of the growing panic regarding syphilis. It was the incidence of syphilis in these children and the spread of the disease by them that first drew attention to the problem. Like their older sisters, child prostitutes were seen as the harbingers of disease and it was usually within that context that the subject was raised by reformers.

From the 1830s and 1840s prominent medical specialists working at major city hospitals had voiced a growing chorus of alarm at the incidence of child prostitution and at the ages of the children so engaged. Dr Michael Ryan, for example, was horrified by the existence of child prostitution, but he was especially stunned by the age of some of his patients with venereal diseases. As honorary surgeon to several metropolitan Rescue Homes, Ryan confronted the reality of street prostitution on a daily basis, yet he felt the necessity to record his shock at the precocious depravity of 'beardless boys or rather children' presenting themselves to him for advice on venereal disease.[1] Mr Miller, Professor of Surgery at the University of Edinburgh, also bemoaned the fact 'that many vagrant boys and girls were prowling about the streets'. He was most concerned about this problem as he had known of 'girls of the tender age of from 10 to 12, certified by the surgeon as diseased'.[2] Although Miller spent much time ministering to prostitutes, he was quite horrified by the youth of some of his charges. The case of an eight-year-old girl who visited the Lock Hospital received special attention as the girl had been seduced in her 'own mother's house'. The Reverend Ralph Wardlaw condemned the widespread existence of child prostitution, largely because of the number of children with venereal disease and the threat they posed to society.[3] Basing his evidence predominantly on figures from the London Society for the Protection of Females and the Prevention of Juvenile Prostitution, Wardlaw claimed that between the years 1835 and 1842 London's three major hospitals treated some 2,700 children between the ages of ten and sixteen for syphilis.

The Edinburgh surgeon Dr William Tait also speculated about the number of children with acquired venereal diseases. He stated that for the year 1835, of the 1,000 patients in his Lock Hospital 42 were under fifteen years of age. He believed that the figures of children with VD cited by Lock Hospitals as an indication of the low level of juvenile prostitution were incorrect. He maintained that they were very inadequate as many doctors became incredulous when faced with venereal disease in young children.[4] This in turn led to its under-reporting. He used the example of a nine-year-old girl brought into his hospital suffering from the early stages of syphilis. '[C]onsiderable doubt existed in the minds of several professional gentleman who saw her at the time' as to whether or not they were dealing with a venereal disease. 'Such doubts were erased,' he claimed, when she returned to the hospital 'labouring under the secondary symptoms of that complaint'. There can be little doubt that Tait was quite correct about this. As we have seen, many doctors had little more than a rudimentary grasp of these diseases. Few doctors could be depended on to correctly diagnose it and when it was recognized it was often reasoned away.

Tait was baffled by these young girls living on the streets. He considered that it was exploitative and dangerous for girls as young as nine to prostitute themselves as he believed sexual desire was 'feeble before the age of puberty'. He believed that some sort of protection should be given to girls so young. Like later reformers, Tait believed that exposure to sexual activity was 'the abuse' that formed 'so remarkable a feature in the history of all prostitutes'. Few child prostitutes, he argued, would have entered prostitution wholly voluntarily. He maintained that many brothel-keepers employed housekeepers who ferreted out young girls to work in the brothel. Some were coerced into the life, others were openly kidnapped. He mentioned a traffic in 'white slaves', but being Scottish, it seems that he believed London was their foreign destination.[5] While Tait's evidence showed quite clearly the coercive measures used to force girls into prostitution, it did little to dispel the notion of childhood depravity that such images evoked.

Several years after the publication of his *Magdalenism*, James Talbot, Secretary of the London Society for the Protection of Young Girls, was commissioned by the House of Lords to compile all the evidence in his possession on the nature and extent of prostitution in Great Britain. Much of the evidence he put forward came from earlier writers. He too stressed the horrors of dealing with children with venereal disease, claiming that at the Lock Hospital he was connected with, they had to treat 360 prostitutes who were under fifteen. Some were 'not more than nine or ten'. He also provided information on the whole structure of prostitution. Tait and other earlier writers had hinted at the possibility of organized rackets for procuring children into a life of prostitution. Talbot provided proof that this was indeed happening. He referred to the case of a woman charged with decoying a child of eleven years of age away from her parents and into a brothel that was prosecuted successfully by his London Society. He discussed other evidence, such as letters sent by brothels through the penny post to 'gentlemen' to inform them of new and young inmates. Talbot clearly believed that it was necessary to restrict the operation of brothels in order to protect girls from a life of vice. It was men, he argued, that necessitated the demand for prostitution and it was men who should be held responsible for the spread of disease.

Many reformers believed that the only way it was possible to prevent children from becoming prostitutes was to raise the age of consent. Calls for reform of this situation during the 1840s however were not widely heeded. In late 1844, a Bill for the Effectual Suppression of Brothels and Trading in Seduction was introduced to the House of Lords. It did not produce much interest and the debate in the House of Lords was interrupted when discussion turned to whether or not it was morally acceptable for Lord Byron to be memorialized in Westminster Abbey.[6] The Bill failed its third reading. Enquiries such as the Poor Law Commission on the Employment of Women and Children in Agriculture in 1843 and the subsequent Annual Reports of the Children's Employment Commission, and Chadwick's Report on the Sanitary Conditions of the Labouring Population, influenced the discussions of child immorality and prostitution. From the evidence given at these enquiries it was shown that not only was the procuration of children causing the ranks of prostitution to swell, but that incest was also a major contributing factor.

Reformers continued to lobby the government to improve the facilities for the protection of young girls. An Associate Institute for Improving and Enforcing the Laws for the Protection of Women was established in 1844. At the time, the age of consent was ten and had not been reviewed since 1576.[7] Many hoped that by raising the age of consent it could be guaranteed that the act of becoming a prostitute would be made 'a deliberate and voluntary act'.[8] The desire to suppress brothels and prosecute procurers was the main concern of those involved in rescue and reform work. The age of female consent remained a contentious issue because the age to which it should be raised could not be decided upon. Many believed that laws should be brought in to punish seduction and others were critical of changes in bastardy laws brought in under the New Poor Law. In 1849 an Act to Protect Women Under Twenty-One from Fraudulent Practices for Procuring their Defilement was passed. This Act represented an uneasy compromise between the sponsors of the Bill in Parliament and non-political reformers and rescue workers. It was vaguely worded and ineffective. It made it a misdemeanour for any person to procure by false pretences, false representations, or other fraudulent means, a woman or child to have illicit carnal knowledge with any man. The Act did not represent a startling change in legislation, nor did it raise the age of consent which was effectively still only ten years of age. It was rarely enforced. The Attorney-General called it a 'homeopathic dose for a great problem'.[9]

Concern about child prostitution continued during the 1850s and the focus of concern remained the relationship between child prostitution and venereal disease. Such concerns were heightened by attempts to implement a system of regulation. The publicity given to the issue of regulation meant that prostitution was more regularly discussed and the question of dealing with child prostitution under a system of regulation was often raised. W.R. Greg, one of the first proponents of regulation, also called for serious law reform when it came to procuring children. Although Greg cited environmental reasons as the principal cause of prostitution and his arguments were firmly based on the idea that prostitution was a necessity, due to the biology of men, he claimed that sexual desire for children was an aberration. He stated that all those informed about the problem of prostitution agreed, 'that carnal connexion with children of tender years, *with or without consent*, is a high crime and misdemeanour'.[10] Even William Acton, who considered himself the 'father of the CD Acts' wrote in horror of the spectacle of child prostitution. He considered the 'extreme youth' of the prostitutes he saw as unique to London. While he believed that few of these children were 'victims of panders and old *debauchees*' he saw the problem of child prostitution as 'strange and sad' and 'worth amending'.[11] *The Lancet*, which had been calling for some state control of prostitution throughout the 1850s, called attention to the problem of child prostitution in one of its many articles on regulation. The editor claimed that 'no female from the age of eight upwards' was safe from the snares of procurers and likened such goings-on to the massacres of English civilians in Cawnpore.[12]

In 1861 the Offences Against the Person Bill was enacted in an attempt to clarify the age of female consent. The Act provided that it should be a misdemeanour to procure the defilement of any woman or girl by threats, by fraud or by administering stupefying drugs or to abduct a girl under the age of sixteen. It also provided that to abduct a woman of fortune, for the sake of her fortune and against her will or, if she was under twenty-one, to take her by fraud and against the will of her parents for the purpose of marriage or defilement, be made a felony. This Act did very little, merely re-enacting the provisions of earlier Acts.[13] Effectively, it offered no protection for the working-class children who were more readily procured and merely created additional protection for heiresses.

It was not until the system of regulation was introduced that real concern about how to prevent widespread child prostitution was voiced. Many of those who supported the CD Acts believed that not only would they control the spread of syphilis, but they would also cause child prostitution to decline. There was very little evidence to support such a belief. Through-out the Continent where prostitution was regulated, many children were found on the police rolls.[14] In France and Belgium, the registration of minors was quite a regular occurrence. Since the institution of this system in Paris, girls as young as ten had been placed *en carte* by the *Police des Mœurs*, even though the age of female consent was twenty-one. Far from discouraging child prostitution, the French system positively fostered it. Children found prostituting themselves were taken to the prison hospital of St Lazare. While they were detained the Prefect of Police was meant to write to the *maire* of the parish in which they were born, in order to contact their parents. This was not often done in practice and if the girls were not released into the custody of their parents they were apprenticed to registered brothels.[15] The British Act provided no specific provisions for the treatment of child prostitutes; it was merely hoped that increased police surveillance would have the desired effect. The British system, however, acted in much the same way as the French system by promoting child prostitution.

Those who opposed the CD Acts were quick to point out that minors were brought into Lock Hospitals and registered. There was no differen-tiation between the treatment of women and that of girls under the age of sixteen. The mingling of women who had spent many years on the streets with girls scarcely in their teens was a frequent source of anguish to rescue workers. A speaker at a meeting to protest the Acts in Birmingham de-clared that 'the forced association of aged prostitutes with young and comparatively innocent girls, at the periodical examinations, and for the long periods of hospital treatment' was 'a most fruitful source of moral contamination' and tended to render such girls 'irreclaimable'.[16] It was claimed that registration increased the number of women engaged in pros-titution, especially when girls who were not prostitutes and 'clandestine prostitutes' were picked up. Many argued that the men who policed the Acts restricted the freedom of young women rather than protecting them. It was said that often girls could not go to work or night-school for fear of police harassment.[17] If falsely accused of being a prostitute, such girls would find it difficult to gain honest employment. A letter to *The Shield*, the journal of the NA and LNA, claimed that in their region

A policeman here, who is fond of a servant girl near St.-'s . . . cautioned his friend lately as to the danger of going out any evenings because of a law lately come into force saying, 'of course it does not apply to you, but I advise you to keep at home!' He gave no other explanation, but the girl had heard of the C.D. Acts and comprehended the dangers which any young girl may now encounter for venturing to breathe God's air at the only time when it is possible for her to enjoy it.[18]

It was also asserted that the Acts encouraged brothelkeepers and procurers, which meant a further increase in juvenile prostitution. The Annual Report of the London Rescue Society for 1869 expressed this fear most explicitly claiming the CD Acts would

> increase the crime of seduction, and make personal immorality a matter more insignificant than it is even thought at the present. . . . It will produce conjugal infidelity, and wring parents' hearts with anguish over the fall and degradation of sons and daughters. . . . It will fill the base spirits of procurers and brothel keepers with an infernal joy, and give them an avowed sanction for the continuance and extension of their evil trade.[19]

Those who sought to repeal the CD Acts were adamant that the system of registration worked to encourage girls into the profession, while those who supported the Acts believed that not only would they control the spread of syphilis, they would also cause child prostitution to decline and the seduction of children to cease. Yet in reality the Acts heightened the vulnerability of young children to sexual exploitation and effectively punished them as well. The system offered no protection for juvenile prostitutes and, in many cases, hastened the decline of young girls into prostitution by policing behaviour usually ignored by authorities.

The failure of the government to do anything to prevent minors being registered relates to the fact that the rationale of the Acts was entirely based upon ideas of male sexual privilege. The purpose of the Acts was primarily to service the sexual needs of men and to protect them from venereal disease at the expense of the personal liberty of women and children. Many who favoured a system of regulation saw prostitution as the inevitable outcome of the differing sexual needs of men and women. Men were assumed to have sexual needs that could only be satisfied by resorting to prostitutes. This was particularly true for soldiers and sailors, whom the Acts were specifically designed to protect. In the 1850s, the English soldiers were understood to be 'helplessly subjected to their irrepressible licentious natures'.[20] Any concern about the plight of children registered under the CD Acts was overshadowed by the desire to protect men from venereal infection. Such inequity was obscured by the rhetoric of masculine biological necessity.

It was not until the 1871 Royal Commission Regarding the Administration and Operation of the CD Acts that the government was forced to consider the implications of the Act for child prostitution. The Royal

Commission came as a response to a Repeal Bill introduced by William Fowler and was no doubt influenced by the loss of several Liberal seats at by-elections to pro-Repeal candidates. It would seem that the government did not intend to disband the system but hoped to make changes within it in order to limit the growing opposition to the Acts. Several prominent Repealers were called to give evidence before the Commission.

The problem of child prostitution was very much on the agenda of the inquiry. Government witnesses such as William Henry Sloggett, Inspector of Certified Hospitals under the CD Acts, claimed that regulation diminished child prostitution in the districts covered under the Acts. He added, however, that it would be better if police had special powers to send prostitutes under the age of fifteen or sixteen to reformatories or industrial schools. His evidence on this point tended to support Repealers who claimed that once a child was registered she was forever doomed to a life of prostitution.[21] The suggestion of reformatories or industrial schools for juvenile prostitutes marks the interest in changing the way juvenile offenders were dealt with. Since the 1840s, reformers such as Charles Dickens and Mary Carpenter had been trying to inform the public of the scandalous situation of children sentenced to prison. In 1856, 1,990 children under twelve occupied English gaols.[22] In 1857, some 10,000 prisoners incarcerated in both England and Wales were under sixteen.[23] Industrial school legislation was created in 1854 and 1857. Mary Carpenter, along with Benjamin Waugh and Ellice Hopkins, lobbied throughout this period for more humane treatment of child law-breakers. It was not until the Industrial Schools Act of 1880 that the law allowed children under sixteen to be removed from parents or employers running a disorderly house.

It would appear that the Commissioners expected the pro-Repeal witnesses to be content with such piecemeal alterations to the existing system of regulation. They asked both Josephine Butler and Daniel Cooper if they would object to an Act that would allow the state to arrest young persons under the age of sixteen found engaging in prostitution and send them to a government-run institution. Both objected strongly to this suggestion. Butler asserted that all young children should be removed from a life of vice, but resisted the idea of state intervention. 'Every girl of that tender age should be taken into a home or industrial school,' she answered, 'but there should be nothing penal or legislative.'[24] In this statement Butler encapsulated the primary dilemma of these reformers. On the one hand, they bitterly rejected the intervention of the state into the private lives of its citizens. This was one of the grounds on which they opposed the CD Acts. Yet on the other hand, it was impossible effectively to rescue and reform victims of the system without such intervention.

Both Butler and Cooper claimed that the institution of the Acts had led to an increase in child prostitution. Butler argued that the British legislation was even worse than that of 'wicked France', where at least technically the law would not allow for the registration of girls under sixteen. In Britain, according to the evidence provided by Dr Sloggett, girls as young as eleven and twelve were registered.[25] Once registered, like their French counterparts, these girls would have to continue in prostitution. As in France, the system was really predicated on the idea that such girls were potential prostitutes. Therefore, rather than protect them or prevent their further demise, the law effectively secured them a fulltime career in prostitution.

Such children, it was claimed, once registered were too brutalized to be reformed. Butler argued that the problems supposedly alleviated by the Acts could better be controlled by creating laws to punish seduction. Both the attempt to thwart the spread of venereal disease and to reduce the levels of child prostitution would be better served, she maintained, if the age of consent were raised. 'Seduction,' she told the Commissioners, 'must be punished.'

At present for the purpose of seduction, and of seduction only, our law declares every female child a woman at 12 years of age. I am ashamed to have to confess to such a shameful state of the law before you gentlemen, but a child is a woman for that purpose and that purpose alone, at twelve years of age. I know from my experience amongst this class of women, that many have become so from that cause.[26]

Daniel Cooper was called to give evidence to the Royal Commission in late April 1871. Much of his evidence repeated Butler's opinions. He believed that juvenile prostitution was increased because many girls were falsely accused of prostitution. He claimed that the Acts positively promoted vice, citing the example of a prostitute who showed her registration certificate as proof of her good health. The aspect of the Acts which most disturbed Cooper, and which he believed had a direct influence on juvenile prostitution, was the parade of 'Queen's Women' through the streets. The spectacle of girls as young as nine or ten being rounded up with the other women he found particularly cruel. This scene, he told the Commissioners, could only brutalize any child who saw it. Both Butler and Cooper spoke of their horror at seeing children playing at examination outside the government Lock facilities. They both claimed that the system of regulation necessarily brutalized children, making them more vicious and corrupt than the older prostitutes.

Such evidence was in keeping with that provided by witnesses in favour

of the CD Acts. Mr Westbrook, Inspector of Metropolitan Police at Portsmouth, claimed that regulation had a very bad effect on young girls,

> because a young girl is almost sure to take the disease, and she is taken
> into the hospital. There is a young girl of 18 in hospital now who has
> been in 17 times, and in such hospitals as they are, it is like turning
> young pick-pockets among housebreakers. They are ruined after having
> been in hospital, because there are such things going on there.[27]

Implicit in this statement is the suggestion that young girls were both
more receptive to disease and more liable to corruption than older women.
When asked about the children he saw in his ministration as the Chaplain
of the Royal Albert Hospital Devonport, the Reverend Isaac Hawker said
that they were worse than the older women, 'far worse . . . more shameless
and hardened'.[28] Such evidence shows how ideas about the innate depravity of such children influenced the way child prostitutes were perceived.
Even reformers who sought to save these children were influenced by the
image of youthful depravity. The treatment of child prostitutes under the
Acts was in many ways a self-fulfilling prophecy. Girls were brought in
to be registered because of their potential for sexual immorality and the
spread of disease and then, due to the system, were forced to live up to
this potential.

The Majority Report of the Commission recommended a continuation
of the Acts. The evidence of the Repealers must have made some impact
as the Report also encouraged the government to pass additional reforms
to raise the age of consent, to send prostitutes under sixteen to industrial
schools and to suppress brothels and procurers more actively. Far from
heeding these recommendations, the government sought to control the
problem by institutionalizing the child prostitute: in effect, punishing her
for the crime that befell her. This attitude reflects the contradictory position of the child prostitute. On one level, she was the epitome of innocence
betrayed and was treated with more sympathy than her adult counterparts.
Yet the ambiguity surrounding the age of consent and the ineffectual attempts made by government to deal with the problem of child prostitution
reflect the fact that the state assumed a potential sexual pathology in the
female that could manifest itself even in the child.

In 1872 H.A. Bruce, the Home Secretary, introduced a Bill that would
have implemented many of the desired reforms. The Bill was intended to
supersede the CD Acts and also sought to raise the age of consent to
fourteen and to provide harsher penalties for harbouring girls under fifteen
for the purposes of prostitution and summary convictions for brothelkeepers.[29] Both those involved in the Abolition movement and those active

in the campaign to reform the protective legislation for girls were deeply divided over the Bill. While on the one hand it addressed some of the reforms they had demanded, in effect it maintained the same elements of compulsion that were found in the CD Acts, which they greatly opposed. In the end it was not passed. The following year another Bill was introduced into the House of Commons which also attempted to raise the age of consent to fourteen. It was later withdrawn. In 1875 the age of consent was raised to thirteen and the seduction of a child under the age of twelve was made a felony (38 & 39 VIC c94 s3).

While the government was proceeding with more protective legislation for girls, the call for the repeal of the CD Acts was growing stronger. Between 1870 and 1882 a Select Committee was held to investigate the workings of the regulation system and two Select Committees were held on the laws relating to the protection of young girls. The Select Committee on the Contagious Diseases Acts was very much a face-saving device for the government. Its purpose was to examine several contentious issues raised by the Acts, particularly whether they breached the Constitution, whether they treated women unfairly and whether they had any effect on child prostitution. The Committee found that juvenile prostitution 'was the principal source by which the supply of fallen women is kept up', but claimed that the Acts had diminished the number of child prostitutes. Several causes were cited for this reduction in the subjected districts, among them the suggestion that want of parental control was remedied by the information that police gave parents as to the dangers of the streets and by the authority which police exerted in attempts to reclaim young girls. The system itself was said to act as a deterrent and it was claimed that police were very effective in preventing brothelkeepers from habouring young girls.

The evidence of the police confirmed the worst suspicions of reformers. Police witnesses such as Alfred William Cosser, Chief Constable of Portsmouth, implied that action taken by police was haphazard and based upon the individual officer's notion of duty. Cosser claimed that he thought his officers should intervene in situations that appeared dangerous for young girls. Girls found in 'dangerous situations' should be sent to private, charitable institutions. When asked what he considered a dangerous situation, he said merely being alone in the streets at night was enough. Such intervention was outside the scope of the Act and was not the sort of reform that rescue workers believed was required. Frederic Wheeler, member of the Society of Friends and Chairman of the Committee of the Chatham Refuge for Unfortunate Women, said such intervention amounted to little more than harassment: so many girls worked long hours that they were often on the street at night. Such 'friendly' intervention from 'kindly' police officers could and did lead to girls being falsely labelled as prostitutes. Nor did pro-Repeal witnesses believe that the level of juvenile prostitution was reduced. Figures on juvenile prostitution shown to the Committee by Daniel Cooper directly contradicted those given by the police. Cooper showed that in the subjected district of Devonport for the years 1870 to 1881 his society had rescued twenty-nine girls under the age of seventeen, five of whom were diseased, while Captain Harriss's report for the same district showed only one girl under sixteen and only six girls between the age of sixteen and seventeen were registered. Cooper's evidence showed that this was not unique to Harriss's district. Harriss's report from all eighteen subjected districts showed only sixty-eight registered prostitutes under the age of sixteen. Yet Cooper's returns for only Devonport, Plymouth and Stonehouse showed that seventy-nine girls under sixteen had been rescued from those districts.

It seems clear from this evidence that the indiscriminate and irregular methods used by the police were ineffective either in preventing juvenile prostitution or in reducing the number of children with venereal disease. This was certainly the opinion of the Select Committee of the House of Lords regarding the Law relating to the Protection of Young Girls in 1882 which stated that 'juvenile prostitution, from an almost incredibly early age' existed to an appalling extent throughout England. This Committee and the Select Committee to Investigate into the Traffic of English Girls to Foreign Destinations resulted from a series of scandals that developed in the late 1870s.

The situation regarding the traffic of English children to foreign destinations was brought to a head in early May 1880. In defiance of all her advisers, Josephine Butler published a scathing letter titled 'The Modern Slave Trade' in *The Shield*. She regretted that she might scandalize the readership but argued that it was necessary to bring these matters to the public notice.

> We are sometimes entreated not to speak of these things, and even the ears of some of our best friends and fellow workers are too sensitive to endure the bitter cry of these outraged ones. . . . But Sir, I can no longer refrain from echoing that cry. . . . I consider it to be a duty, even at risk of scandalizing some of your readers, to tell them the results of this illegal and cruel system.[30]

In the letter she told of the terrible trade in human flesh that was carried on on the Continent. In such brothels, she claimed, there are immured little children, English girls of from twelve to fifteen years of age, lovely creatures (for they do not care to pay for any who are not beautiful) innocent creatures too, stolen, kidnapped, betrayed, got from English country villages by every artifice. These little creatures never leave these rooms . . . *they never see the sun.*[31]

Butler's letter was generally ignored in England, but in Europe it caused a sensation. The Belgian authorities sought to extradite Butler to repeat her statement on oath before a magistrate. Many of her friends warned her not to take up this challenge, but she remained steadfast. She sent a sworn deposition to the Home Office. At the same time her Federation prepared to mount a private prosecution against several Belgian brothelkeepers for prostituting girls under the age of twenty-one. They were to use the evidence of four of the girls rescued from Belgian brothels by a young Quaker missionary called Alfred Dyer. Under cross-examination these girls told of their systematic kidnapping, the prison-like conditions they were kept under, their regular beatings and brutalization. In the course of giving their evidence, they all suggested police complicity with brothelkeepers, thus incriminating the *Police des Mœurs.*

In England the results of this trial caused quite an uproar. Lord Granville introduced a motion in the House of Lords to inquire into the state of the law relative to the protection of young girls. The Select Committee was set up in mid-1881. While this committee had been established to examine the 'white slave trade' to the Continent, most of the witnesses spoke of the flourishing trade in child prostitution in London. One witness stated that older women were forced to dress as children in order to get any trade.[32] Further scandalous accusations were made at the Select Committee the following year.

While the intention of reformers and rescue workers was to play upon the spectre of helpless innocence corrupted by a brutal system of vice in order to force improvements to the law, this was not the image of the child prostitute that came across at the hearings. Committee Members were incredulous when faced with evidence that girls as young as twelve could and did find lodgings in which to take clients, that girls as young as thirteen 'kept' young men of their own class, and that twelve-year-old girls solicited elderly gentlemen. The police witnesses were particularly cynical in their reporting of cases of child prostitution. One policeman describing his experience with a thirteen-year-old prostitute, said, '[H]er fingers were covered with rings . . . she waited till "her man" went away in the van, and then she hurried up to the police court to see him there'.[33] Inspector Joseph H.Y. Dunlop, Superintendent of C Division of the Metropolian Police, told the Committee:

I had a warrant to execute a short time ago, to arrest some brothel keepers, and I went with my Chief-Inspector, and in each of the rooms I found an elderly gentleman with two of these children. I asked their ages and got into a conversation with them. They knew perfectly well that I could not touch them in the house; and they laughed and joked me [*sic*] and I could get no direct answers whatsoever.[34]

While some witnesses maintained that seduction was the principal cause of child prostitution, most suggested that it was merely the inevitable outcome of the culture of poverty. The image of the street-smart, working-class girl, negotiating with police and accustomed to the depraved culture of the streets, was a far cry from the portrait of helpless babes falling into the snares of evil procurers of the 1850s but it was not necessarily any more or less realistic.

This confusion relates to the image of the depraved child prostitute that had been developing throughout the period. In part it reflected the inability of middle-class reformers to correlate their ideal of untainted childhood with the reality of working-class existence. But more significantly it represented the shift away from the idea of the child prostitute as the reformer's idealistic model of innocence corrupted, to its opposite, that of innate depravity. Earlier reformers had suggested that there was little hope for some children, given the dreadful conditions they were forced to live in. The Reverend Ralph Wardlaw, writing in the early 1840s, suggested that the practice of child prostitution was due solely to the 'unnaturalness' of working-class parents. Such parents brought up their daughters in 'licentious habits', their primary concern being to what profitable account their children could be turned. 'When their girls grow up,' he reported, 'prostitution is regarded, both by parents and children . . . not in its sinfulness and its dishonour, but as one amongst other means in their choice of getting a livelihood.'[35] Mr Miller, writing in 1856 of the case of an eight-year-old girl seduced in her mother's house, claimed that

[A]n abundant source of prostitution, in the lower ranks, is the force of early habits and education – education, not in knowledge but in vice and crime. Children are born to unchastity. Their parents are the offscourings of the earth: the first words a daughter hears are those of cursing and blasphemy; the only example her childhood sees is that of obscenity and vice; such youth is an apt learner, and at the age of ten or twelve, she may be a prostitute and a thief – her lapsed state having proved rather a simple progress than a fall.[36]

Such claims suggested a lack of consent in these children as there were no other options open to them. By the 1880s, the child prostitute was being portrayed not as a hapless victim of the system but as a keen manipulator of the sexual and economic options available to her. This is very much the image of the child prostitute presented by the witnesses before the Select Committees of 1881 and 1882. Such children were described as being 'addicted to prostitution'. They became prostitutes 'spontaneously'. The notion that girls were forced onto the streets by their parents or lured into brothels was hotly disputed. Mr Dunlop, when asked what he considered to be the general cause of the fall of these girls, stated:

> It is only an opinion; but it appears to me that influence has much to do with it. There are a lot of little servant girls in my division in lodgings, and other places; they are of every kind; they get small wages; they come out on errands; they see girls walking about the streets, their equals in social standing; they see them dressed in silks and satins; they do not think of the way they get the money; they say, 'You can go and dress in silks and satins while I am slaving'; they talk to the girls and they are influenced.[37]

Mr Daniel Morgan, Inspector of Criminal Investigations, X Division Paddington, stated that girls as young as eleven and twelve become accustomed to being 'accosted in the streets by men, who offer money and make improper overtures to them, and so they are led on by the evil association of other girls . . . [and] drift into a life of immorality'.[38] When asked by the Bishop of London whether he believed girls fell into prostitution from poverty, Morgan replied that he had never met with an instance of a girl who became immoral due to poverty.

Child prostitution came to be considered not the result of abject poverty or the behaviour of wicked seducers, but as merely the natural course of a working girl's life. This shift had been developing since the interest in child prostitution began. The lack of real interest in doing anything to effectively reduce the number of girls on the street reflected the underlying assumption of medicine and the law that the child prostitute was simply another variation of pathological female sexuality. Fear of the spread of venereal infection by the child prostitute far outweighed any concern raised about the seduction of minors. While in theory many sympathized with the plight of such children, the sexualized girl-child was widely considered an aberration and responsible for her own demise. Fear of syphilis meant that the contaminating role of the prostitute outshone the notion of innate childhood innocence.

PART IV
Syphilis, Male Sexuality and Female Degeneration

We must remember that the diseased state of the spermatozoa and, consequently of the embryo, proceeds primarily from the vices of the male. Alcoholic, nicotic, and syphilitic poisons were first engendered in the male organism and then transmitted to the offspring. The first drunken woman was the daughter of a male drunkard. The ferments of male animals are not poisons to the female – they are potent, not noxious. The human race is suffering from over-fertilization and enforced reproduction. Man, the destroyer, has been at work, not woman the constructor. When man is continent, the mysterious origin of cancer will be solved. . . . Sexual germs are not confined to the reproductive organs; they permeate the whole body. Assimilation and absorption by the female organism cannot divest them of their potential properties of stimulation and disintegration, of decay and corruption.

Frances Swiney, *The Bar of Isis*

8 The Sins of the Father

Most historians who have examined the subject of venereal disease in nineteenth-century Britain tend to conclude their studies with the repeal of the Contagious Diseases Acts in 1886. The period between 1886 and the Royal Commission into Venereal Disease has only been of interest to historians of first-wave feminism investigating the suffragette interest in syphilis and social purity.[1] That is not to say that interest in venereal disease faded during this time, but it did shift focus away from a direct connection to prostitution. This was largely due to a renewed interest in the question of congenital or hereditary syphilis. If the medical profession in Great Britain turned a blind eye to children with acquired syphilis in the nineteenth century, they positively ignored children with symptoms of congenital syphilis. To a certain extent this was due to mistaken ideas about the gravity of the condition that can be directly attributed to the work of John Hunter, but the basis of this error was the ever-increasing belief in the feminine responsibility for the spread of the disease. Syphilis and gonorrhoea were largely treated as the product of the diseased female body; the question of male responsibility in the spread of the disease was generally ignored in the medical literature. Moreover, in practice, doctors considered venereal disease only to be the product of immorality. This meant that medical discourse tended to overlook the possibility that men could pass on the disease, especially to 'innocent' wives and children. Increased concern about the problem of congenital syphilis at the turn of the century meant that many doctors shifted their attention briefly to the role of men in the spread of syphilis. This reflected not only the impact of feminist and eugenicist ideas on medical discourse but was also related to growing doubts within the medical establishment about the transmission of congenital syphilis.

As more became known about venereal disease generally, doubts about the transmission of congenital syphilis arose. Some doctors came to believe that it was possible for men to pass on syphilis to their children without infecting their mother. Such an idea challenged the connection between femininity and disease and implicated men in the spread of syphilis. The idea of male responsibility had been advocated by those feminists such as Josephine Butler during the campaign to repeal the CD Acts and was taken up with increased enthusiasm by many of those women demanding suffrage. Eugenicists who were greatly concerned with the decline of the race also promoted the idea that men could and did infect

143

unsuspecting wives and children. For a time, the medical establishment
endorsed this idea and sought ways to limit the possibility of such disastrous unions occurring. It would appear that the concerns of the medical
profession remained primarily the defence of traditional family values and
male sexual privilege. This of course limited the effectiveness of any
action on the part of doctors to prevent the transmission of congenital
syphilis. It did not take long for the prostitute to resurface in the medical
literature as the 'source' of both acquired syphilis and congenital syphilis.
This time, however, the notion of congenital defect was incorporated into
the disease model. During the nineteenth century, it was argued that the
capacity to infect was inscribed on the body of the prostitute. In the early
years of the twentieth century, this notion was elaborated upon – not only
were prostitutes considered inherently infectious, but it was argued they
were born that way. In other words, congenitally syphilitic prostitutes
were held responsible for the transmission of congenital syphilis. Not only
did this allow male responsibility for the spread of the disease to be ignored but, in suggesting that some women were 'born prostitutes', it was
possible to avoid any question of male responsibility for the sexual exploitation of these women.

There is considerable doubt about when congenital and hereditary syphilis
were first recognized. Theodore Rosebury, writing on the antiquity of
syphilis, has suggested that both hereditary and congenital syphilis are re-
fered to in the Bible.[2] The problem of hereditary syphilis had been reported
shortly after the siege of Naples. In 1498 Gaspar Torella, the Valencian
doctor-bishop, mentioned its existence in the offspring of syphilitic parents.
He and other contemporary observers believed it was possibly transmitted
during birth or through the mother's infected milk. Paracelsus, writing in
1529, was the first to recognize the hereditary nature of the disease for
he recognized it at birth, thus showing that it must have been contracted
in utero. His description of the transmission of the disease, 'fit morbus
hereditarius et transit a patre ad filium', reflects the common opinion at the
time that the responsibility for the disease in the child rested upon the
father, as the mother often appeared in good health. Ferrier, writing in
1553, extended this idea, claiming that the noxious agent could be attached to either the paternal or the maternal germ cell. He also recognized
that syphilis could be acquired at conception or after conception. By the
end of the seventeenth century, doctors had noted that even years after a
dose of primary syphilis parents could produce syphilitic children, that
syphilitic children could infect their wet-nurses and that inherited syphilis
often did not show up in infants until they were five or six years old.[3]

In Britain, there was much discussion of both congenital and hereditary syphilis before the publication of Hunter's treatise. James Handley, Surgeon to the Royal Navy, wrote in 1743 that 'a person can be infected with the grand pox' by 'impure embraces' and from 'pocky parents'. He also recognized that infants could infect wet-nurses and wet-nurses could infect infants.[4] A text published around the same time by the English physician Nicholas Robinson made explicit references to the effects of both congenital and hereditary syphilis. He wrote extensively on the subject stating:

> The third and last way of getting the Infection, is when the Infant received the Disease from its Parents in Embryo; and the Child in such a Case is said to be hereditarily affected: This is the most deplorable Case that can Happen, yet certain I am that such Objects are but too frequently met with in Practice, now-a-days: Sometimes a Child is so rotten with the Pox, that it dies before the Birth, sometimes it expires as soon as born; but if such Infants live, then, in a little Time, there arise hard, fetid Pustules in the Head, Face and Mouth, which in some are diffused all over the Body, in a most frightful Manner; nor is it scarce possible to relieve such Objects; for the Children thus affected if they live, are born Heirs to Pills, Potions and Powders all the Days of Their Lives.[5]

As late as 1757, the anonymous author of *Every Man Is His Own Physician in Venereal Cases* makes reference to the effects of both congenital and hereditary syphilis when he wrote:

> [I]t is notorious from Experience not only children are often infected by their Nurses, but that Nurses are infected by their Sucklings; and that in the former case when this Disease hath continued some Time unobserved without medical help the tender Bones of Children have been eroded by its Virulency.[6]

All discussion of congenital syphilis was dismissed by John Hunter and indeed, because of his great authority, there were few advances on the subject until the end of the nineteenth century. Hunter's failure to recognize the possibility of inherited syphilis was perhaps the most tragic of his errors, both for his wife and children and for countless other women and children. Because Hunter held that it was only the primary lesion that was infectious he would not admit the possibility of intrauterine transmissions of the disease to the infant. He held that infants who showed signs of syphilis shortly after their birth must have been infected during their path through the birth canal by a local primary sore. The possibility of recognizing congenital syphilis was further hampered by Hunter's failure to acknowledge the infectiousness of secondary lesions and his dismissal of

Morgani's evidence showing that syphilis could affect the internal organs. Hunter recommended that men were safe to marry a year after their dose of primary syphilis had disappeared and suggested that men with gonorrhoea were safe to engage in intercourse so long as they wiped any offending 'matter' off the penis beforehand.[7] Hunter, being a 'man of conviction', married some three years after his unfortunate experimentations with syphilis, having put off his marriage until his infection could be controlled. Several of his biographers have suggested that three years was not long enough, as he lost two children in infancy and one of his children who did survive showed signs of mental imbalance in adulthood.[8]

Despite the lack of interest in England, doctors in France and Ireland continued to work on the problem of hereditary syphilis. In 1780 a special hospital was established for venereally infected expectant mothers and their infants and in 1810, Bertin, a physician from this hospital, published a book specifically dealing with babies infected with syphilis. In this work, Bertin provided a detailed account of the symptoms of venereal disease in infants. He placed particular emphasis on ophthalmia which he believed could end in blindness.[9]

The Dublin surgeon, Abraham Colles, wrote a treatise on syphilis in 1837 in which he observed that he had never witnessed an instance where a child with syphilitic ulcers had infected an asymptomatic mother, though the healthiest of nurses would be infected. This observation became known as Colles' Law and was widely misunderstood.[10] It was taken by many doctors during the late nineteenth and early twentieth century that Colles' dictum meant that the mothers did not have syphilis and they had developed antitoxins from the syphilitic foetus. For example, George F. Still, Professor of Diseases, Kings College Hospital, writing of Colles' Law in 1914 stated emphatically:

> This immunity, however, cannot in the light of recent pathology be taken as proof that the mother has had the disease. It is quite conceivable . . . [that] the mother may absorb from the syphilitic foetus some antitoxin and so gain immunity herself, partial or complete. Whether or not the *Spirochaete pallidum* proves to be the specific cause of this disease or not, the theory of maternal immunity from the foetus seems at least to be a plausible one.[11]

It is clear now that the correct explanation for Colles' observation is that the mother suffers from latent syphilis and has a degree of immunity to super-infection from her child.[12] It is also true that the longer the duration of untreated syphilis in the mother, the less likely that the foetus will die *in utero*, and the more likely a syphilitic infant will be born. Recent medical findings have indicated that pregnancy has a benign effect on syphilis in the mother. The pregnant syphilitic presents few symptoms of the disease and after a series of pregnancies, though untreated, she may appear to be cured, with negative blood tests in approximately twenty per cent of cases.[13]

In 1834, the Irish doctor William Wallace noted the infectiousness of secondary syphilis. The medical profession in Germany took advantage of this observation, but in France and England the authority of Hunter and Ricord held sway. Wallace died of typhus in 1837 before he could complete his research on syphilis.[14] Had he lived to finish his work it is quite possible that studies of congenital syphilis might have benefited from his knowledge but it was not until the 1850s, when Paul Diday and Rollet of Lyons were challenging Ricord's authority on the question of the infectiousness of secondary syphilis, that much interest was taken in congenital syphilis.

In 1854, Diday, a student of Ricord's, published his work on syphilis providing a full description of the deformities found in infants born of syphilitic parents. The mother, he believed, generally infected the foetus after being infected by the father.[15] Around the same time in Great Britain, Sir Jonathan Hutchinson began working in this area. He was the first to describe the pegged and notched teeth characteristic of congenital syphilis and he noted that these were often seen with interstitial keratitis and nerve deafness. These three signs became known as the Hutchinsonian triad.

Hutchinson's work created much interest in Great Britain. In 1876, all the reports of the London Pathological Society in *The Lancet* were devoted to a discussion of his works. Yet there was little agreement on the nature of acquired syphilis, and none on hereditary syphilis. The importance of hereditary syphilis continued to be overlooked. The report of the Skey Committee in 1867, for instance, recognized that a dose of syphilis might recur regardless of the form of treatment and that no person who has been the 'subject of true syphilis' could be promised immunity from a relapse. Yet the vast majority of doctors called before the Committee maintained that it was safe to marry a year after the infection had passed.[16] While it was maintained that asymptomatic parents could produce a syphilitic child, most doctors went along with Hunter's idea that most syphilis in infants was the result of active syphilis in the mother. In the Majority Report of the 1882 Select Committee into the workings of the CD Acts there was no mention of hereditary syphilis. This is hardly surprising as many of those in favour of the Acts believed that it was a credit to the system of regulation that many diseased prostitutes quit the streets and married.

Many doctors favoured the idea that it was the mother who infected the child. The question of the father infecting the child at conception had been dismissed by Dr Thomas Ballard, President of the Harveian Society of London, who stated '[I]f the causes of death resided in the germ, it surely would not grow. The defective state of the soil seems sufficient to account for the blight of the young creature, which is so dependent on it for nourishment.'[17] A contrary view was expressed by Sir Jonathan Hutchinson in 1876, when he declared that hereditary syphilis was for the most part derived from the father exclusively. He was 'firmly of the opinion that in a large majority of instances in English practice, the inheritance of syphilis is from the father, the mother having never suffered before conception'.[18] While this theory explained why some women could give birth to congenitally syphilitic children while appearing 'untainted', it raised more questions than it answered. For instance, if fathers were predominantly to blame for congenital syphilis, how was it that asymptomatic women gave birth to healthy infants, who were then afflicted by syphilis shortly after birth? Hutchinson's explanation for this – that 'the child may manifest symptoms of syphilis in some such manner as chlorophyll is developed in leaves of a plant or as a tadpole is developed into a frog by the same influence' – was hardly convincing.[19] Yet those who criticized Hutchinson usually came up with equally implausible explanations.

During the 1870s, the systematic dangers of syphilis were being rediscovered. Rudolph Virchow, one of the leading figures in the development of germ theory, showed that syphilitic infection could be transferred through the blood to the internal organs and that syphilis was, in fact, a systemic condition. By 1876, doctors had re-established that syphilis could affect the cardiovascular system and the spinal cord. As Allen M. Brandt has noted, the 'discoveries of the nefarious spread of syphilis to the internal organs made clear that the disease was much more dangerous than many doctors had previously assumed'.[20] This was also true of gonorrhoea. In 1872, the American physician Emil Noeggerath demonstrated the dangers of latent gonorrhoea in men. He believed that many men married while they still had gonorrhoea but were asymptomatic and subsequently infected their wives. He attributed ninety per cent of sterility in women to this cause. Around this time, it was also discovered that gonococcus could cause blindness in newborn babies. Acknowledging the significance of these ideas for the health of women and children was, however, resisted in England.[21]

The work of J. Alfred Fournier confirmed the growing fears of the more enlightened members of the medical profession. Fournier was a pupil of Ricord. He inherited Ricord's private practice and married his daughter.[22] He had written extensively on many aspects of syphilis before turning his attention to the tragedy of the disease in infants. Fournier stressed the importance of syphilis as a cause of degenerative change. He was among the first to show the relationship between *tabes dorsalis* (a degenerative condition of the spine), general paralysis of the insane (GPI) and syphilis. His emphasis on degenerative change allowed him to describe in considerable detail the conditions of 'congenital syphilis' in which children are born healthy but suffer from serious effects of the disease years later.

Until this time, there had been considerable resistance to the idea that children who showed no obvious symptoms of syphilis could develop syphilis-related disorders later in life. Moreover, if a baby developed syphilis shortly after birth and survived, many doctors were unaware of complications that might occur later in life. Fournier emphasized the distinction between syphilis acquired after conception, which became known as 'hereditary syphilis' and syphilis acquired at conception, which was called 'congenital syphilis'. He maintained that congenital syphilis was far more serious than hereditary syphilis. Fournier demonstrated the predisposition of children with congenital syphilis to meningitis, severe mental retardation, hydrocephalus and other constitutional disorders. Indeed, Fournier was the first to attempt a systematic discussion of congenital syphilis.

Fournier's chief mission in life was to promote an understanding of the dangers syphilis posed, especially within marriage. In his work *Syphilis and Marriage*, published in France in 1880, Fournier stressed the need for syphilitic men to be particularly careful when entering upon matrimony. Fournier did not suggest that syphilitic men should be barred entirely from marriage; he merely indicated that they should wait until at least four years after the initial outbreak of symptoms. Fournier was greatly concerned about the dangers faced by women in such a situation. However, unlike later feminists who took up his ideas, Fournier did not challenge the patriarchal dominance of fathers over their offspring; rather, he attempted to remedy men's ways with an appeal to their duty as patriarchs. He wrote, '[N]ow to my mind, as I understand the question, a man who, before marriage has contracted syphilis, may become dangerous in marriage in three directions; – *firstly* as husband; *secondly* as father; *thirdly*, as head of the social community which he constitutes by his marriage'.[23] He did not believe that men should be prevented from marriage due to a bout of syphilis; rather, he maintained that it was a man's duty as husband and father to wait until he was entirely cured to embark on procreation.

While Fournier's intention was not to focus attention on middle-class men as the primary source of venereal misery, his contributions to the discussion of congenital syphilis did just that. Indeed, Fournier's major contribution to the late nineteenth-century discussion of syphilis was the reassertion of the importance of the paternal origin. Swediaur had suggested this possibility in the late eighteenth century but it had been generally ignored. During the 1850s, Diday had mentioned the possibility of paternal infection in his work *Infantile Syphilis*. Diday maintained that many women gave birth to congenitally infected children yet remained apparently free from the disease themselves. For Diday the imprint of the paternal was omnipresent. For instance, he cites the case of the wife of a syphilitic man who gave birth to a child who became syphilitic. The woman, however, suffered no symptoms of the disease. The woman on becoming a widow, married a healthy man, but again gave birth to a syphilitic child. Diday supposes in this case that an impression was left behind on the woman by her first husband, 'as the subsequent foals of a mare once covered by a zebra are sometimes impressed with the markings of a zebra'.[24]

The importance of recognizing paternal infection had been pronounced in England by Hutchinson and had been hotly debated. Fournier took a much stronger stance. He rejected claims that the birth of the paternally infected congenital syphilitic was 'only a very rare thing'. He felt it absurd to admit that the 'state of a diseased father' could be 'inoffensive to his progeny'.

> What! When we see, so repeatedly and so manifestly, paternal heredity revealing itself in the child by so many resemblances of all kinds. When we see this attested not only by moral and physical analogy, but also by the most striking pathological analogy, can we believe that inheritance will not exercise itself with regard to a malady such as syphilis, a malady especially diasthetic, especially chronic, affecting the organism so deeply as to have the double power of affecting the whole system and of developing its manifestations at almost any period, at any lapse of time, even up to thirty, forty, fifty years from its origin![25]

In this way, Fournier reasserted Hutchinson's explanation of how children could be born with syphilis while their mother appeared free from the disease. Fournier also popularized the notion of syphilis by conception which had first been put forward by both Ricord and Diday. Hutchinson and other doctors had puzzled at the idea of whether it was possible for a woman to become syphilitic without a primary lesion, without chancre, and become diseased by contact with a husband exempt since marriage from all contagious lesions. To this query Fournier stated that it was possible if the woman was pregnant, had just been confined or had recently miscarried.

> The wife-mother infected in this manner, that is to say become syphilitic without primary symptoms, and become so by contact with a husband

long since freed from all exterior indications, is a patient who contracts syphilis, not from her husband *but from her child*.[26]

Fournier asked: if it was possible for the mother to communicate it to her infant, *in utero*, why was it not possible for the reverse to be true? The most common explanation of this was Hutchinson's idea of foetal blood contamination.[27] Opponents of this theory claimed that the placenta acted as a filter which prevented the passage of contagious germs in the direction of the mother.[28] Fournier argued that in the case of syphilis by conception 'it would be remarkable if the mother remained free with such chances of contagion'.[29] Fournier rejected the idea that infection could be passed on through semen, claiming that experimental evidence proved that syphilitic semen inoculated on healthy subjects would not result in syphilis.[30] It was conception that allowed the disease to develop in the mother. Later observers, such as Fournier's American protégé Prince Albert Morrow, described the phenomenon in terms of the specific action of an infected sperm on the ovum.

A woman may be inundated with the sperm of a syphilitic and remain healthy, but if one of her ovules be fecundated by this same sperm the virulent principle is kindled into action, in some mysterious and inexplicable way there is engendered a syphilitic being, which, through the agency of fetal [*sic*] blood, will contaminate the mother.[31]

Certain observers had claimed that while they accepted that fathers could infect their children they believed that this resulted in less serious cases of congenital syphilis than if the mother infected the child. Fournier would have none of this. Indeed, he maintained that the 'syphilis of the father' was far more dangerous to the child. Foetuses infected by the father, Fournier said, suffered from an 'inaptitude for life, showing itself as death, which takes place either *in utero* or very shortly after birth'.[32] Fathers were also to blame for constitutional weakness, morbid tendencies, degenerations, congenital malformations and arrested developments. Worse symptoms followed if both parents were infected. Again Fournier blames men for this. The children of two syphilitic parents, Fournier maintains, were exposed to 'certain morbid conditions, [and] to certain morbid inclinations'. Such children, he claimed, were recognizable by their 'inherent weakness'.

They come into this world diminutive, mean-looking, sickly, of poor constitution, wrinkled, shrivelled, stunted-looking, 'like little old men' as is said, with skins too large for their little bodies.[33]

More than anything else, Fournier's work stressed the importance of the paternal in heredity. While it had long been recognized that the father contributed much to the child's heredity at the moment of conception, many scientific and lay observers maintained that foetus and nursling remained labile and malleable until weaning. Subsequently, much emphasis had been placed on the mother's physical, moral, mental and emotional state.[34] If Fournier's ideas were correct, the condition of the father at the moment of conception could seal a child's fate irrevocably. The concept of congenital error had become incorporated into the disease model.

The idea of paternal infection created a model of degeneracy that presumed that some acquired pathology in the father was the direct cause of the stigmata of degeneracy in the next generation.[35] The pendulum of blame had swung the other way. The fact that a father could transmit the disease to his innocent children proved a more ghastly idea than that women could generate the disease within themselves. This shifted the impact of blame away from the women and onto men, most especially middle-class men. The result of the double standard of sexual morality no longer meant that sometimes men were afflicted with a loathsome and troublesome disease, but that their whole life and that of their children could be affected. To use Alain Corbin's terms, in discussing Fournier's impact, it seemed as if he were translating the contemporary bourgeois into scientific language:

> Even more serious in nature than syphilis, hereditary syphilis struck most often in the upper classes since, according to Alfred Fournier, the fatal diasthesis was essentially of paternal origin. This was because in the bourgeoisie, male infidelities were much more common than female ones. The lower classes thus transmitted to the bourgeois male, via their womenfolk, a virulent syphilis which metamorphosed into a germ fatal to the whole line. Despite the purity of the wife-mother, the race – for which one should read the 'bourgeois family' – finds itself threatened by a rot which has its origins in the street or sixth floor.[36]

In such a scenario, the purity of the middle-class female stood for nothing as it appeared the father infected the line without noticeably infecting the mother. The basis for this belief was a misunderstanding of Colles' Law. Doctors explained women's immunity to syphilis in this situation as having developed antitoxins from the foetus. They found little to challenge this assumption. Given the almost complete ignorance of women on such matters at this time, it is very likely that many suffered from syphilis without being aware of it and also that many consulted doctors but were not treated in order to prevent them from knowing the real cause of their affliction.[37] As Sir Jonathan Hutchinson stated:

> It is improbable in the highest degree that a large number of married women should acquire syphilis in its primary form, pass through to its secondary stages and yet never know it. Yet this is the supposition which we must adopt, not once nor twice, but being an everyday occurrence, if we reject the belief that a syphilitic father may beget a syphilitic child quite independently of any previous infection in the mother.[38]

The general standards of modesty further confused the issue by preventing the physician from performing a complete examination on women unless the patient was a prostitute. Doctors usually accepted a patient's statement that she had never suffered from a chancre or disseminated rash. This failure led to the further strengthening of the concept of paternal transmission.[39]

The medical profession in Great Britain was slow to accept Fournier's idea that the father could infect the foetus at the moment of conception. Until the early twentieth century, the question of the father transmitting the disease to his wife and offspring was generally ignored. Doctors continued to blame women for the transmission of syphilis to the child and continued to advise men that it was safe to marry after a short interval. A 'Junior Member' wrote to the *British Medical Journal* in 1885 asking how to advise one of his patients, 'a young man, aged 25, of fair social position' and in the throes of secondary syphilis, who wished to marry. The editor advised that while it was not safe to marry immediately, after an interval of a year 'there would be much less risk' providing the patient underwent a course of mercury treatment.[40] During the most (in)famous divorce of the 1880s, that of Lord and Lady Colin Campbell in 1886, the Court was told that in 1882 Lord Campbell's surgeon, Mr William Allingham, FRCS and author of *On Diseases of the Rectum, their Diagnosis and Treatment*, advised him that sex with his wife would be beneficial to him while he was recovering from stricture of the urethra, caused by syphilis.[41] Even Sir Jonathan Hutchinson, who pioneered the idea of paternal infection, stated in his introduction to the English edition of Fournier's *Syphilis and Marriage*:

> No one can doubt that many patients who seek medical advice on this point receive permission to marry far too early, and under conditions when such permission had much better been withheld. Having said this, however, I must next in honesty add, that I feel scarcely prepared to go the full length which M. Fournier suggests, in the direction of caution and of prohibition. With his medical reasoning I fully agree, and what

of difference of opinion there may be between us concerns rather questions of social expediency than of pathological science.[42]

Hutchinson's comments related to a growing dilemma amongst doctors at this time as to what was the best approach to take in such cases. Hutchinson believed that the effects of prohibiting marriage for some syphilitic patients would result in more social evil than it would prevent, leading to 'the formation of illicit connections, or yet more degrading immorality'. He maintained that 'where . . . a social institution as vast as marriage is at stake, the surgeon must not push medical scruples too far'.[43] Such discussion raised other issues such as whether it was ethical to warn women, especially future wives, of such dangers. Many doctors maintained a 'conspiracy of silence' on the question, preferring that women should be kept ignorant for the greater benefit of society.[44] Other doctors, however, warmly welcomed Fournier's work on the subject. Frederick W. Lowndes, Surgeon to Liverpool Lock Hospital, in a review of *Syphilis and Marriage* dismissed Hutchinson's claims stating:

I must express my regret at the following sentence of Mr Hutchinson's: 'The surgeon who, on account of syphilis, forbids marriage to an otherwise eligible man, must remember that he forbids it at the same time to some woman who possibly, if well informed as to the risks, would willingly encounter them.' Now I maintain that no woman should be permitted to encounter such risks, and neither man or woman is justified in exposing to this risk an unborn child.[45]

While there is little evidence to suggest that women consulted their doctors on how soon they could marry after a dose of syphilis, doctors began to advise against it entirely. For instance, Dr C.R. Drysdale, physician to the London Rescue Society, thought that men might marry some three to four years after a dose of syphilis, but cautioned 'that a woman who had primary syphilis should never marry'.[46] It would seem that here Drysdale's medical opinion was influenced by his ideas of morality. It was the fact that the woman was immoral rather than that she was syphilitic that led him to this conclusion. He admitted this when he revealed that he was troubled by the problem of how to advise widows who wished to remarry but had innocently acquired the disease during their previous marriage. In 1885 Drysdale reviewed his position on men, claiming that he once thought it was safe to marry two years after the initial outbreak of syphilis but now suggested five years would be adequate. He remained adamant that syphilitic women should never marry.[47]

It was still possible in 1889 for Mr Lawson Tait, an eminent gynaecologist, to present a paper before the Nottingham Medico-Chirurgical Society claiming that the threat of congenital syphilis was not serious.[48] Throughout the 1890s, however, the British medical establishment came to recognize the risks to wives and children posed by syphilis and an increasing concern developed for those who 'innocently' acquired syphilis. This related to a growing recognition of symptoms hitherto unrelated to congenital syphilis.

During this time there was much debate as to which parent contributed the most to the infection of the child. Many doctors rejected the notion of maternal infection by conception, suggesting that it was very possible that symptoms of the disease had been ignored prior to conception.[49] Some doctors favoured the possibility of maternal syphilis in every case.[50] Other doctors retained the notion that fathers were primarily responsible for the transmission of the disease to the offspring and even claimed that it was possible for mothers to be infected by suckling their own congenitally infected infant.[51] By the first decade of the twentieth century, however, Dr R.J. Lee estimated that in Great Britain, in about ninety-five per cent of cases of congenital syphilis the mother was free from all symptoms of syphilis.[52] This belief in the immunity of mothers from the disease did not lessen, but rather strengthened the notion of male responsibility. Sayings like the 'sins of the father are visited upon their children' and 'the father has eaten sour grapes and set his children's teeth on edge' (referring to the characteristic teeth noted by Hutchinson) abounded in the literature on congenital syphilis.

The idea that sperm was the carrier of the infection became quite popular in both the medical and feminist texts on the subject. 'The commonest mode of transmission,' Still wrote, 'is that to which the name "sperm infection" has been applied'.[53] This led some more radical observers to suggest it was sperm itself that was the weak link. Some claimed that not only syphilis but a multitude of other skin diseases were caused by sperm being deposited in the pregnant woman's womb. The author of *Modern Researches* stated:

Those parents who have well-defined and positive convictions on the subject of sex-relations that there should not be any co-habitation after pregnancy is assured . . . in such cases there is no *vernix caseosa* found on the child at birth. . . . I believe it to be an indication of a disturbance in the maternal organism, that is a signal-light which Nature holds out so that he who runs may read, to warn mankind that there has been something at work that has been detrimental to the race . . . I repeat, that cheesy mess is not found on infants born to parents who believe that motherhood is a sacred and, as it were, a holy state.[54]

The feminist writer Frances Swiney took this idea one step further, claiming that in men who were alcoholics or syphilitics, not only the initial fertilising sperm brought disease to the ovum, but 'if sexual relations continue during gestation, the embryo [became] covered with toxic matter'. Nature, she mused,

> in vain warns and protests against any infringement of her decrees. Inexorably she demands the penalty to the third and fourth generation. The mortality of infants is thus more than often accounted for. They are often conceived in iniquity, of drunken, lustful parents; and developed in the rankest poison; they become stunted, malformed, diseased and prematurely old before they see the light.[55]

Historians who treat such claims by feminists as ill-informed and hysterical rantings have ignored the fact that much of what they wrote was derived from the medical debates around congenital syphilis at the time.[56]

By the 1890s, doctors in Britain were gradually accepting the fact that the symptoms of hereditary syphilis might be delayed longer than adolescence. Tom Robinson, doctor at St Andrew's Hospital, in consultation with Sir James Paget, wrote to *The Lancet* in 1895 on the dangers of 'delayed inherited syphilis'. Inherited syphilis he suggested, had 'three epochs of activity': where it manifests itself at or about birth; where it manifests during childhood; and where the disease is delayed until after puberty. 'If inherited syphilis will lie dormant for six years,' he asked, 'why should not the period be prolonged to thirty-six?'[57] The possibility that congenital symptoms could be delayed until adulthood added a new terror to syphilis.

Fournier had written in 1886 that it was 'a well-authenticated fact, albeit little-known and not generally accepted that the progeny of syphilitic subjects are sometimes intellectually deficient'.[58] He maintained that syphilis could be transmitted from generation to generation in the form of a predisposition to all kinds of other diseases or malformations, such as scrofula, tuberculosis, idiocy and rickets.[59] In France this phenomenon was referred to as *l'hérédité syphilis* and in England it was called parasyphilis or occult syphilis. Elizabeth Lomax has suggested that British doctors resisted these ideas but there is evidence to suggest that many treated them seriously. In 1892, the work of Drs Barlow and Judson Bury was presented to the London Medical Society. These doctors claimed that every variety of nervous affection of acquired syphilis had its parallel among congenital examples.[60] Other doctors were proposing a link between syphilis and cerebral palsy in children and claimed that syphilis was an important agent in the aetiology of such infantile disorders as hemiplegia and posterior basal meningitis. On the idea that idiocy and feeble-mindedness could be linked to syphilis, doctors in Britain had mixed opinions. Much of the discussion in the 1880s and early 1890s was negative. Dr Langdon-Down, writing in 1887, stated that his inquiries had confirmed that 'syphilis is not an important factor in the production of idiots'.[61] In 1892, Drs Shuttleworth and Beach examined the family histories of 2,380 cases of idiocy and imbecility in the Royal Albert Asylum and in Darneth Asylum and found only in twenty-eight cases an undoubted history of congenital syphilis.[62]

Such ideas about congenital syphilis must be placed within the context of discussion of degeneration that had begun in the 1850s with the publication of Bénédict-Augustin Morel's highly influential texts, *Traité des dégénérescences physiques, intéllectuels et morales de l'espèce humaine* in 1857 and *Traité des maladies mentales* in 1860. Morel's ideas stemmed from research he had undertaken on cretinism.[63] Cretinism, a condition caused by thyroid gland deficiency, presents a picture of mental retardation, dwarfism and other developemental defects from birth or early infancy. Morel was the centre of a debate on cretinism in the *Annales médico-psychologiques*. Unlike his counterparts who argued that cretinism was due to environment, Morel maintained that the problem lay in heredity. He stressed the incurability of certain types of cretin and argued that they were victims of a 'constitutional pre-disposition to the disease'. The historian Daniel Pick has suggested that the cretin's body defined the degenerate's body.[64]

It could also be argued that the syphilitic body became the degenerate's body. Morel's theories had wide-reaching implications. He defined degeneration as pathological deviations from the normal type, which are transmissible through heredity and which develop progressively until death. According to Morel's thesis, degeneration could be due to intoxication, social milieu, pathological or congenital insults of various kinds.[65]

The link between syphilis and degeneration was Morel's Law of Progressivity. This law stressed that in hereditary transmission from generation to generation, not only was the 'bad seed' passed along, but each new generation received a heavier and more destructive dose of whatever the evil influence was. Morel's work provided detailed examples of this process. The first generation was characterised by a nervous temperament and a tendency toward cerebral vascular congestion, as well as irritability, quick temper and resulting violent behaviour. The second generation ran the risk of illnesses of the central nervous system such as cerebral haemorrhages, epilepsy and the neurotic disorders of hysteria. In the third generation, degeneracy manifested itself in the form of insanity. As Eric T. Carlson records, by the fourth generation '[I]nfants were born with markedly reduced vitality, demonstrated a congenital weakness of their faculties and were sterile, imbeciles or idiots'.[66]

In Great Britain these ideas were taken up by the psychiatrist Henry Maudsley, who introduced the degeneracy theory into the debate on habitual criminals. Maudsley's ideas around degeneration went further than Morel's, combining the medico-psychiatric theory of *dégénérescences* with Social Darwinist theories of evolution and a positivist theory of criminal inheritance.[67] He came to believe that pathologies were inscribed upon the body. According to Pick, he described the body 'as a tree . . . whose age, history and health could be seen in cross-section'.[68] Integral to such thinking was the theory of progressive degeneration through inherited defects of the constitution.[69] Congenital syphilis, with its obvious physical signs, clearly leant itself to such an analysis.

The idea that pathology was inscribed on the body came to greatly influence the discussion of congenital syphilis. As Claude Quétel has pointed out, the notion of hereditary syphilis was extended by Fournier and other French clinicians to cover dementia and psychoses.[70] The question as to whether there was a causal connection between congenital syphilis and idiocy or mental degeneration remained a somewhat thorny one. During the 1890s, support was increasing for another of Fournier's theories – that general paralysis of the insane was actually a terminal form of syphilis. The apparent confirmation that GPI was related to syphilis and the notion of parasyphilis began to be more accepted. As George Rosen has noted, the 'theory of predestination in terms of an original biological sin exerted a powerful attraction on many psychiatrists and directed their attention away from any concept of specific aetiology'.[71] Consequently, epidemiological theories were framed in vague environmental terms. Doctors used language wonderfully evocative of degeneration to describe the onset of GPI and other related illnesses. *Tabes dorsalis*, for instance, was described as 'a slow process of decay and death of the intra-spinal portion of the sensory protoneurones'.[72] Indeed, Frederick Mott's description of general paralysis as the 'smouldering destruction of neural elements, the latter conflagration often fanned into flames by circulatory disturbances', could be described as apocalyptic.[73]

GPI had long been assumed to be a somatic illness with distinct physiological, pathological and psychological characteristics which could be triggered by a diverse list of causes such as 'brain exhaustion', irritation, excesses in drinking, overwork, vice or physical injury.[74] The discovery that GPI was related to syphilis conclusively connected it with the accepted nosography of degeneration, hereditary tendency to vice and disease. The German psychiatrist Richard von Krafft-Ebbing's description of GPI as a 'disease of civilization and syphilization' is illustrative of these connections. Such beliefs received further confirmation with the discovery of juvenile tabes and general paralysis in congenital syphilitics.

In both France and England, doctors argued over whether congenital syphilis could be passed onto the third and fourth generation. Sir Jonathan Hutchinson claimed that he had never seen an authenticated case of third-generation congenital syphilis.[75] But other doctors disagreed. Some used the Biblical authority that God would visit misfortune 'unto the third and fourth generations of them that hate me' to sustain their case.[76] Others maintained that the reason such cases were not blatantly apparent was the fact that sometimes the signs of the disease became less obvious, although no less insidious.

Sir Victor Horsley, Surgeon to the University College Hospital, suggested that a syphilitic taint in the family hit everybody 'more or less'. In language borrowed directly from degeneration theory he claimed, '[T]hey are all hit more or less. The infection at one end of the family or the other may be slight, but you cannot say that any child of such a family who you can trace escapes during his whole life and is really a healthy individual'.[77]

By the end of the nineteenth century it was generally assumed that both syphilis and congenital syphilis were responsible for numerous dystrophic afflictions, malformations of the body, arrest or retardation of physical and intellectual development, infantilism, dwarfism, inborn lack of vitality, cachexia, rickets, hydrocephalus, meningitis, certain forms of epilepsy, tabes and general paralysis. The syphilitic body was set to become the quintessential degenerate's body.

9 The Syphilitic as Moral Degenerate

It emerges from recent research that syphilis can because of its hereditary consequences, debase and corrupt the species by producing inferior, decadent, dystrophic and deficient beings. Yes, deficient . . . or they can be mentally deficient, being, according to the degree of their intellectual debasement, retarded, simple-minded, unbalanced, insane, imbecilic or idiotic.

Alfred Fournier, 1904

If medical authorities were not fast to catch on to the connection between congenital syphilis and degeneration, other observers, especially eugenicists and feminists, were. Public health officers, eugenicists, feminists and social purity organisations combined in the last years of the nineteenth century to form a broad movement for social hygiene. The aspirations of this social hygiene movement were many and varied. At the heart of it was the belief that the British race was in decline. Several factors influenced this thesis. First, throughout the Western world observers were shocked by what they claimed was a drastic decline in the birthrate. In Great Britain fears about the declining birthrate and the increase in infant mortality had begun in the 1880s. For many social commentators it seemed that the British population was not increasing fast enough to fill the empty spaces of Empire. But it was not only quantity at which such commentators were alarmed. It was a question of quality. To add to the panic, the infant mortality rate for the 1890s was higher than that of the 1880s.[1] Such statistics fuelled ideas of degeneration. The nascent eugenic movement called attention to such issues by suggesting that it was only part of the population that was in decline. The 'racially unfit' were said to be on the increase.

Eugenics, came from the Greek, *eugenes*, meaning 'well-born' and was coined by Sir Francis Galton, cousin of Charles Darwin.[2] From the 1860s, Galton had been developing theories based around the idea that a wide range of traits, mental, moral and physical were inherited. The eugenic theories that developed from Galton's work were loosely based on Darwin's theory of 'natural selection' but they were also influenced by other theories of heredity, especially Mendelism and Morel's *dégénérescences*.[3] By the end of the century, those interested in eugenics had formed a movement seeking to present scientific solutions to Britain's social problems. Eugenicists sought to pre-empt 'natural selection' by programmes of controlled breeding, promoting 'eugenic marriages, encouraging the 'well-born' to procreate and discouraging 'the unfit'.

The idea of eugenic marriage was shared by both feminists and eugenicists. Feminist concern about venereal disease had not ceased with the repeal of the CD Acts. Fear of 'innocently acquired' syphilis had prompted renewed interest from feminists. For feminists, 'eugenic marriage' meant that women should be prevented from marrying syphilitic men. For eugenicists, there was a variety of taints that made someone unfit to marry. In an article entitled 'The Cry of the Unborn', eugenicist writer Evelyn Hunt graphically illustrated the problem, in terms corresponding to Morel's laws of degeneration:

> We look around and see the sickly girl uniting herself with an equally sickly man. We know that in the families there are fatal tendencies to horrible disease. We see cousins marrying, we *know* how fatal this will prove to their helpless offspring. And even worse. We see the nervous hysterical woman marrying a worn-out, vicious man. . . . Heredity. We may call it a catch word, cant, what we will. It exists, nevertheless, and the time has come when it can no longer be ignored. In the smiling, innocent baby may be the fatal taint that will wreck it, body and soul, in spite of all education and environment can do.[4]

Taking a slightly different tack, feminists maintained that it was male lust that was responsible for racial decline and advocated chastity, marital continence and measures to protect wives and infants from becoming the 'innocent victims' of syphilis. The feminist writer Ellis Ethelmer wrote in a warning tone:

> [T]hat from the most virulent forms of syphilis there may be grave hereditary consequences through two or three generations is incontestable, though the amount and severity of such hereditary suffering is utterly insignificant by comparison with the exaggerated reports of the alarmists. . . . Meanwhile if a man had indeed more than an affected concern for his wife and offspring, he can refrain from spreading it.[5]

In the early 1890s, the feminist newspaper *Shafts* consistently drew attention to these issues in articles such as 'Enforced Maternity'[6] and 'Immoral Marriage'.[7] Readers were warned that 'the death rate of infants can be shown to be almost entirely due to the *incontinency of married persons*'.[8] Others suggested that feminine ignorance was the heart of the problem.

If every young person knew the true meaning of marriage, thousands at
least, would refuse to ally themselves in wedlock. If our morals were
not based upon immorality, and upheld by deception, few women would
marry without love. Does the girl who marries the dotard fully compre-
hend all the obligations of the state of cohabitation? Has she any pre-
monition of the loathing, disappointment, or despair, which accrue from
the close mental and physical proximity between fervent youth and
decadence?[9]

The new knowledge of the pathological impact of syphilis combined
with discussions of racial degeneration raised the spectre of male guilt in
the public imagination. Much has been written about the scandal that the
first (and only) performance of Ibsen's *Ghosts* created in London in 1891
and the attention that it brought to the question of hereditary syphilis.[10]
Some five hundred reviews of the play were published in England in the
year following this single performance. As Elaine Showalter has pointed
out, the language of the critics 'confused the play and the disease and
vilified it in the traditional rhetoric used for prostitution'.[11] The *Daily
Telegraph* called the play 'an open drain . . . a lazar house with all its
doors and windows open'. This was clearly a reference to syphilis and
demonstrated the critic's unease at the subject of the play, as lazar houses
were originally built for lepers and then syphilitics.[12] Showalter maintains
that conventional readers were threatened by Ibsen's intimations that the
principles of conjugal obligation, feminine purity and religious inhibition
were not the forces of spiritual evolution but of degeneration.

It could also be suggested that what the conventional reader was object-
ing to was the new concept of the male syphilitic as model of pathological
sexuality. In *Ghosts* it is the philandering father Captain Alving, and his
innocent son Oswald, who are the syphilitics in this drama of biological
decay. Hence it is they who represent pathological sexuality. This is so,
despite the fact neither Mrs Alving nor the servant girl Regine could be
said to represent an ideal of feminine purity, as both women attempt to
initiate sexual relationships outside of marriage. In the past this flirtation
with unorthodox relationships would have necessarily led to ruin, but in
Ghosts it is the women who are spared. The fact that Mrs Alving remained
untainted by the disease relates to Fournier's belief that fathers could pass
the disease onto their children without infecting their wives.

Ibsen's play paralleled the feminist interest in social purity and racial
degeneration in stressing the role of men in the transmission of syphilis.
This meant that for the first time since the eighteenth century the source
of syphilitic contagion was represented iconographically as a man. This

was particularly true in feminist novels of the period, where the debauched degenerate male replaced the hapless disease-ridden fallen woman. In Sarah Grand's novel *The Heavenly Twins*, both her heroines, Evadne and Edith, marry men with 'pasts'. Evadne is warned of her husband's premarital incontinence on the day of their wedding. Because she has secretly read her father's medical books, Evadne realizes the seriousness of her situation and leaves her husband. While she is eventually coerced into moving back to his home, she does so on the proviso that they will not sleep together. Her husband, Major Colquhoun, is described as not quite human. Grand tells the readers, '[He] had always cultivated an inscrutable bearing as being "the thing" in his set. . . . His attitude was however due to the want of proper healthy feeling, for he was a vice-worn man with little capacity for any great emotion.'[13] Colquhoun is not a terrible man despite his past failings and he and Evadne share a trouble-free companionate marriage, he improving under Evadne's influence. Thus, while he is described as 'vice-worn' and 'the thing', there is a sense that he is redeemable and not too far set apart from other men: a quaint inversion on the unfortunate fallen woman theme.

Such is not the case for Edith's husband Sir Mosely Menteith, a world-weary debauchee. Edith, a bishop's daughter, marries Sir Mosely despite Evadne's warning that he is a 'moral leper'. Evadne is aware of his corruption because it was worn like stigmata on his face. 'She noticed something repellent around the expression of Sir Mosely's mouth . . . his eyes were small and peery and too close together and his head shelved backwards like an ape's.'[14] Edith's fate is to bear a baby with all the classic signs of congenital syphilis, 'a little old man baby . . . with a cold in his head'. She dies in a fit of madness after her husband's infidelities are revealed to her by a chance meeting with a similarly afflicted woman and her congenitally syphilitic child, who appears slightly older than Edith's boy: 'small and rickety with bones that bent beneath his weight, slight as it was'. The boy's name was Mosely Menteith, 'after his father'.

The idea of men being responsible for degeneracy is even more forcefully stated in Emma Frances Brookes's *A Superfluous Woman*, written in 1893. In this novel the beautiful heroine, Jessamine Halliday, rejects the possibility of a poor but happy life as wife of an honest Highland farmer, and marries the rich but tainted Lord Heriot. She marries for material comfort and vanity, but eventually her callousness and the repulsion she feels for her husband give way to the higher emotions evoked by expectant motherhood. All such bright hopes are dashed with the birth of not one, but two 'degenerate children'.

Explicit in the description of these children is the sense that they personify the sins of their father. 'On those frail, tiny forms lay heavily the sins of heritage of the fathers. The beaten brows, the suffering eyes, expiated themselves the crimes and debauchery of generations.'[15] More grounded in eugenic ideas than Grand, Brookes was stressing that degeneracy breeds further degeneracy. Such catastrophes of birth were not only due to congenital syphilis but a heritage of vice. Her description of the lineage of Lord Heriot is worth quoting at length as it raises many concerns that both feminists and eugenicists brought to public attention, especially the questions of degeneration, survival of the fittest and the control of reproduction.

> There had been a sameness in the history of the Heriots for generations. . . . Violence and excessive animalism, in the first instance, the unabashed and muscular tiger who founded the family – had, in the inevitable process of time, degenerated into meanness, irritation and vices in such members who did not reap their heritage in insanity, disease and shocking malformation. . . . That the Heriots had survived at all was the result of the extraordinary advantages in sick-nursing which wealth had permitted them to enjoy – that is, the hot-bed fostering care which go to cherish an enfeebled stock. That cause and one other, had prevented their extinction, the other cause being the alliances into which their wealth and titles had tempted England's fair daughters from time to time.[16]

Unlike other feminists who stressed the need to rehabilitate men, Brookes took a more eugenicist approach. Her demand for reform was not for the good of the individual, but to benefit the whole race. 'The important thing,' she insisted, 'was not that Heriot should reform, but that his race should pass into annihilation. Virtue itself meets some too late, and the best to be hoped for is painless extinction.'[17]

Feminist writers such as Grand and Brookes were rejecting the belief that women were unaffected by syphilis and forcefully showing that women and children were being sacrificed on the 'altar of male lust'. That a man could marry an innocent young woman, infect her and cause her to bear weak and degenerate children became emblematic of women's unequal position in society as knowledge and power were denied her. Feminists argued that marriage was a dangerous trade, and like other dangerous trades its negative aspects should be more widely advertised.[18] As the actress and writer Cicely Hamilton so eloquently stated:

> Women, like men, when they enter upon a calling, have a perfect right to know exactly what are the dangers and drawbacks to their calling;

you do not, when you turn a man into a pottery or a dynamite factory, sedulously conceal from him the fact that there are such things as lead poisoning or combustion. On the contrary you warn him – as women are seldom warned.[19]

By the early twentieth century, many doctors would agree with eugenicists and feminists. Doctors became very fearful lest racially sound women should team up with racially unsound men. Fournier had raised such questions in the 1880s but they were taken up with renewed vigour in the early years of the twentieth century. American doctors seem to have been the most zealous in promoting the idea of eugenic marriage. The publication of *Syphilis in the Innocent (Syphilis Insontium)* in 1894 by American physician L. Duncan Buckley marked a shift in the way syphilis was treated by the medical profession. Central to Buckley's thesis was the idea that syphilis was not primarily a venereal disease. He maintained that genital contact was only one of a multitude of ways syphilis could be acquired, claiming that a shared cup or towel were in fact more likely to act as an agent of transmission. He also stressed, however, that many of its victims, women and children especially, acquired the disease 'innocently'.[20]

Prince Albert Morrow, a student of Fournier's and Emeritus Professor of Genito-Urinary Diseases at the University Medical College New York, championed the idea of eugenic marriages within medical circles. He claimed that '[I]t is especially in the legitimate union between the sexes that the prophylaxis of these diseases becomes a social and sanitary duty of the highest interest and importance.'[21] Morrow maintained that seventy-five per cent of all men in America had had gonorrhoea at some time and that five to eighteen per cent had or had had syphilis. Emil Noeggerath provided similar figures, claiming 800 out of every 1,000 men in New York City had or had had gonorrhoea. Medical research in the late nineteenth century had confirmed that gonorrhoea was not limited to the urinary tract but that the infection could spread to the cervix, uterus, fallopian tubes and throughout the bloodstream of its victims. Morrow estimated that fifty per cent of women infected with gonorrhoea would become sterile. He challenged the notion that women were deliberately having fewer children and asserted his belief that much sterility in marriage was involuntary. On the basis of the 1890 Census, Morrow estimated that one in seven marriages proved sterile as a result of some form of venereal disease.[22]

In Great Britain, members of the medical profession, eugenicists and feminists were greatly alarmed by Morrow's work and immediately began to act upon it. For feminists, the syphilitic man was seen as chiefly responsible for the spread of the disease and the decline of the race. It was men who refused women access to knowledge, who denied them a political voice, who paid them wages they could scarcely live upon and then tempted them with vice. These same men demanded pure wives, and then brought disease and dishonour on them and on their children. Doctors too, expressed their concern about the problem of 'syphilis of the innocent'. Articles such as 'The Duty of the Medical Profession in the Prevention of National Deterioration' and 'The Effect of Venereal Disease on the Decay of the Race' began to appear regularly in journals such as the *British Medical Journal* and *The Lancet*. While many doctors were more concerned over ethical issues involved, such as whether to tell a wife of the husband's disease, others made genuine attempts to disseminate information about the dangers. Some eugenicists were equally concerned with male sexual misbehaviour, but many took a more conservative line, blaming middle-class women for limiting their family size.

Not surprisingly, concern about the prostitute resurfaced. Medical discourse had effectively pathologized the prostitute during the nineteenth century, emphasizing the idea that prostitutes created venereal disease within themselves. Medical intervention in the policing of prostitution was premissed on the idea that prostitutes were innately diseased and hence different from other women. The failure of regulation meant that medical authorities sought different ways to deal with the threat of prostitution. Doctors found the most effective way of doing this was to incorporate the idea of congenital weakness into the disease model. Feminists who in the nineteenth century had shown compassion and caring for 'the fallen' joined with doctors and eugenicists in this endeavour.

Prostitutes began to be considered as physically degenerate: the product of poor breeding. The notion that the physiognomy of the prostitute was different from that of other women related back to the work of Alexandre Parent-Duchatelet in the 1830s. From these descriptions of the physical attributes of the prostitute it was but a small step to use such catalogues of signs as a means of categorizing those woman who appeared to have an aptitude for prostitution. Throughout Europe this medical anthropology became a tool of public health officials. The prostitute began to be seen not merely as a pathological female but as an atavism.

The first major study based on these principles was carried out by a Russian physician, Pauline Tarnowskii, in the 1880s. In her work Tarnowskii went into Russian prisons and examined the mental and physical state of many incarcerated women. Like Parent-Duchatelet, Tarnowskii presented a detailed inventory of the physical attributes of prostitutes – excessive weight, dark hair, low fecundity – but she added signs of degeneration to her description such as asymmetry of the face, misshapen nose and low forehead. Where Tarnowskii differed from Parent was in her belief that the physical appearance of the prostitute and her sexual identity were pre-established by her heredity.[23] Tarnowskii concluded from her research that the prostitute was, as a rule, a 'degenerate being, the subject of an arrested development, tainted with morbid heredity, and presenting clear signs of physical and mental degeneracy'.[24]

Other such studies followed. The work of the Italian criminologists Cesare Lombroso and William Ferrero in Italy borrowed heavily from Tarnowskii's research. For these men, the prostitute became the model of moral degeneracy. They claimed that a large proportion of women were born with certain traits that made them more susceptible to prostitution than other women. For Lombroso this had its roots in atavism. He wrote:

> Atavism helps to explain the rarity of the criminal type in woman. The very precocity of prostitutes – the precocity which increases their apparent beauty – is primarily attributable to atavism. Due to it also is the virility underlying the criminal type; for what we look for most in the female is femininity, and when one finds the opposite in her we conclude as a rule that there must be some anomaly. And in order to understand the significance and atavistic origin of this anomaly, we have only to remember that virility was one of the special features of the savage woman. [25]

Simultaneously, Lombroso argued that the normal woman was 'deficient in moral sense, and possessed of slight criminal tendencies, such as vindictiveness, jealousy, envy, malignity, which are usually neutralized by less sensibilities and less intensity of passion'.[26] In a sense he was merely replicating the idea that all women were inherently diseased, but placing it in a different theoretical framework. Lombroso's theories were predicated on the idea that women were abnormal because the norm was male. Femininity itself was suspect. But in order to explain the fact that men more than women committed crimes, he maintained that it was those women who were excessively masculine or excessively feminine who were 'born' criminals or prostitutes.[27]

Lombroso's proposal of a biological explanation of prostitution was taken quite seriously in Britain, although his theories on male criminality were rejected.[28] His idea that prostitution had its roots not in sensuality but in innate 'moral insanity' struck a chord with the British medical establishment. The idea of moral insanity had been pioneered in Britain by James Cowles Prichard. In 1835 he wrote that madness was a 'morbid perversion of natural feelings, affections, inclinations, temper, habits, moral dispositions, and natural impulses, without any remarkable disorder or defect of the intellect, or knowing and reasoning faculties'.[29] The concept of moral insanity became one of the cornerstones of Victorian psychiatry, re-defining madness not as a loss of reason, but as a deviance from socially accepted behaviour.[30] The work of Henry Maudsley from the 1870s had attempted to posit an organic cause of this insanity. It was his conviction that there was a hereditary predisposition to madness or 'moral insanity'. Other Social Darwinist psychiatrists came to argue that the hereditary organic taint combined with the habits of vice caused congenital moral insanity.

The possibility of a relationship between syphilis and general paralysis of the insane seemed to be the causal link many observers, both medical and non-medical, had been seeking. General paralysis of the insane (GPI) became the perfect example of a Darwinian disease as it linked immoral behaviour to hereditary causes.[31] The ability to catch a venereal disease suggested a tendency to vice; a degenerative disease such as GPI seemed to confirm it. It was generally men who showed symptoms of GPI and in this capacity they became symbols of moral degeneracy. Some doctors, however, could not avoid blaming women for this condition. Dr George Savage for instance noted that there were

> many patients admitted yearly to Bethlehem whose diseases I believe to be chiefly produced by sexual excesses; but such men are generally not only living lives of general excitement, but are wedded to women of a specially amatory nature; and although it would be unscientific to connote excess as necessarily associated with certain types of women, I have been struck by the frequency of the occurrence of general paralysis in the husbands of women of voluptuous nature.[32]

Despite its lack of scientific objectivity, the idea that certain types of women were more likely to indulge in sexual excess became a common idea during this period. One keen observer, the American eugenicist Eugene Talbot, used the example of the ancestry of Marie Duplessis, heroine of Alexandre Dumas' *La Dame aux Camélias* to prove his point. He wrote that her

> paternal grandmother, who was half prostitute, half beggar, gave birth to a son by a country priest. This son was a country Don Juan, a pedlar by trade. The maternal great-grandmother was a nymphomaniac, whose son married a woman of loose morals, by whom a daughter was born. This daughter married a pedlar, and their child was Marie. She died childless, early in life, of consumption.[33]

Blurring the distinction between fiction and fact, Talbot used the hapless Marie as 'scientific' proof of the degenerative process. Usually such women were said to be feeble-minded and the result of syphilitic heritage. Congenital syphilis came to be equated with hereditary moral degeneracy. The disease was not only seen to cause degeneracy of the constitution, but to affect the moral sense. The feeble-minded, idiots, imbeciles and the insane were all targeted as moral degenerates. The symptoms of congenital syphilis were read as the signs of degeneracy. This resulted in a vastly different idea of the prostitute. The infectious model of disease that had characterized the body of the prostitute earlier in the century was abandoned and the idea of congenital defect was incorporated. In this way, the prostitute's difference from other women was no longer based on moral judgement or on the presence of disease but inscribed on her body as congenital deformity.

Such concerns became explicit in the 1904 Inter-Departmental Committee into Physical Degeneration. The Committee was established following the problems the government had recruiting troops for the Boer War, as three-fifths of those who volunteered were declared unfit.[34] The Report of the Committee confirmed that the imperial race was indeed in decline. Alcohol was posited by the Report as the major cause of degeneration with syphilis a distant second. This was not the opinion of the medical witnesses who were called to give evidence. Each of these specialists maintained that syphilis in one form or another was responsible for untold amounts of degeneration. Sir Alfred Cooper, President of the Royal College of Surgeons, told the Committee that in the first generation syphilis was responsible for

insanity; idiocy; diseases of the bones, producing deformity and disfigurement; diseases of the eyes producing blindness; diseases of the ear producing deafness; diseases of the internal organs causing defective nutrition and deficient development; diseases of the nervous system, producing insidious forms of paralysis and locomotor ataxy.[35]

In the second generation the symptoms were far worse. The disease, Cooper claimed, appears in the form of 'disseminated sclerosis and degeneration of the nervous system'. While he could proffer no proof of congenital syphilis in the third generation, he was 'quite prepared to find it'. He concluded by stating that syphilis was a major 'source of general physical deterioration' and 'one of the principal elements in the manufacture of the insane'.[36] Professor Cunningham, Professor of Anatomy, University of Edinburgh and Chairman of the Anthropometric Committee of Britain, told the Committee that 'syphilis and alcohol were the worst forms of excess to transmit to your children'. While he believed that the hereditary taint of syphilis became less with each generation, it 'would come out in various forms'.[37] Sir Victor Horsley, Surgeon to University College Hospital, told the Committee that he believed that there was a 'very large class of mentally deficient children whose condition is due to congenital syphilis alone'.[38]

Perhaps the most damning evidence came from Dr Frederick Mott. Mott was the pathologist to the Asylums of London County and would later conclusively prove the relationship between syphilis and GPI.[39] At the Committee, he maintained that a large amount of insanity was due to syphilis. He also claimed that the living offspring of a congenitally syphilitic parent would be 'more likely to be stunted and to be bodily and mentally weak'.[40] What is of most interest here is his discussion of the problem of prostitution and the transmission of syphilis. On the subject of men infecting prostitutes, he told the Committee,

> I do not think they would affect the prostitute class, because I think the prostitutes are already immune. The danger is, I think, that they would infect the young women who are in shops and so on, who have not gone on the streets yet. In fact, that class of person, I think, is more dangerous than the prostitute because after a year or two the prostitute has already had the disease and is not likely to infect others.[41]

The problem of clandestine prostitution had always bothered those attempting to check the spread of venereal disease. Now medical experts were positing the 'amateur' prostitute as the major source of the disease. Such ideas were doubly alarming as the new evidence about syphilis was suggesting that syphilis was the cause of moral degeneracy; the amateur prostitute was then both the victim of syphilis and the most dangerous agent in its transmission.

Eugenicists had been heralding such ideas since the 1890s and by the first decade of the twentieth century the contention that the most dangerous class of prostitutes, in terms of syphilis, was made up of feeble-minded moral degenerates was gaining widespread acceptance. The findings of the Royal Commission on the Feeble-Minded did much to incite this discussion. The Commission had been set up to consider the care and control of those who had 'lost the power of managing their affairs'. The term 'feeble-minded' had first been used by Sir Charles Trevelyan, a member of the Council of the Charity Organization Society, in 1876. He had used the term to distinguish 'improvable idiots', that is, those who responded to institutional care and idiots and imbeciles who were considered to be in the lower ranges of intelligence.[42] Other authorities used the term to suggest those with 'tainted' constitutions. By the end of the nineteenth century, the term 'feeble-minded' had become increasingly linked with the problem of the 'unfit', the physically or morally degenerate.[43]

The Commission was appointed in 1904 and reported in 1908. The Commissioners included the Earl of Radnor, W.P. Byrne, Principal Clerk to the Home Office and F. Needham, Commissioner in Lunacy. The Commission estimated that of the whole population of England and Wales, there were 149,628 mentally defective persons. For many, the fact that 0.46 per cent of the population could be classified as 'feeble-minded' (not including certified lunatics) was proof of national decline.

The Report of the Commission indicated what many authorities feared, that syphilis was the cause of much idiocy, imbecility and insanity and that many prostitutes were drawn from the ranks of the idiotic, the imbecilic and the insane. A closer look at the Minutes of Evidence would suggest that the cause for alarm was not so great. For instance, an Inquiry made by the National Association for the Welfare of the Feeble-Minded as to the number of feeble-minded inmates in Magdalene Homes between 1905 and 1908 showed that from the answers received from over a hundred such homes throughout Britain, it could be discerned that some 14,725 women passed through their doors. Of these, some 2,521 women were regarded as feeble-minded (16 per cent). Despite fears of their enormous fertility, only one-third of the feeble-minded inmates had illegitimate children. Some 588 had one illegitimate child (25 per cent); only 198 of these women had more than one illegitimate child (8 per cent).[44] The Commission reported that many feeble-minded children were apt to commit offences of a sexual or perverted sexual nature. Some authorities suggested that up to 30 per cent of prostitutes were feeble-minded, while others claimed the figure was more likely around 10 to 15 per cent. Part of the problem lay in the question of how one defined feeble-mindedness. As Mrs Rupini of the Church Penitentiary Association stated, 'there are so many degrees of feeble-ness in *mind* and *will* – some verge on idiocy and others only show their weakness by infirmity of purpose'.[45]

Figures presented to the Commission by W.A. Potts, Lecturer in Pharmacology at the University of Birmingham and Honorary Physician to the National Association for the Feeble-Minded, illustrate this difficulty of definition. In his study of one hundred consecutive cases of teenage girls admitted at the Edgbaston Magdalene Home, he found twenty-six cases of 'feeble-mindedness; seven cases of moral insanity; one epileptic; one lunatic; and one deaf and dumb'. He stated that he used the term moral insanity to describe 'girls who were sharp and intelligent, but without any sense of honour or modesty, and who were not susceptible to moral and religious training, thereby differing markedly from the majority; nothing could stop them from lying or stealing'.[46] All these women, he believed, were degenerate and should be under permanent control.

Given the breadth of his category of moral insanity, it is surprising that Potts did not discover more such women. Certainly, eugenicists were keen to suggest that most prostitutes were feeble-minded. Dr Robert Rentoul, a leading eugenicist, defined prostitutes as 'degenerates composed of sexual perverts, drunkards, confirmed loafers, thieves and those so degraded as to prefer to make their living by hiring out their sex organs and not by honest toil'.[47] Gone were the economic explanations for prostitution and the image of the helpless seduced woman: biology now explained the propensity for vice. Women who engaged in prostitution were considered by virtue of that necessarily morally degenerate.

Despite the somewhat mixed findings of the Commission, eugenicists feared the worst. The first edition of the *Eugenics Review*, published in 1909, dealt almost exclusively with the Royal Commission. Alcoholism and syphilis were dubbed the 'twin racial poisons' as alcohol led to vice and vice to syphilis. The feeble-minded were generally targeted as a threat to the race but the feeble-minded prostitute was considered a national disaster.

A further cause of alarm was the supposed high fecundity of such women. In the 1880s, it was quite possible for a doctor to suggest in the *British Medical Journal* that one cause of the sterility of prostitutes was that the class of prostitutes was 'largely recruited from women who are naturally sterile'.[48] By the period immediately prior to World War One, it was argued that far from being sterile such women were very fertile. It was claimed that the 'unfit' were out-breeding the 'fit'. Indeed, the vast majority of illegitimate births were said to be the result of the union of degenerates.

This was said to be leading to 'race suicide'. Prior to the Commission, leading eugenicists of the period such as Dr Robert Rentoul had been sounding alarms:

> If this total of diseased humanity were afflicted with sterility, the present sad conditions would disappear. But unfortunately fertility is common among degenerates. They are in fact, 'the weeds in the garden' and have an enormous power of reproduction.[49]

Following the Commission, eugenicists sounded warnings and demanded action. A vigorous campaign was conducted by *The Times* and various pressure groups to get the government to pass mental deficiency legislation.[50] A.F. Tredgold, the Royal Commission's chief medical investigator, wrote that 'national degeneracy is no myth, but a very serious reality'. He had told the Royal Commission that the average number of children born to normal parents was four, but the average number of children born to degenerate families was 7.3.[51] He claimed that in Great Britain there was one mentally defective person for every 248 normal persons. He saw the central problem of degeneracy as being the fact that feeble-minded women were both extremely promiscuous and extremely fertile. He stated:

> [A]s an example, I may say that in Somersetshire, I found that out of a total number of 167 feeble-minded women, nearly two-fifths had given birth to children, for the most part illegitimate. Moreover it is not uncommon as a rule for these poor girls to be admitted into the workhouse maternity wards time and time again.[52]

Given the theme of degeneracy that underscored eugenic thinking, it was impossible for men such as Tredgold to conceive the possibility that a child of such a union could be 'normal'. The double burden of feeble-minded parentage and illegitimacy would brand the child as degenerate. The idea of 'degenerate families' horrified eugenicists, who claimed that such a phenomenon would bring a 'tide of regression'. As Dr Clouston, Physician Superintendent of the Royal Edinburgh Asylum, had told the Royal Commission:

> [O]f late years I have been devoting special attention to the previous history of the feeble-minded who have been sent to the asylum as certified patients, especially the young women. . . . I have come to the conclusion that such persons in a large city are subject to overwhelming temptations and pressure towards sexual immorality. Many of them have illegitimate children and this often at a very early age. One had seven such children. I look on this source of immorality as an extremely grave one in our social life. When illegitimate children are born, by such young women, the chances are enormously in favour of their turning out to be either imbeciles, or degenerates, or criminals.[53]

What frightened eugenicists even more was the possibility of degenerates breeding with non-degenerates. Bastardized theories of genetics convinced many that if the feeble-minded bred only amongst themselves then they would eventually die out. Tredgold concluded his article suggesting the possibility of colonies for the 'mentally defective', stating:

> For mark you it is not as if these degenerates mated solely amongst themselves. Were that so, it is possible that, even in spite of the physician, the accumulated morbidity would become so powerful as to work out its own salvation by bringing about the sterility and extinction

of its victims. The danger lies in the fact that these degenerates mate with *healthy* members of the community and thereby constantly drag fresh blood into the vortex of disease and lower the general vigour of the nation.[54]

The sexologist Havelock Ellis was another who championed controls being placed on the mentally defective. He proposed such 'simple and practical' solutions as 'confining them [the feeble-minded] in suitable institutions and colonies and by voluntary sacrifice of procreative powers by those who are able to work in the world'. He asserted that by so doing, 'we shall be able, even in a single generation, largely to remove one of the most serious and burdensome taints in our civilization, and so mightily work for the regeneration of the race'.[55]

The question of enforced sterilization vexed the Eugenics Movement. In America, the State of Indiana had passed an Act for the sterilization of 'confirmed criminals, idiots, imbeciles and rapists' in 1907. Many felt that Britain should pass similar legislation. The eugenicist Arnold White, writing in the *Eugenics Review*, claimed that such action was necessary for 'national efficiency':

[A]dult men and women who exhibit homicidal, perverted, sexual or animal propensities dangerous to the public may justly be segregated and prevented from propagating their kind, for the same reason the runaway engine is sidetracked and upset.[56]

Prostitutes and, indeed, any women who stepped outside the restrictive norms of sexual behaviour were now considered not merely models of aberrant femininity but as a threat to the race. The linking of moral degeneracy with congenital syphilis created a vicious circle in which prostitutes were not merely vectors of the disease because they spread infection but because they 'bred degeneracy'. While feminists of the period attempted to put forward the idea that prostitution was the product of male vice, they did little to challenge the image of the prostitute as feeble-minded and morally degenerate. Ultimately eugenicists, feminists, the medical establishment, social puritans and legal reformers were all in agreement that prostitution was the main cause of venereal disease and consequently the principal source of physical and moral degeneracy.

Many of these concerns were reflected in the debate leading up to the enactment of the Mental Deficiency Bill in 1913. The primary aim of the Act was the compulsory institutionalization of certified mental defectives. Since the publication of the Report of the Commission in 1908 there had been calls for such legislation. What underlay these demands was the great concern about disease, prostitution and illegitimacy. In one of the debates the MP A. Lyttelton stated:

> These women have no control over themselves. In the summer months when they go out they are a source of temptation, and they are the prey of dissolute minded men. They transmit loathsome diseases throughout the country, and year after year, they reappear in workhouses, and give birth to children begotten by parents, from time to time who are unsound.[57]

Women were the primary target of this legislation. One of the amendments proposed to extend the legal definition of feeble-mindedness to include 'sexually feeble-minded persons, that is to say, female-persons who do not belong to any of the above mentioned classes, of mentally defective persons, but who are feeble-minded and on account of their mental condition fail to exercise due self-control or due self-respect to sexual morality'.[58] While this amendment was not passed, another clause was added which made any woman pregnant with, or giving birth to an illegitimate child whilst on poor relief liable to compulsory segregation in an asylum as mentally defective. As the legal historian Lucia Zedner has pointed out, feeble-mindedness in women 'became a description that could be applied not only on the basis of psychiatric judgement, but on that of morally determined criteria'.[59]

At the First International Congress of Eugenics held at the University of London in July 1912, the medical section of the conference was entirely taken up with the question of the effects of alcoholism and syphilis on racial decline. Not surprisingly, those doctors who spoke before the Congress claimed that both 'vices' were seriously damaging racial vigour. Later that year, the Royal Society of Medicine and Eugenics formed a joint Committee to study venereal disease. A year later, a large group of prominent doctors published a plea in the *Morning Post* for a Royal Commission on venereal disease. Calls for a Royal Commission had begun as early as 1896 and the Report of the Inter-Departmental Committee on Physical Degeneration had recommended in 1904 that a Committee should be established to investigate the problem of venereal diseases. The memory of the bitter public debate over the CD Acts seems to have prevented the government from acting upon this suggestion. Mounting public pressure pushed the Government to act and a Royal Commission on Venereal Disease was appointed in late 1913.

The Royal Commission on Venereal Disease has received considerable attention from historians, especially in regard to the question of the debate over prevention or prophylaxis and the impact of the First World War on the Commission.[60] Yet the concern about the connection between prostitution and mental degeneracy has only been hinted at. Certainly, those historians who have dealt with the Royal Commission and the impact of the First World War on discussions of venereal disease are aware that the women who were of most concern during this period were not the 'professional' prostitutes, but the 'swarms of amateurs' whom observers claimed to be 'infesting' military camps.[61] It would seem that many of these 'amateurs' were the same women that were being defined elsewhere as 'feeble-minded' or victims of 'moral insanity'.

This was certainly the opinion of some of the witnesses before the Commission. The Right Honourable Miss Albinia Broderick, Representative of the National Council of Trained Nurses of Great Britain and Ireland, told the Commission that in her opinion venereal disease was spread through the community by the feeble-minded, alcoholics and tramps.[62] Dr E.B. Sherlock, Medical Superintendent of Darenth Industrial Colony, agreed, claiming that 'mentally deficient' persons were more likely from ignorance, from pressure of economic conditions and from deficient moral sense to contract and spread the disease.[63]

More telling perhaps was the evidence put before the Commission on the incidence of congenital and acquired syphilis in institutionalized populations such as prisons, Poor Houses and Borstals. The theory that levels of both acquired and congenital syphilis were higher in institutionalized populations than in the general population had been reported in various American studies during this period.[64] The Report of the Royal Commission likewise indicated what it considered to be a high rate of syphilis and gonorrhoea in incarcerated populations. The figures presented were less than conclusive. For instance, the recorded incidence of venereal disease amongst prisoners in local prisons in England sentenced to terms of imprisonment not exceeding two years between November 1913 and March 1914, was under 2 per cent. Of convict prisoners serving terms of three years or more, 13.3 per cent showed signs of suffering from syphilis, 11.67 per cent acquired syphilis, 2.16 per cent congenital syphilis. Out of 941 young prisoners in Borstal Institutions, especially selected as likely to become habitual criminals, some 153 presented one or more signs of congenital syphilis and five had acquired syphilis.

Such statistics must be treated with some scepticism as the Report states that these figures only relate to cases where there were evident and manifest symptoms. The Wassermann blood test for syphilis was not applied. What they do indicate, however, is the grave concern many observers felt about the amount of disease amongst the working classes and how threatening this was to British imperial greatness. Yet for all this, the Royal

Commission really added very little to the discussion of the connections between degeneracy, syphilis and prostitution.

This was due to the effect of the outbreak of the First World War on the Commission. The war affected the issues raised before the Commission in three ways. First, it meant that the Commission, which had been established ostensibly to look at the impact of venereal disease on the civilian population, rapidly had its terms of reference changed. The memory of the CD Acts had made the government extremely cautious when establishing the Commission to distance itself from the military. When it was first set up none of the Commissioners had a military background. The coming of war and the subsequent rise of venereal diseases in the armed forces meant that syphilis was no longer predominantly a civilian problem. Protection of soldiers became paramount.[65]

Secondly, while issues of imperial greatness and the supremacy of the British race remained important throughout the war, the means by which the government could foster them were greatly limited by obvious wartime restrictions. The war greatly impeded the efforts of the Board of Control to set funds aside for the construction of specialized institutions for the feeble-minded.[66] But, most importantly, the war marked a return of the image of the prostitute as an infectious site. Concerns about heredity, about moral degeneration and racial decline were superseded for the duration of the war as most of the efforts of those engaged in the prevention of venereal disease focussed again on restricting the body of the prostitute solely for the protection of men.

As the historian Lucy Bland has pointed out, the war had barely started before moves were made to introduce oppressive legislation for women in the name of protecting the troops.[67] As early as October 1914, the Plymouth Watch Committee had made a request to the Government to reintroduce regulation.[68] In November of the same year, it was claimed in the House of Commons that venereal disease had incapacitated from 30 to 40 per cent of men in some units. Lord Claude Hamilton, of the War Office, demanded power to commit prostitutes to hospitals and reformatories. While legislatively the government did nothing at this stage, in December of 1914 military authorities had taken the law into their own hands. In Cardiff, for instance, a curfew was placed on all women, banning them from all public houses in the city between 7 p.m. and 8 a.m. Five women were arrested and committed by a military court martial to 62 days' imprisonment.[69] This prohibition was adopted in London, where the Commissioner of Police forbade publicans to serve women before 11.30 a.m. Throughout Britain, military police imposed such curfews and raided houses they believed to be of 'ill repute'.[70]

While the Royal Commission was debating issues of prevention versus prophylaxis, the military establishment was determined that further restrictions upon prostitutes, or indeed upon any women who were believed to be sexually promiscuous, be implemented. The Report of the Commission was published in 1916 and resulted in the passing of the Venereal Diseases Act which, among other things, forbade the treatment of venereal disease by other than qualified persons. But many observers, both civilian and military, demanded a more comprehensive approach to the spread of venereal disease. Attempts were made by the Home Office to draft a new Criminal Law Amendment Act in 1917 which combined clauses for the protection of young girls and repressive measures against prostitutes. By 1918 the government, pressured by the Allied forces, introduced an amendment to the Defence of the Realm Act (DORA) which effectively meant the reintroduction of the CD Acts.[71]

DORA was part of the initial burst of emergency legislation created in early August 1918. The original aim of the Act was to prevent persons communicating with the enemy or obtaining information for that purpose or from jeopardizing the success of His Majesty's forces or assisting the enemy and to secure the safety of any means of communication.[72] Amendment 40d made it an offence punishable with six months' imprisonment for a woman suffering from venereal disease to have sexual intercourse with any member of the armed forces or to solicit or invite any member of the armed forces to have sexual intercourse with her. If a woman was charged under this regulation, she could be remanded for a period of not less than a week for the purpose of medical examination, as this might be required for ascertaining whether she had the disease or not. As with the CD Acts, prostitutes' bodies were again seen as the source of the disease and were again treated as sites of infection to be policed. Prostitution and syphilis became synonymous and were now being being posited as the 'enemy within'.

There was a storm of protest about the regulation but it failed to be repealed until the end of the war. The connection between prostitution, syphilis and degeneration was not forgotten. Outside government and military circles many social puritans, feminists and eugenicists argued that control of the 'feeble-minded' would greatly diminish the spread of venereal disease and other social problems brought on by the wartime conditions, such as 'war babies'. Many reformers writing on prostitution during the war stressed the fact that prostitutes were generally mentally defective. Some authorities claimed that over half the prostitutes in Great Britain were 'mentally defective'.[73]

Even those observers such as the Anglican feminist Maude Royden,

who were sceptical of figures given for feeble-minded prostitutes, claimed
that there was a definite change in prostitutes found in Rescue Homes
during the war. 'We find the strong hardworking woman who used to
come to us a thing of the past . . . and replaced by a . . . weak minded,
pleasure loving girl unable to do battle with the difficulties of life'.[74] The
sexologist Havelock Ellis regarded protection of the feeble-minded woman
as of major importance if prostitution and venereal diseases were to be
diminished. In his essay on the white slave trade Ellis wrote:

> Certainly there are many among us – and precisely the most hopeless
> persons from our point of view – who can never grow into really re-
> sponsible persons. Neither should they ever have been born. It is our
> business to see that they are not born; and that, if they are, at least
> placed under due social guardianship, so that they may not be tempted
> to make laws for society in general which are only needed by this feeble
> and infirm folk.[75]

If the war had reinforced the notion of the prostitute's body as an
infectious site, it did not take long for the idea of congenital defect to be
reincorporated into the disease model. In the period up to the war, many
observers claimed that most prostitutes were feeble-minded but, as has
been shown, the definition of feeble-mindedness was generally based on
moral criteria and was subsequently a questionable diagnosis. After the
war, however, there was an attempt to make a more overt connection
between mental and physical degeneracy on the one hand and moral degeneracy on the other.

The war had changed the way that the connection between prostitution
and disease was viewed. For the first time a majority of observers had
claimed that professional prostitutes were not the primary source of venereal disease. In the years following the war, it was the sexually promiscuous 'amateur' who provided civil and medical authorities with most concern.
It was the amateur who became the model of pathological female sexuality. As Maude Royden stated, it is 'the young girl whom hardly anybody
would have the heart to register as a licensed prostitute, who is most
actively infectious'.[76] The professional prostitute was no longer linked
with moral degeneracy, as her behaviour was viewed as an occupational
choice in which she would exercise proper precaution. Experts believed
that the professional prostitute was more willing to make use of condoms
in order to prolong her working life. Increased sales of condoms in the
immediate post-war period was viewed as confirmation of this trend.[77] Yet
such distinctions meant very little in reality, as any prostitute who failed
to take 'precautions' was labelled a weak-minded amateur.

In 1921, in the evidence put before the Parliamentary Committee on the Prevention of VD, such concerns become explicit. The Committee, like its predecessors, voiced concerns about the birthrate and the decline of the race. It was also concerned with the spread of venereal disease as the chief cause of sterility and degeneracy and with its increase during demobilization. Many of those interviewed by the Committee believed that moral standards had declined during the war and that venereal disease was on the increase. Witnesses before the Committee were unanimous in believing that most venereal disease both during and after the war was spread by amateur prostitutes. The rationale for this was circular. It was considered that professional prostitutes were safer because their livelihood depended on their trade and therefore they used some form of prophylaxis. Amateurs, however, were assumed to be safe by men who feared venereal disease and were therefore more likely to be diseased.

Many of the witnesses before the Committee believed that amateurs were more dangerous because they were mentally deficient. Sir Frederick Mott told the Committee that 'the professional prostitute was less dangerous than the amateur' as most amateurs were 'moral degenerates or high grade imbeciles'.[78] Dr Maurice Craig FRCS told the Committee that he thought the vast majority of amateur prostitutes were both morally deficient and high-grade imbeciles, who could not be controlled morally.[79] Not surprisingly, many of these medical experts claimed that syphilis was the chief cause of this degeneracy. Acquired syphilis was said to 'greatly decrease their moral position' while congenital syphilis was said to be the cause of their mental and physical degeneracy. As Dr Charles Bond stated before the Committee:

> a vicious circle exists, the degenerate condition of the population tends to the increase of venereal disease and the contracting of venereal disease brings about degeneracy.[80]

By suggesting that the congenital syphilitic woman was the most likely agent in the spread of acquired syphilis, medical experts were merely continuing the process of pathologizing prostitutes that had begun at the end of the eighteenth century. By incorporating the idea of congenital defect into the disease model it was but a small step to suggest certain women appeared to have an aptitude for prostitution. Such a conception of the prostitute married well with ideas of eugenics and allowed state and medical authorities to avoid the harder questions about society's responsibility for prostitution. Once it was believed that certain women were born prostitutes, the question of how to prevent prostitution ceased to involve any social reform. The problem of the sexual coercion of working-class girls could be ignored because only already morally degenerate girls would be corrupted. Moreover, when necessary, it was possible for such authorities to invoke the idea that such women needed protection from themselves in order to justify repressive legislation.

The connection between congenital syphilis and prostitution also marked a major shift in ideas about prostitution since the Enlightenment. Until the passing of the CD Acts, much of what was written about venereal disease implied that all women were inherently diseased. The CD Acts, however, emphasized that it was only prostitutes who were diseased and it was their disease that set them apart from other women. The connection between congenital syphilis, degeneracy and prostitution further distanced prostitutes from other women. Prostitutes became completely pathologized. By the 1920s it was impossible to consider that a prostitute was in any way a 'normal' woman. Instead, she was viewed as a carrier of disease who bore all the signs of a mental, moral and physical degenerate.

Until the Second World War the prostitute remained a symbol of dangerous sexuality and the archetypal pathological female. While condom use increased during the interwar period, many still believed that policing prostitution was the only way of restricting the spread of venereal disease.[81] With the outbreak of the Second World War, the government again acted to police prostitution in order to reduce the threat that venereal disease posed to the armed forces. In November 1942 the British government introduced Defence Regulation 33B. This Regulation provided that if a person was named by two or more separate patients as the suspected source of infection they could be required by the Medical Officer of Health of the county in which they lived to attend a medical examination. If they refused to be examined they could be arrested and imprisoned. The fact that both men and women could be compelled to undergo inspections was no doubt due to the history of protest such previous provisions provoked.

Despite the fact that the provision applied to both men and women, prostitutes remained the focus of attempts to control venereal disease. In the prevention propaganda devised by the government it was avoidance of prostitutes that was advised. Sometimes the Gonococcus and the *Treponema pallidum* were represented as 'good-time girls' in prevention posters and in other war propaganda prostitutes were depicted as 'the enemy within'.[82] After six months of Regulation B being in operation, the Ministry of Health reported to the House of Commons that only 28 persons (one man and 27 women) had been reported twice. Only two people had refused treatment. It was generally agreed that the provision had not the slightest effect on the diminution of venereal disease.[83]

The end of the Second World War saw the development of the widespread use of penicillin to treat both syphilis and gonorrhoea. As the dangers appeared to be greatly reduced by the use of penicillin, the prostitute came to be seen not as a threat to society but as a threat to herself. Theorizing about the pathology of prostitutes became the realm of psychologists and psychiatrists. The idea of the prostitute as 'contaminated other' began to disappear from the medical discourse around venereal disease.

The idea that women are innately pathological and represent the contaminated other has, of course, resurfaced with the onset of the AIDS epidemic. The idea of feminine pathology has pervaded the disease model of HIV/AIDS within bio-medical discourse since the early 1980s. This is despite the fact that, at least within Western society, the person with the virus has predominantly been represented as male. In part, this reflects historical continuities in the medical understanding of sexually transmissible disease but it also suggests the adaptability and tenacity of ideas around feminine pathology.

PART V
Conclusion

10 Trapped in a Woman's Body? The Persistence of Feminine Pathology in Biomedical Discourse around HIV/AIDS

In the *Scientific American* of October 1988, an issue entirely devoted to the question of HIV/AIDS, an article entitled 'HIV Infection: The Cellular Picture' was accompanied by a diagram purporting to show the distribution of tissues in the body that can be infected with HIV. A superficial look at the diagram would present nothing problematic. A skinless body is shown with the affected viscera highlighted and surrounded by microscopic representations of the impact of HIV on the tissues. A more than cursory glance, however, would indicate something more curious, that is, that this anatomically correct male body has lymphocytes found in his blood, semen and vaginal fluid.

Is it being pedantic to point out this gender confusion? This diagram of the infectious body, with both a penis and vaginal fluids is very much a cultural product of biomedical discourse around HIV/AIDS and a remnant of older representations of sexually transmissible diseases. Until the Enlightenment, the sexually diseased body and sexual disease were represented in gender-specific ways. Sympathetic representations of the leper or the syphilitic have generally been represented by a male figure, usually a parody of the suffering Christ figure, 'the exemplum of masculinity'.[1] The iconography of such diseases was primarily masculine. The disease itself however was always represented as female. Monumental and morally random diseases may have received regal and hence masculine stature, such as 'King Cholera', but sexually transmitted diseases were invariably feminized.

During the nineteenth century men tended to disappear entirely from representations related to sexually transmitted diseases. Women took on the dual role of representing both sufferer and contaminator. The shift from male 'victim' to female 'source' related to both aetiological and nosological developments around syphilis as well as changing conceptions regarding the construction of the sexed body.

185

In the diagram from *Scientific American*, all such gender distinctions are blurred. It would seem that there is no historical precedent for such an image. Whether the body shown is the source of the disease or merely susceptible to it, is not apparent. The conflation of the penis and the vagina prevents any one-dimensional analysis. It illustrates both the continuities and changes in the medical construction and representations of AIDS and other sexually transmitted diseases. In part, it marks the ongoing influence of ideas about feminine pathology on any discourse surrounding sexually contagious diseases. At the same time, however, it marks a break and a shift away from ideas that the female body is inherently pathological that is unique to the discussion of HIV/AIDS.

Such an image is possible due to what Simon Watney has called the 'crisis of representation' created by HIV/AIDS. Watney argues that not only has AIDS posed an unprecedented medical crisis, but 'a crisis over the entire framing of knowledge about the human body and its capacities for sexual pleasure' has developed.[2] Yet while Watney has announced this 'crisis in representation', for the most part he and other theorists of the AIDS epidemic have charted the development of representations around AIDS only in relationship to older disease models, most particularly syphilis.[3] This resembles not so much a 'crisis in representation' as a replication of older representations.

Watney, for instance, has argued that, like syphilis, AIDS is framed by a moral aetiology of disease. Unlike syphilis, however, it is not female depravity that constitutes this medicalized metaphor of contagion, but rather homosexual desire. 'AIDS,' Watney writes, 'is read as the outward and visible sign of an imagined depravity of will.' As he points out, this returns us to a 'pre-modern vision of the body, according to which heresy and sin are held to be scored in the features of their voluntary subjects by punitive and admonitory manifestations of the disease'.[4] Here Watney relates representations of people living with HIV/AIDS to the iconography that developed first around the leper and then around the male syphilitic. While such images are ambiguous, suggesting both sinner and penitent, they hardly mark a 'crisis'.

Another dimension needs to be examined before the 'crisis' in representation can be fully explored. The disease model constructed in early biomedical discourse around HIV/AIDS is ambiguous and contradictory. On one level it remains deeply influenced by earlier ideas of feminine pathology and pathological femininity, even when only dealing with the gay male body. It is, if you like, 'trapped in a woman's body'. But while the gay male body is feminized and the anus replaces the vagina as the source of disease, women's bodies do not disappear from the aetiological discussion of the disease. Rather, they serve as a foil to the gay male body, acting simultaneously as its opposite and its twin. This becomes more apparent as the medical focus shifts from the gay male body to the heterosexual female body.

At the same time, the vagina does not merely replace the anus as the source of both the disease and of medical anxiety. Rather, they are conflated, as in the diagram from *Scientific American*. It is this that marks the 'crisis in representation'. The resurfacing of the female body as 'contaminated other' in recent medical discourse around HIV/AIDS does not displace the gay male body; rather, they are positioned together, so as to present the heterosexual male body as invulnerable and as the standardizing model of health.

Such an analysis raises many questions. How is discussion of HIV/ AIDS informed by discourses that feminize the homosexual body? Is it analogous to older ideas about feminine pathology? How is the female body represented? In order to answer such questions it is necessary to engage in a discussion of representation and HIV/ AIDS that goes beyond the teleological male victim to female source approach and demonstrates the maelstrom of conflicting discourses that have come together in the biomedical theories around HIV/AIDS.

The fact that in the West, at least initially, gay men appeared to be the most widely affected group, has made a lasting impact on the nosological and aetiological theories of AIDS. It meant that on some level the male body was constructed as pathological. This has been perceived as a drastic reconceptualization of the way the male body has been represented in biomedical discourse. This, however, is slightly misleading as medical discourse had already pathologized this type of male body.[5] Since the mid-nineteenth century, homosexuality was no longer constituted as a set of practices but as a condition, a way of being. This represented a transition from notions of sin in ecclesiastical law to notions of deviancy and disease. Following the publication of Carl Westphal's famous essay on the 'contrary sexual instinct' in 1870, sexologists and psychiatrists began to discard old anatomical taxonomies of sexual type and look to new theories such as degeneration in order to explain homosexuality.[6] The gay male was morbidified, his sexual practices were constructed as pathological and his constitution (mental, moral and physical) was defined as diseased. Essential to the construction of the homosexual as pathological was the idea that he was a 'feminized' male. Richard Davenport-Hines has argued, 'the possibility of sexual intercourse between any but abnormal men was dismissed as a diseased fantasy: as part of this process it was insisted that homosexuals were effeminate in manner and feeble in physique'.[7]

The belief that gay men were necessarily effeminate was the one constant feature of the vastly different sexological accounts of male homosexuality from this period. Even sympathetic observers such as Karl Ulrich and Edward Carpenter, who pioneered the idea of the 'intermediate sex', claimed that male homosexuality was the result of 'a female mind in a male body'.[8] Perhaps the most influential theorist of homosexuality during this period, Havelock Ellis, drew on such ideas in his work. Ellis combined the theories of Westaphal, Ulrich and Carpenter, that stressed homosexuality as a congenital abnormality, with the theories of Krafft-Ebbing and Lombroso that named homosexuality as a degenerative condition. In this way he characterized homosexuality as a form of sexual inversion.

Co-existent with the idea that homosexual men were 'feminized' and hence pathological was an understanding that such men were also more susceptible to venereal disease. Such discussion marked a strange sort of reversal. With prostitutes it was considered the more filthy and depraved the woman was, the more likely she was to have a venereal disease. While in men the more effeminate a man was, the more likely he was to contract the disease. Such notions exemplify the very gendered nature of the medical discourse on venereal disease. Just as it was believed that the most 'unfeminine' of women were the most likely to transmit the disease, so the 'unnatural', 'feeble', 'unmanly' man was also seen as a high risk.

There is nothing new then, about the notion of 'the lethal character of male homosexuality' that resurfaced so readily in the popular and medical discourse around HIV/AIDS. Homosexuality was considered a feminizing condition and femininity was a disease. AIDS merely reinforced these connections. Indeed, the feminization of the gay male body became a central trope in the first narratives of the epidemic. Where this differed from earlier discussions was that this feminization was represented in ways that related specifically to sexual practice. Previous discussion of the homosexual body tended to avoid any direct comparisons between the anus and the vagina. Discussions of homosexuality and HIV/AIDS, however, were premised on this connection.

Even prior to the first reports of AIDS, there is evidence to suggest that the medical profession was already pathologizing the anus of homosexuals in much the same way as the vaginas of prostitutes or other promiscuous females were pathologized in the nineteenth century. The visibility of gay men following the 'sexual revolution' of the 1960s and the increased knowledge of gay sexual practice allowed the medical profession to present new insights into old conditions. Cancer of the anus and the rectum, hepatitis B and other proctological complications came to be seen as the result of anal sex between men.

Just as doctors in the nineteenth century constructed their understanding of the diseases syphilis and gonorrhoea in terms of promiscuous femininity, doctors in the 1970s related pathologies of the anus and rectum to promiscuous homosexuality. In part, this meant that the anus replaced the vagina as source of sexual disease within medical discourse. It also meant that at times the anus and the vagina were conflated. New ideas regarding pathological masculinity were of course informed by older ideas of pathological femininity. The correlation between cancer of the anus and rectum and homosexuality received considerable attention from the late 1970s onwards. For instance, in an article on carcinoma of the rectum presented to the Royal Society of Medicine in January 1981, Drs R.D. Leach and H. Ellis argued that:

> as the female cervix is derived from the same cloacagenic membrane as the transitional cells of the anorectal junction, there might be a common aetiological factor.

While appearing to structure a connection between these cancers in terms of transitional cell changes, in fact the aetiological commonality is based largely on moral concerns. They continued:

> Carcinoma of the cervix is associated with early experience in sexual intercourse in conjunction with a multiplicity of partners. Male homosexuals are well recognized for promiscuity, many having more than a hundred casual contacts each year.[9]

The connection between cancer of the rectum and cervical cancer in this case is most probably Human Papillomavirus (HPV) or 'wart virus'. Yet Drs Leach and Ellis have structured their discussion in terms of a moral aetiology. The feminization of the gay male body functions here on two levels. First, and most obviously, this is seen in the conflation of the vagina/cervix with the anus/rectum. The connection between sexual promiscuity and disease is also clearly derived from older moral constructions of sexually transmissible diseases.

These connections become both more explicit and more ambiguous in relation to AIDS. Clearly, in early biomedical discourse around HIV/AIDS gay bodies and the nature of gay sexuality are represented as both diseased and disease-producing. In the first article confirming the deaths of five gay men of *Pneumoncystis carinii* pneumonia (PCP) in Los Angeles, it was suggested that '[T]he fact that these patients were all homosexual suggests an association between some form of homosexual lifestyle or disease acquired through sexual contact'.[10] A year later these connections were made more obvious when *The Lancet* reported that there were 'some theoretical grounds for believing that the nature of homosexual coitus can cause immunosuppression'.[11] The idea that the disease related to homosexuality or gay sexual practice came to inform both the medical and popular presses. The group of symptoms associated with AIDS were first described as GRID (Gay Related Immune Deficiency). PCP became 'gay pneumonia' and Kaposi's Sarcoma became 'gay cancer'.

But as more became known about the disease, less was certain in both medical and moral terms. The scramble to discover the cause/cure of the disease produced a series of ambiguous and contradictory meanings for the disease. This is particularly evident in the discussion around the male body, gay sexual practice and the disease. Most of the earliest theories that developed around the incidence of Kaposi's Sarcoma and PCP in gay men tended to focus on and pathologize gay sexual practice. Excess was the primary factor that interested medical researchers at this time. Excessive sex, excessive drug and alcohol use, excessive numbers of sexual partners, excessive amounts of venereal disease were all put forward as explanations for the development of these new syndromes. As the authors on one of the first medical text books on AIDS reported:

> Male homosexuals have accounted for 71 per cent of all AIDS cases in the United States. AIDS patients in this risk group have commonly had histories of extreme promiscuity and extensive use of illegal drugs. When compared to sexually active male homosexuals without AIDS, the male homosexual AIDS victim had had more sexual partners, more anonymous sexual activity, greater involvement in anal sex, greater use of illicit drugs, and a greater history of sexually transmitted diseases such as syphilis and diarrhoeal diseases such as amebiasis and giardiasis. In sum many homosexual men with AIDS have had 'Fast track life-styles with well-known risk for infectious diseases.'[12]

The idea that those gay men affected with AIDS were hyper-promiscuous, drug users with long histories of sexually transmitted diseases came to inform much of the early theorizing around AIDS aetiology. Experiments were set up along these lines with 'non-promiscuous' gay men as the control samples.[13] The major theory to develop from this line of inquiry suggested that AIDS developed as the result of multi-aetiological factors. Some of the first exponents of this theory argued that there were two distinct phases in the development of AIDS. They maintained that during the first stage promiscuity was important because it was associated with an accumulation of effects that would eventually lead to the second, self-sustaining stage.[14] Immune impairment, they predicted, would peak around the fourth decade of life resulting from cumulative exposures to *Cytomegalovirus*

(CMV), sperm and other infectious agents. A self-sustaining condition – that is, AIDS – would then develop as the result of the increasing burden of active infectious agents, immune complexes, auto-antibodies, immune regulatory impairment, and diminished cytoxic T-cell and NK-cell activity.[15]

Such theories were clearly derived from earlier medical research on cancer of the rectum and anus. AIDS activists such as Randy Shilts and Larry Kramer have suggested that such theories derived from a deep-seated homophobia within the medical community.[16] Indeed, certain doctors such as the editor of the *Southern Medical Journal* had no qualms in pronouncing that the disease was a punishment from God.[17] Those promoting these theories maintained that the disease was not due to homosexuality but to promiscuity. The (then) non-existent rate of infection amongst lesbians was cited as proof that homosexuality was not necessarily lethal. As the editor of the *New England Journal of Medicine* asked rhetorically, 'Were the contemporaries of Plato, Michelangelo and Oscar Wilde subject to the risk of dying from opportunistic infections?'[18] Such an approach to homosexuality of course did not make it *not* homophobic. Indeed, when such ideas were translated from medical jargon into layman's terms the distinction between homophobia and cautious calls to moderation were distinctly blurred. Margaret Fromer, for instance, in one of the first popular texts on AIDS noted:

> The whole question of promiscuity is a thorny one. Surely one cannot attach any credence to the accusations of the moral majority and other homophobes that this is God's punishment for sin. . . . No rational and ethically responsible person would hold such a view. . . . But by the same token, we cannot ignore the link between lifestyles and AIDS any more than we cannot ignore the link between cigarette smoking and cancer.[19]

Such discussion only thinly masked the fact that much of the early medical discourse on AIDS was informed by deep cultural ideas about the deadly character of male homosexuality.[20] Far from creating a new disease model, doctors were merely reinventing an older one.

By stressing promiscuity and excess rather than homosexuality, medical authorities were doing more than making calls for moderation. This emphasis on promiscuity clearly linked any discussion of AIDS with earlier ideas regarding pathological femininity and promiscuity. On one level, the connection between excess, AIDS and femininity is made because the female body itself represents excess. Feminine promiscuity has long been considered both diseased and disease-producing. Excessive sexual desire in women not only led men into temptation but was considered enough to spontaneously create venereal disease. Victorian doctors linked femininity and sexual promiscuity to disease through other forms of excess such as alcoholism and opium addiction. These forms of immoderation, it was said, predisposed women to sexually transmitted diseases.

The representation of the gay male body as feminized in such medical discourse went beyond the connection between promiscuity and femininity. Certain medical authorities came to suggest that AIDS was due to certain 'feminizing practices' that gay men engaged in. The use of steroid and oestrogen creams was posited by medical authorities in several journals as the possible cause of AIDS.[21] Drug use, particularly use of amyl nitrate as a sexual stimulant, was believed to be a factor. While not directly seen as a feminizing practice, drug use suggested a body out of control, and was related back to 'hyper-promiscuity' amongst gay men.

While within this discourse the gay male body was represented as a feminized site, its maleness was not entirely obscured. In certain circumstances this 'maleness' was seen as a distinct risk factor for AIDS and other sexually transmitted diseases. Semen, for instance, became suspect and certain doctors claimed that men, as opposed to women, were immunologically unequipped to absorb large quantities of it, either anally or orally. One correspondent reported to the *New England Journal of Medicine* that human semen was 'an antigenic nightmare' as well as a 'potent immunosuppressor'.[22] Such fears were rapidly translated from medical jargon into the popular press. The English newspaper *The Observer* reported in June 1985:

> Semen contains antigens, foreign elements that stimulate the production of antibodies. The female body has ways of deactivating semen; the male body has no such strategies. At each reception the immune system goes on red-alert. Ironically, it too becomes paranoid and repeated *trauma* prolongs the crisis until the cells lose their capacity to correct their own over-correction.[23]

The maleness of the gay body is always constrained by heterosexist and gendered considerations. In this example, semen is only dangerous to men as they are not considered the appropriate receptacles for it. While the medical press framed their ideas about the danger of semen in terms of CMVs and semen-related carcinomas, much of the discussion was underpinned by a belief in the 'naturalness' of the vagina as the receptacle for sperm. Not only did this obscure the possibility of heterosexual transmission by sanitizing the vagina, it also positioned the heterosexual male body as a locus of safety.

It is particularly interesting to consider how the penis was treated in this context. Certainly, medical observers represented the penis as a transmitter of disease: the male urethra, for instance, was seen as a significant factor in transmission of 'its ability to penetrate into cavities with the forceful ejaculation of semen, make the urethra an excellent transmitter of infection'. Medical discourse shaped ideas about transmission around the ejaculatory properties of the penis. As one reporter put it, HIV infection 'requires a jolt injected into the blood-stream'.[24] Needles and penises were objects of infection due to their projectile capacities. Again, such discussion is always constrained by heterosexist assumptions about gay sexual practice. The penis is a potent transmitter of disease between gay men, because gay sexual practice, as one medical observer suggested, 'involves many orifices, including the urethra, mouth, and anus'.[25] It is the belief in the 'naturalness' of heterosexual intercourse and the 'unnaturalness' of homosexual intercourse that gives rise to this rather spurious discussion of the differences between homosexual and heterosexual practices. Heterosexual, gay and lesbian sexual practices all tend to involve 'many orifices'. Yet this discussion is framed in a way that pathologizes gay sexuality, while simultaneously obscuring the possibility of heterosexual transmission.

Much has been made of the John Langone article in the December 1985 issue of *Discover* magazine in which he argued that the virus entered the bloodstream through the 'vulnerable anus' and the 'fragile urethra'. Women were not at risk, according to Langone, because in contrast 'the rugged vagina' was designed to be abused by blunt instruments such as penises and small babies and provided a barrier too tough for the virus to penetrate.[26] Langone's subsequent reversal in his book published in 1987 has been seen as a watershed in biomedical discourse around HIV/AIDS and as a marker for when medical attention shifted focus away from gay men's bodies and onto women's bodies. Langone's reversal has come to symbolize the fact that the female body was no longer viewed as a site of safety but as a reservoir of disease.

The suggestion that Langone's article marked the time when 'rugged vagina' theories were being phased out of biomedical discourse and were replaced by theories of innate feminine pathology is somewhat problematic. While certainly the primary focus of biomedical discourse up until the late 1980s was the gay male, by 1983 medical authorities were aware that 'risks groups' included haemophiliacs, Haitian nationals, and women. The women who were seen principally to be at risk were sex workers and I-V drug users. Medical concern for such women was, however, somewhat obscured by the fact that as 'prostitutes' and 'drug addicts' they were readily lumped into the pathological model that was used for gay men. For instance, doctors from Saint-Pierre University Hospital, writing in *The Lancet* about prostitutes in Rwanda, claimed that:

> As expected, the prostitutes were highly promiscuous. Penis–vaginal intercourse was most commonly described, suggesting that the frequency of sexual contacts with different partners is more important than the type of intercourse with respect to HTLV-III infection. . . . Although the population sample was small, it appears that heterosexual promiscuity, especially with prostitutes, should be discouraged; with more than 40 different partners per year, the risk of exposure to HTLV-III increases sharply.[27]

While this indicates a shift in interest away from anal intercourse, the emphasis on promiscuity is very much in keeping with earlier disease models that focused on pathological femininity as well as those developed in order to explain HIV/AIDS. As with gay men, doctors set up experiments comparing promiscuous and non-promiscuous women. As Joyce Wallace, a doctor in charge of one such experiment, stated: 'Because frequent diverse sexual contact is not unique to male homosexuals we set out to determine if women who have frequent sexual intercourse with diverse partners, are also developing T-cell abnormality.'[28]

Such comparisons were not restricted only to 'lifestyle' explanations of the disease. The pathological nature of the female body resurfaced easily as an explanation for heterosexual transmission. As the critic Frank Browning explained in a review of AIDS literature in 1988:

> Gay men get it because during anal intercourse infected semen can mix with blood once the penis has caused an abrasion on the rectal wall. And women are at greater risk because their reproductive systems are generally more subject to infections than are men's. Men who generally do not have bleeding sex organs, are not usually exposed during intercourse because the virus, which may be present in vaginal fluids, does not seem to survive in the urinary tract as do other venereal diseases.[29]

Such an analysis of the transmission of HIV draws on traditional representations of the (heterosexual) male body as the healthy body and the female body as the diseased body. Women's unique biological functions are represented as morbid and polluting. Ideas about the infectiousness of bleeding sex organs are reminiscent of the earliest theories of the aetiology of syphilis that suggested that the poison was introduced to men through menstrual blood.

Such evidence suggests that the interest in women's bodies was not so much a new development as an inevitable progression. The disease model for HIV/AIDS was after all one that was essentially feminized; consequently, the vagina was readily conflated with the anus as the source of disease in biomedical discourse. What then is the purpose of drawing together these factors? It is important for both feminists and gay theorists who write and critique medical history to recognize the deep-seated misogyny and homophobia that informs biomedical discourse around HIV/AIDS as the cultural product of an hegemonic masculinity that, to paraphrase Judith Butler, 'sets up pathologizing practices and normalizing sciences in order to produce and consecrate its own claim to originality and propriety'.[30] To suggest that ideas of 'feminine pathology' were simply replaced or merely resurfaced is to ignore the fact that the heterosexual white man remains as much the standard of health today as he was one hundred, two hundred or even a thousand years ago.

Notes

INTRODUCTION

1. Cited in Linda Mahood, *The Magdalenes: Prostitution in the Nineteenth Century* (London, 1990), p. 20. It should be noted that such primitive ideas regarding the stigmatization of those with disease persist into the late twentieth century. William F. Buckley, the conservative critic, wrote in the *New York Times* in 1987: 'Everyone detected with AIDS should be tattooed on the upper forearm, to protect common needle users, and on the buttocks to prevent the victimization of other homosexuals.' Cited in Daniel M. Fox, 'AIDS and the American Health Policy' in Elizabeth Fee and Daniel M. Fox, *AIDS: The Burden of History* (Berkeley, 1988), pp. 328–9.
2. Linda Mahood, *The Magdalenes*, p. 20.
3. Mary Poovey, *Uneven Developments: The Ideological Work of Gender in Mid-Victorian England* (London, 1989), p. 214.
4. See, for instance, Lesley Dean-Jones, *Women's Bodies in Classical Greek Science* (Oxford, 1992), pp. 110–47.
5. Marina Warner, *Alone of All Her Sex: The Myth and Cult of the Virgin Mary* (London, 1978), pp. 40–1.
6. Thomas Laqueur, *Making Sex: Body and Gender from the Greeks to Freud* (Cambridge, Mass., 1990), p. 4.
7. Lesley Dean-Jones, *Women's Bodies in Classical Greek Science*, pp. 44–6.
8. See, for instance, Janice Delany *et al.*, *The Curse: A Cultural History of Menstruation* (Chicago, 1983), p. 20; Emily Martin, *The Woman in the Body: A Cultural Analysis of Reproduction* (London, 1987); Barbara Duden, *The Woman beneath the Skin* (Cambridge, Mass., 1991).
9. D. Jacquart and C. Thomasset, *Sexuality and Medicine in the Middle Ages* (Princeton, 1988), p. 191.
10. Patricia Crawford, 'Attitudes towards Menstruation in Seventeenth Century England', *Past & Present*, No. 91 (1981), p. 50.
11. Claude Quétel, *The History of Syphilis*, trans. Judith Braddock and Brian Pike (London, 1990), p. 25.
12. Sander L. Gilman, *Disease and Representations: Images of Illness from Madness to AIDS* (Ithaca, 1988), p. 254.
13. Claude Quétel, *The History of Syphilis*, p. 23.
14. Cited in William Acton, *Practical Treatise on the Venereal Diseases and Their Immediate and Remote Consequences* (London, 1841), p. 3.
15. *Ibid.*, p. 3.
16. Edward Shorter, *A History of Women's Bodies* (London, 1982), p. 12.
17. D. Jacquart and C. Thomasset, *Sexuality and Medicine in the Middle Ages*, p. 188.
18. George Luys, *Textbook on Gonorrhoea and Its Complications* (London, 1922), p. 8.
19. When cases of syphilis were first reported in Europe, many believed that the

196

disease had been brought back from the Americas by Columbus. Since then there has been considerable debate as to whether syphilis was a new disease or whether it was merely a more dreadful manifestation of an older disease such as yaws.

20. Sander L. Gilman, *Disease and Representation*, p. 248.
21. W.A. Pusey, *The History and Epidemiology of Syphilis* (Springfield, 1933), p. 33.
22. Cited in Harvey Gideon, *Great Venus Unmasked, Or a More Exact Discovery of the Venereal Evil* (Cornhill, 1672), p. 4.
23. *Ibid.*, p. 4.
24. Etienne Lancereaux, *A Treatise on Syphilis: Historical and Practical* (London, 1868), p. 16.
25. J.R. Whitwell, *Syphilis in Earlier Days* (London, 1940), p. 34.
26. Claude Quétel, *The History of Syphilis*, p. 33.
27. Anna Foa, 'The Old and the New: The Spread of Syphilis 1494–1530' in *Sex and Gender in Historical Perspective* (Baltimore, 1990), p. 33.
28. Edward Shorter, *A History of Women's Bodies*, p. 257
29. In so doing I want to expand on the Foucauldian idea that the body is only inscribed by discourses of power. See, for instance, Michel Foucault, *The History of Sexuality*, Vol. 1, An Introduction, trans. Robert Hurley (London, 1978); *Discipline and Punish: The Birth of the Prison*, trans. Alan Sheridan (London, 1977); *Language, Counter-Memory and Practice: Selected Essays and Interviews*, Donald Bouchard (ed.) (Oxford, 1977). Rather, I want to see the body more in terms of the Nietzschean notion of the body as a surface of social incision.
30. See, for instance, Carroll Smith-Rosenberg, *Disorderly Conduct: Visions of Gender in Victorian America* (New York, 1978); 'The Hysterical Woman: Sex Roles and Role Conflict in Nineteenth Century America', *Social Research*, Vol. 39 (1972); Carroll Smith-Rosenberg and Charles Rosenberg, 'The Female Animal: Medical and Biological Views of Woman and her Role in Nineteenth Century America' in Judith Walzer Leavitt (ed.) *Women and Health in America: Historical Readings* (Madison, 1984); Elizabeth Fee, 'The Sexual Politics of Victorian Social Anthropology' in Mary Hartmann and Lois Banner, *Clio's Consciousness Raised: New Perspectives on the History of Women* (New York, 1976); 'Psychology, Sexuality and Social Control in Victorian England', *Social Science Quarterly*, Vol. 58 (1978); Elaine Showalter, *The Female Malady: Madness and English Culture 1830–1980* (London, 1987).
31. Mary Poovey, *Uneven Developments*.
32. *Ibid.*, p. 49.
33. Mary Poovey, *The Proper Lady and the Woman Writer* (Chicago, 1984), p. ix.
34. Nancy F. Cott, 'Passionlessness: An Interpretation of Victorian Sexual Ideology 1790–1850', *Signs*, Vol. 4, No. 2 (1978) p. 219.
35. Randolph Trumbach, 'Modern Prostitution in *Fanny Hill*: The Libertine and Domesticated Fantasy' in G.S. Rosseau and Roy Porter (eds), *Sexual Undergrounds of the Enlightenment* (London, 1978), p. 219.
36. Leonore Davidoff and Catherine Hall, *Family Fortunes: Men and Women of the English Middle Class 1780–1850* (London, 1987), p. 19.

37. Nancy Cott, 'Passionlessness: An Interpretation of Victorian Sexual Ideology 1790–1850', p. 222.

38. Thomas Laqueur, *Making Sex*, pp. 1–24.

39. Carol Christ, 'Victorian Masculinity and the Angel in the House' in Martha Vicinus (ed.), *A Widening Sphere: Changing Roles of Victorian Women* (London, 1980), p. 146.

40. *Ibid.*, p. 162.

41. *Ibid.*, p. 162.

42. Mary Poovey, 'Speaking of the Body: Mid-Victorian Constructions of Female Desire' in Mary Jacobus *et al.*, *Body Politics: Women and the Discourses of Science* (New York, 1990), p. 35.

43. Steven Marcus, *The Other Victorians* (London, 1964). See also Ron Pearsall, *The Worm in the Bud: The World of Victorian Sexuality* (London, 1969); Michael Pearson, *The Age of Consent: Victorian Prostitution and its Enemies* (London, 1972); Eric Trudgill, *Madonnas and Magdalenes: The Origins and Developments of Victorian Sexual Attitudes* (London, 1976); Fraser Harrison, *The Dark Angel: Aspects of Victorian Sexuality* (London, 1977).

44. Frances Finnegan, *Poverty and Prostitution: A Study of Victorian Prostitution in York* (Cambridge, 1979).

45. Paul McHugh, *Prostitution and Victorian Social Reform* (London, 1980); Judith Walkowitz, *Prostitution and Victorian Society: Women, Class and the State* (Cambridge, 1980).

46. Walkowitz's work on prostitution was steeped in the tradition of E.P. Thompson's *The Making of the English Working Class*. Consequently, prostitutes are viewed as part of working-class culture, and working-class culture is viewed as the ultimate expression of human agency. Recently this conflation of culture and agency has been critiqued. Peter Way, in his book *Common Labour* (Cambridge, 1994), has suggested that such an analysis of power ignores the experience of the vast majority of workers. Working-class culture reflects the alienation of the workers as much as their sense of community. He writes 'Workers' culture's rough dimension has received far less attention from historians, but was equally important, being the negative side of class struggle in which class antagonisms were submerged and subliminated by labourers, to be vented on themselves and co-workers,' pp. 5–6. Ostensibly, Way is suggesting that there are certain elements of the working class, such as common labourers, who cannot become agents. I would argue that the common prostitutes were in much the same situation as common labourers. While I do not wish to view them only as victims, I feel the very negative aspects of their existence should not be overlooked.

47. See, for instance, W.R. Greg, 'Prostitution', *Westminster Review*, Vol. 53, (1850); William Acton, *Prostitution*, Peter Fryer (ed.) (London, 1968); Eugene S. Talbot, *Degeneracy: Its Causes, Signs and Results* (London, 1898).

1 THE SICK ROSE

1. Freeman J. Bumstead, *The Pathology and Treatment of Venereal Diseases*, (Philadelphia, 1893), p. 34.

2. *Ibid.*, p. 34. The meaning of this phrase is in fact quite ambivalent. There has been discussion of the meaning of this phrase recently that suggests that Herodotus was actually referring to transvestism. See Ann Rosalind Jones and Peter Stallybass, 'Dismantling Irena: The Sexualising of Ireland in Early Modern England' in Andrew Parker, Mary Russo, Doris Sommer and Patricia Yaeger (eds), *Nationalisms and Sexualities* (New York, 1992), pp. 158–63.
3. J.E.R. McDonagh, *Venereal Diseases: Their Clinical Aspects and Treatment* (London, 1920), p. 272.
4. Freeman J. Bumstead, *The Pathology and Treatment of Venereal Diseases*, p. 35.
5. George Luys, *Textbook on Gonorrhoea and Its Complications*, p. 2.
6. F. Buret, *Syphilis in Ancient and Prehistoric Times* (Philadelphia, 1891), p. 56.
7. C.F. Marshall, *Syphiliogy and Venereal Diseases* (London, 1914), p. 3.
8. A.C. Mangian, *The Practitioner's Manual of Venereal Disease* (London, 1919), p. 72.
9. C.F. Marshall, *Syphiliogy and Venereal Diseases*, p. 1.
10. *Ibid.*, p. 2.
11. Geoffrey Eatough, *Fracastoro's Syphilis*, p. 12.
12. C.B. Godfrey, *An Historical and Practical Treatise on the Venereal Disease* (London, 1797), p. 51.
13. Anna Foa, 'The Old and the New: The Spread of Syphilis 1494–1530', p. 33. See also Mary B. Campbell 'Carnal Knowledge: Fracastoro's *De Syphilis* and the Discovery of the New World' in Daniel Segal (ed.), *Crossing Cultures: Essays in the Displacement of Western Civilization* (Tuscon, 1992).
14. Ernest Finger, *Gonorrhoea* (New York, 1894), p. 5.
15. Kenneth Flegel, 'Changing Concepts of the Nosology of Gonorrhoea and Syphilis', *Bulletin of the History of Medicine*, Vol. 48 (1974), p. 573.
16. George Luys, *Textbook on Gonorrhoea and Its Complications*, pp. 7–8.
17. Freeman J. Bumstead, *The Pathology and Treatment of Venereal Diseases*, p. 35.
18. Claude Quétel, *The History of Syphilis*, p. 23.
19. Sander L. Gilman, *Disease and Representation*, p. 248.
20. Susan Sontag, *Illness as Metaphor* (New York, 1977), p. 58.
21. D. Jacquart and C. Thomasset, *Sexuality and Medicine in the Middle Ages*, p. 186.
22. Etienne Lancereaux, *A Treatise on Syphilis: Historical and Practical*, Vol. 2, p. 214.
23. Cited in D. Jacquart and C. Thomasset, *Sexuality and Medicine in the Middle Ages*, p. 189.
24. Jean Astruc, *A Treatise on Venereal Disease in Nine Books* (London, 1754), p. 121.
25. John Martin, *A Treatise of all the Degrees and Symptoms of Venereal Diseases in both the Sexes* (London, 1708), p. 17.
26. Cited in Claude Quétel, *The History of Syphilis*, p. 77.
27. Ernest Finger, *Gonorrhoea*, p. 6. See also D. Barlow, *Sexually Transmitted Disease: The Facts* (Oxford, 1979); J.T. Crissey and C.P. Lawrence, *The Dermatology and Syphilology of the Nineteenth Century* (New Jersey, 1981);

Ambrose King *et al.*, *Venereal Disease* (London, 1981); R.S. Morton, *Gonorrhoea* (East Sussex, 1977).

28. See, for instance, John Martin, *A Treatise of all the Degrees and Symptoms of Venereal Diseases in both the Sexes*, p. 17.
29. George Luys, *Textbook on Gonorrhoea and Its Complications*, p. 22.
30. Iwan Bloch, 'The History of Syphilis' in D'arcy Power and J. Keogh Murphy, *A System of Syphilis*, Vol. 1 (Oxford, 1914), p. 32.
31. William Allen Pusey, *Syphilis as a Modern Problem* (Chicago, 1915), p. 23.
32. John Hunter, *On the Venereal Disease* (London, 1810), pp. 24–66.
33. R.S. Morton, *Gonorrhoea*, p. 11.
34. L.S. Jaycna, 'Images of John Hunter in the Nineteenth Century', *History of Science*, Vol. 21, Pt. 7 (1983), p. 87.
35. Russell C. Maulitz, *Morbid Appearances: The Anatomy of Pathology in the Early Nineteenth Century* (Cambridge, 1987), p. 117.
36. *Ibid.*, p. 116.
37. Michael Kelly, 'Swediaur: The Vicious anti-Hunter Rheumato-Venereologist', *Medical History*, Vol. 11 (1967), p. 172.
38. Sir D'arcy Power, 'John Hunter's Experiment', *British Journal of Surgery*, Vol. 22, No. 85 (1934), p. 1.
39. John Hunter, *On the Venereal Diseases*, p.vi.
40. *Ibid.*, p. 65.
41. *Ibid.*, p. 28.
42. *Ibid.*, pp. 28–9.
43. *Ibid.*, p. 27.
44. *Ibid.*, pp. 69–75.
45. *Ibid.*, p. 27.
46. *Ibid.*, p. 27.
47. F.X. Swediaur, *Practical Treatise on Venereal Complaints* (New York, 1788), p. 10.
48. Berkeley Hill, *Syphilis and Local Contagious Disorders* (London, 1881), p. 9
49. C.C. Dennie, *A History of Syphilis* (Illinois, 1962), p. 82.
50. Kenneth M. Flegel, 'Changing Concepts of the Nosology of Gonorrhoea and Syphilis', p. 584.
51. C.C. Dennie, *A History of Syphilis*, p. 93.
52. Richard Carmichael, *An Essay on Venereal Disease* (London, 1814).
53. Ambrose King and Claude Nicholls, *Venereal Diseases* (London, 1975), pp. 20–5.
54. John Abernathy, *Surgical Observations on Diseases Resembling Syphilis* (London, 1826). I have used this text as it provides the most detailed view of Abernathy's ideas; he had however been writing on the question of syphilis and pseudo-syphilis at least as early as 1805.
55. *Ibid.*, p. 5.
56. *Ibid.*, p. 4.
57. *Ibid.*, pp. 6–7.
58. 'Mr Evans on the Ulceration of the Genital Organs', *Medico-Chirurgical Transactions*, Vol. 4 (1813), pp. 1–3.
59. *Ibid.*, p. 3.
60. Edward Shorter, *A History of Women's Bodies*, p. 257.

61. Dr Burder, 'On Syphiloid Diseases', *Medico-Chirurgical Journal*, Vol. 1, No. 6 (1818), p. 248.
62. *Ibid.*, p. 248. (His emphasis.)
63. Cited in George T. Morgan, 'On the Unity and Plurality of Poisons in Lues Venerea', *Edinburgh Medical and Surgical Journal*, Vol. 47 (1837), p. 169. See also 'Mayo, Skey, Parker and Acton on the Aphroditic Diseases', *Edinburgh Medical and Surgical Journal*, Vol. 78 (1868), p. 431.
64. Richard Carmichael, *An Essay on Venereal Disease*, p. 56.
65. George T. Morgan, 'On the Unity and Plurality of Poisons in Lues Venerea', p. 162.
66. Mr Travers, 'On the Venereal Infections', *Medico-Chirurgical Journal*, Vol. 13, No. 25 (1839), p. 162.
67. Mr Eagle, 'Production of Gonorrhoea and Chancre from Leucorrhoea', *The Lancet*, Vol. 2 (1836), p. 491.

2 THE SOURCE

1. Enid Gauldie, *Cruel Habitation: A History of Working Class Housing 1780–1918* (London, 1974), p. 101.
2. Brenda M. White, 'Medical Police: Politics and Police and the Fate of John Robertson', *Medical History*, Vol. 27 (1983), p. 407.
3. Ludmilla Jordanova, 'Policing Public Health in France 1780–1815' in Teizo Ogawa (ed.), *Public Health*, (Tokyo, 1981), p. 11.
4. Christopher J. Lawrence, 'Sanitary Reformers and the Medical Profession in Victorian England' in Teizo Ogawa (ed.), *Public Health*, p. 146.
5. Ludmilla Jordanova, 'Policing Public Health in France 1780–1815', p. 12.
6. The notion that syphilis was a specific infection caused by a microbe was not pressed until the 1880s by Jonathan Hutchinson and Charles Drysdale.
7. Susan Sontag, *Illness as Metaphor*, p. 59.
8. See Jill Harsin, *Policing Prostitution in Nineteenth Century Paris* (Princeton, 1985).
9. *Ibid.*, p. 102.
10. Alexandre Parent-Duchatelet, *De la Prostitution dans la ville de Paris*, Vol. I (Paris, 1836), p. 4.
11. Alain Corbin, *Women for Hire: Prostitution and Sexuality in France after 1850* (Cambridge, Massachusetts, 1990), p. 5.
12. Judith Walkowitz, *Prostitution and Victorian Society*, p. 32.
13. Charles Bernheimer, *Figures of Ill Repute: Representing Prostitution in Nineteenth Century France* (Harvard, 1989), p. 16.
14. Alexandre Parent-Duchatelet, *De la Prostitution dans la ville de Paris*, Vol. II, pp. 513–14.
15. 'M. Parent-Duchatelet on Prostitution in the City of Paris', *Edinburgh Medical and Surgical Journal*, Vol. 47 (1837), pp. 204–5.
16. Rev. James Marchant, *The Master Problem* (London, 1917), p. 174.
17. David Newman, 'The History and Prevention of Venereal Disease' *Glasgow Medical Journal*, Vol. 81 (1914), p. 95.
18. Philippe Ricord, 'On the Employment of the Speculum in Females Affected with Venereal Disease', *The Lancet*, Vol. 1 (1832–33), p. 587.

19. Cited in Diane Beyer-Perett, *Ethics and Errors: The Dispute Between Ricord and Auzias-Turenne over Syphilization*, PhD Thesis (Stanford, 1977), p. 15.

20. *Medico-Chirurgical Journal*, Vol. 18, No. 36 (1833), p. 234.

21. John C. Egan, *Syphilitic Diseases: Their Pathology, Diagnosis and Treatment* (London, 1853), p. 116. See also the discussion of the speculum in Judith Walkowitz, *Prostitution and Victorian Society*, pp. 56–7, and in Ornella Moscucci, *The Science of Woman: Gynaecology and Gender in England 1800–1929* (Cambridge, 1990), pp. 113–18.

22. Ernest Finger, *Gonorrhoea*, p. 10.

23. *Ibid.*, p. 11.

24. See, for instance, the review of *De la Prostitution* in *Edinburgh Medical and Surgical Journal*, Vol. 47 (1837), p. 226.

25. Sander L. Gilman, *Difference and Pathology: Stereotypes of Sexuality, Race and Madness* (Ithaca, 1985), pp. 94–5.

26. Cited in Derek Lewellyn-Jones, *Sex and V.D.* (London, 1974), p. i.

27. Cited in J.T. Crissey and C.P. Lawrence, *The Dermatology and Syphilology of the Nineteenth Century*, p. 86.

28. F.C. Skey, *A Practical Treatise on the Venereal Disease* (London, 1840), pp. 3–4.

29. While women might have remained symptomless carriers of gonorrhoea for perhaps weeks or even months, they could not remain without infection and symptomless forever. Generally, after a period of time the results of infection would be visible with the use of a speculum. Latent syphilis is only infectious during the very early stages.

30. F.C. Skey, *A Practical Treatise on the Venereal Disease*, p. 8.

31. *Ibid.*, p. 9.

32. *Ibid.*, p. 10. (His emphasis.)

33. *Ibid.*, p. 174.

34. Langston Parker, *Modern Treatments of Syphilitic Diseases* (London, 1845), p. 41.

35. W.R. Greg, 'Prostitution', *Westminster Review*, Vol. 53 (1850), p. 475.

36. James Miller, *Prostitution Considered in Relation to Its Causes and Cure* (Edinburgh, 1856), p. 5.

37. 'Prostitution', *Medical Times and Gazette* (23 January 1856), p. 90.

38. See Peter Fryer's introduction to the 1968 edition of Acton's work *Prostitution*. See also Peter Quennell's introduction to Henry Mayhew's writings, *London Underground* (London, 1969). For a critique of the hallowed position certain historians have given Acton, see M. Jeanne Peterson, 'Dr Acton's Enemy: Medicine, Sex and Society in Victorian England', *Victorian Studies*, Vol. 29, No. 4 (1986).

39. Judith Walkowitz, *Prostitution and Victorian Society*, p. 46.

40. William Acton, *A Complete and Practical Treatise on the Venereal Diseases: Their Immediate and Remote Consequences* (London, 1841), p. 25.

41. *Ibid.*, p. 25.

42. *Ibid.*, p. 227.

43. William Acton, *A Practical Treatise on Diseases of the Urinary and Generative Organs* (London, 1851), p. 36.

44. See Leonore Davidoff, 'The Rationalization of Housework' in D.L. Barker

and S. Allen, *Dependence and Exploitation in Work and Marriage* (London, 1976), p. 128.

45. William Acton, *A Practical Treatise on Diseases of the Urinary and Generative Organs*, p. 35.
46. *Ibid.*, p. 40.
47. *Ibid.*, p. 41.
48. William Acton, *Prostitution*, p. 59.
49. Judith Walkowitz, *Prostitution and Victorian Society*, p. 5.
50. 'Prostitution – The Signs of Reform', *The Lancet* (Vol. 2) 1857, p. 453; 'Diseases of the Camp', *The Lancet*, Vol. 2 (1857), p. 493.
51. For a favourable treatment of *Prostitution* see Peter Fryer's introduction to the 1968 edition of *Prostitution*. See also Peter Quennell's introduction to Henry Mayhew's writings, *London Underground*, and Keith Neild's introduction to *Prostitution in the Victorian Age* (London, 1973). While Judith Walkowitz is critical of Acton, much of her argument in *Prostitution and Victorian Society* is based around many of Acton's misconceptions.
52. William Acton, *Prostitution*, p. 119.
53. Acton's use of Tennyson ('Idylls of the King', ii, 514–18) may also be placed in the context of the Victorian interest in the Arthurian legend and in Guinevere as symbol of adulterous love and masculine anxiety.
54. William Acton, *Prostitution*, p. 60.
55. William Acton, *Functions and Disorders of the Reproductive Organs* (Philadelphia, 1894), p. 208.
56. William Acton, *Prostitution*, p. 67.
57. Holmes Coote, *A Report upon some of the more important points connected with the Treatment of Syphilis* (London, 1857), p. 6.
58. *Ibid.*, pp. 3–6.
59. *Ibid.*, p. 6.
60. *Ibid.*, p. 7.
61. Frank Mort, *Dangerous Sexualities*, p. 28.
62. Holmes Coote, *A Report upon some of the more important points*, p. 20.
63. Dr Gordon, *General Statistics of Local Venereal Ulcers, Syphilitic, Bubo &c.*, npd.
64. 'Diseases of the Camps', *The Lancet*, Vol. 2 (1860), p. 493.
65. Henry Mayhew, *London and the Labouring Poor*, p. 75.
66. Cited in James Greenwood, *Seven Curses of London* (London, 1872), p. 294.
67. William Acton, *Prostitution*, p. 57.
68. 'Necessity for Lock Hospitals', *The Lancet*, Vol. 1 (1853), p. 62.
69. Henry Mayhew, *London and the Labouring Poor*, p. 67.
70. For a more detailed discussion of this see Londa Schiebinger, *Nature's Body: Gender in the Making of Modern Science* (Boston, 1993) or Sander L. Gilman, *Difference and Pathology*.
71. Carol Smart, 'Disruptive Bodies and Unruly Sex: The Regulation of Reproduction and Sexuality in the Nineteenth Century' in Carol Smart (ed.), *Regulating Womanhood: Historical Essays on Marriage, Motherhood and Sexuality* (London, 1992), pp. 25–8.
72. To view syphilis or indeed any sexually transmissible disease as a foreign or imported illness is hardly novel. As discussed earlier, syphilis was always

categorized as an external threat. See also Anna Foa, 'The Old and The New' and Mary B. Campbell, 'Carnal Knowledge'. More recently, HIV/AIDS has received similar xenophobic treatment. For similar discussion around HIV/AIDS see Cindy Patton, 'From Nation to Family: Containing African AIDS' in Andrew Parker *et al.* (eds), *Nationalisms and Sexualities* (New York, 1992); Paula A. Triechler, 'AIDS & HIV Infection in the Third World: A First World Chronicle' in Barbara Kruger and Phil Marian (eds), *Remaking History* (Seattle, 1989); Simon Watney, 'Missionary Positions', *Critical Quarterly*, Vol. 30, No. 1 (1989).

73. W.R. Greg, 'Prostitution', p. 475.
74. *Ibid.*, p. 491.
75. Henry Mayhew, *London and the Labouring Poor*, p. 71.
76. See, for instance, *The Times* (11 November 1847), p. 5.
77. 'Prostitution: The Need for Its Reform', *The Lancet*, Vol. 1 (1853), p. 62.
78. *The Lancet*, Vol. 1 (1855), p. 75.
79. 'Prostitution, the Means for Reform', *The Lancet*, Vol. 2 (1857), p. 504.
80. 'Prostitution and the Reformatories', *The Lancet*, Vol. 2 (1857), p. 588.
81. James Miller, *Prostitution Considered*, p. 28.
82. *Ibid.*, p. 5.
83. Myna Trustram, 'Distasteful and Derogatory? Examining Victorian Soldiers for Venereal Disease' in London Feminist History Group, *The Sexual Dynamics of History* (London, 1983), p. 155.
84. John Gill Gamble, *The Origins, Administration and Impact of the Contagious Diseases Acts from a Military Perspective*, PhD Thesis (University of Southern Mississippi, 1983), p. 4.
85. Myna Trustram, 'Distasteful and Derogatory?', p. 156.
86. F.B. Smith, 'Ethics and Disease in the Later Nineteenth Century: The Contagious Diseases Acts', *Historical Studies*, Vol. 57 (1971), p. 119.

3 IMPLEMENTING THE SYSTEM

1. F.B. Smith, 'The Contagious Diseases Acts', p. 119.
2. Paul McHugh, *Prostitution and Victorian Social Reform*, p. 36.
3. Myna Trustram, *Women of the Regiment: Marriage and the Victorian Army* (Cambridge, 1984), p. 121.
4. F.B. Smith, 'The Contagious Diseases Acts Reconsidered', *Social History of Medicine*, Vol. 3, No. 2 (1990).
5. Report of the Committee appointed to Enquire into the Pathology and Treatment of Venereal Disease, Parliamentary Papers, Vol. 37 (1867), p. iv.
6. *Ibid.*, p. v.
7. See evidence of Langston Parker, Questions 3256–3379; Prescott G. Hewett, Esq., Questions 5097–5199.
8. *Ibid.*, pp. 222–3.
9. *Ibid.*, p. 346.
10. *Ibid.*, p. xiv.
11. *Ibid*, p. 262.
12. *Ibid.*, p. 207.
13. Carol Smart, 'Disruptive Bodies and Unruly Sex', p. 28.

14. Report of the Committee appointed to Enquire into . . . Venereal Disease, p. 106.
15. *Ibid.*, p. 81.
16. *Ibid.*, p. 69.
17. *Ibid.*, p. 81.
18. *Ibid.*, p. 85.
19. *Ibid.*, p. 320.
20. Sander L. Gilman, *The Jew's Body* (New York, 1991), pp. 124–7.
21. See Michel Foucault, *Madness and Civilisation* (London, 1967); *The History of Sexuality*, Vol. 1 (London, 1977); Jeffrey Weeks, *Coming Out: Homosexual Politics in Britain* (London, 1977).
22. Report of the Committee appointed to Enquire into . . . Venereal Disease, p. 289.
23. Sandra Stanley Holton, 'State Pandering, Medical Policing and Prostitution: The Controversy within the Medical Profession concerning the Contagious Diseases Legislation 1864–1886', *Research in Law, Deviance and Social Control*, Vol. 9 (1988), p. 154.
24. Report of the Committee appointed to Enquire into . . . Venereal Disease, p. 52.
25. *Ibid.*, p. 289.
26. *Ibid.*, p. 481.
27. *Ibid.*, p. xviii.
28. *Ibid.*, p. 244.
29. F.B. Smith, 'The Contagious Diseases Acts Reconsidered', p. 209.
30. Frances Finnegan, *Poverty and Prostitution*, pp. 148–9.
31. Cited in Richard Davenport-Hines, *Sex, Death and Punishment* (London, 1990), p. 172.
32. 'Select Committee into the Contagious Diseases Acts', *British Medical Journal* (28 May 1881), p. 862.
33. Royal Commission on Venereal Disease, *Parliamentary Papers, Commissions and Reports* (1916), p. 188.

4   RESISTING THE ACTS

1. John Chapman, 'Prostitution in relation to the National Health', *Westminster Review*, Vol. 36 (1869), pp. 179–80.
2. Josephine Butler, 'An Appeal to the People of England on the Recognition and Superintendence of Prostitution by Governments' (1870) in Sheila Jeffreys (ed.), *The Sexuality Debates* (London, 1987), p. 112.
3. Annie Besant, 'The Legislation of Female Slavery in England' (1876) in Sheila Jeffreys (ed.), *The Sexuality Debates*, p. 91.
4. J.B. Post, 'A Foreign Office Survey of Venereal Disease and Prostitution Control 1869–70', *Medical History*, Vol. 22 (1978), p. 328.
5. John Simon, 'Prostitution: Its Sanitary Superintendence by the State', *Westminster Review*, Vol. 37 (1869), p. 559.
6. J.B. Post, 'A Foreign Office Survey of Venereal Disease', p. 328.
7. Dorothy Porter and Roy Porter, 'The Enforcement of Health: The British

Debate' in Elizabeth Fee and Daniel M. Fox, *AIDS: The Burden of History* (Berkeley, 1988), p. 100.

8. Paul McHugh, *Prostitution and Victorian Social Reform*, p. 65.
9. Judith Walkowitz, *Prostitution and Victorian Society*, p. 229.
10. Letter to the Admiralty, 17 January 1870, Public Records Office, Adml/ 6835.
11. Report of Royal Commission regarding the Administration and Operation of the Contagious Diseases Acts, *Parliamentary Papers*, Vol. 19 (1871), p. 130.
12. *Ibid.*, p. 81.
13. *Ibid.*, p. 130. (My emphasis.)
14. *Ibid.*, p. 130.
15. *Ibid.*, p. 523. (My emphasis.)
16. *Ibid.*, p. 46. (My emphasis.)
17. *Ibid.*, p. 206.
18. Abraham Flexner, *Prostitution in Europe* (New York, 1914), p. 216.
19. Report of Royal Commission (1871), p. 112.
20. *Ibid.*, p. 510.
21. *Ibid.*, p. 637.
22. *Ibid.*, p. 478.
23. *Ibid.*, p. 226.
24. Rev. Ralph Wardlaw, *Lectures on Prostitution: Its Nature, Extent, Effects, Guilt, Causes and Remedies* (Glasgow, 1842), p. 71.
25. Thomas Laqueur, *Making Sex*, p. 230.
26. Report of Royal Commission (1871), p. 11.
27. *Ibid.*, pp. 376–7.
28. *Ibid.*, p. 69.
29. *Ibid.*, p. 479.
30. Josephine Butler, 'An Appeal to the People of England', p. 119.
31. Paul McHugh, *Prostitution and Victorian Social Reform*, p. 65.
32. Glen Petrie, *A Singular Iniquity: The Campaigns of Josephine Butler* (London, 1971), p. 122.
33. Report of Royal Commission (1871), p. 344.
34. Letter to the Right Hon. H.A. Bruce – Memorial of London Physicians, *Parliamentary Papers*, Vol. 47 (1872).

5 THE NEW CAMPAIGN

1. Both Judith Walkowitz and Paul McHugh are critical of what they see as the triumph of social purity over the more liberal components of the Repeal movement; however, they both provide a fairly balanced appraisal of the movement overall. More recently, in an article reconsidering the CD Acts, F. Barry Smith has characterized all those involved in the movement in this manner. He writes '[L]ong before the Acts were repealed, the hard core of the Antis had moved onto demanding 'social purity', censorship, legislation against male homosexuals and school campaigns against masturbation'. See F.B. Smith, 'The Contagious Diseases Acts Reconsidered', p. 215. Here, Smith seems to be conflating all the repressive measures of the 1885

Criminal Law Amendment Act with the views of the Repealers. In so doing, Smith conveniently forgets his own argument regarding the so-called Labouchere's Amendment to the Act, where he suggests that the legislation against homosexuals was added in order that the Bill might fail. See F.B. Smith, 'Labouchere's Amendment to the Criminal Law Amendment Bill', *Historical Studies*, Vol. 17 (1976). His claims about masturbation campaigns at schools have to be treated very carefully too, as such ideas were taken up by many and varied sectors of the community in the 1890s. Moreover, there were many such as Dr William Acton, who regarded himself as Father of the CD Acts, who would have wholeheartedly supported such campaigns. The idea that those who favoured the Acts were liberal in their approach to fallen women belies a total lack of understanding of the functions of the Acts and ignores the fact that far from being oppositional, social puritans and those in favour of the Acts often worked hand in hand. This was certainly the case for Ellice Hopkins, one of the more repressive social puritans, who was warmly greeted by Extensionists in Plymouth and was reprimanded by the Ladies National Association Against the Contagious Diseases Acts (LNA) for her collusion with them. See Judith Walkowitz, *Prostitution and Victorian Society*, p. 238.

2. Sandra Stanley Holton, 'State Pandering, Medical Policing and Prostitution', pp. 154–6.
3. Myna Trustram, *Daughters of the Regiment*, p. 128.
4. *Ibid.*, p. 129.
5. The Report from the Select Committee on the Contagious Diseases Acts, *Parliamentary Papers*, Vol. 8 (1878–79), p. 8.
6. Claude Quétel maintains that during the latter half of the nineteenth century the *méthode expectante* gained renewed impetus from repeated therapeutic failures. This was the idea that syphilis would get better by itself without being treated, perhaps even only on the condition that it was not treated. See Claude Quétel, *The History of Syphilis*, p. 135. I do not want to suggest here that it was impossible for syphilis to spontaneously cure itself as there have been at least two major studies, the Boeck-Bruusgard study in Norway and the Tuskegee Experiment in Alabama, USA, that have shown contradictory results. In the Norwegian study, Dr Boeck, Professor of Dermatology and Venereology at Oslo Hospital, compiled medical records on the course of untreated syphilis in 1,978 patients admitted to his hospital between the period 1891 and 1910. In 1929, Edwin Bruusgaard, his successor, compiled an analysis of the subsequent medical history of 473 of these patients. A massive restudy was conducted between 1948 and 1951 by Trygue Gjestland, who published his findings in 1955. He found that although untreated syphilis was the cause of death amongst some of the sample, 90 per cent died of other causes. In the Tuskegee Experiment, the United States Public Health Service conducted a study of the effects of untreated syphilis on black men in Macon County Alabama between the period 1932 and 1972. The results of this study were inconclusive, although it was noted that the life expectancy of these men was reduced by 17 per cent. When the experiment was exposed in 1972, the US government was forced to pay compensation to the subjects of the experiment and in 1975 the state extended treatment to the subject's wives who contracted syphilis and their children with congenital

syphilis. What I want to highlight is the fact that untreated primary syphilis would necessarily develop into secondary syphilis. Sores that spontaneously cured themselves were not cured syphilis but minor ailments such as 'dirt sores' or herpes. See William J. Brown, *et al.*, *Syphilis and Other Venereal Diseases* (Cambridge, Mass., 1973); James H. Jones, *Bad Blood: The Tuskegee Syphilis Experiment* (New York, 1981).

7. F. Barry Smith has argued that those in favour of repeal were correct in claiming that the Acts would not remove/cure the disease but they 'could not have known that at the time'. I would argue that Repealers had spent considerable time and effort examining the statistics dealing with venereal disease, not only in the subjected districts but throughout Great Britain and the Continent, and had considerable evidence to show that there was little correlation between regulation and decline in the diseases. Moreover, many of the claims pro-Repeal doctors made at the 1881 Select Committee, regarding the nature of gonorrhoea and the difference between soft sores and syphilis, were found to be correct. See F.B. Smith, 'The Contagious Diseases Acts Reconsidered', p. 213.

8. Report from the Select Committee, pp. 63–4.

9. It is worth noting here that this theory has recently been put forward in the *Journal of the American Medical Association* to explain how a US serviceman in Germany, who claimed to have only heterosexual contact and had not used intravenous drugs, came to acquire the AIDS virus. One correspondent wrote that transmission was not really from women to men but was 'quasi-homosexual'. That is, Man A infected with HIV had sexual intercourse with a prostititute, 'she [performing] no more than a perfunctory external cleansing between customers' then had sexual intercourse with Man B; he is infected by way of Man A's semen still in the vagina of the prostitute. As Paula A. Treichler has pointed out, in this description 'the projectile penis could also function as a kind of proboscis, sucking up quantities of the virus from a contaminated pool'. See Paula A. Treichler, 'AIDS, Gender and Biomedical Discourse' in Elizabeth Fee and Daniel M. Fox, *AIDS: the Burden of History* (Berkeley, 1988), p. 208.

10. Report from the Select Committee, p. 63.

11. Holmes Cootes, *A Report upon Some of the More Important Points*, p. 1.

12. *Ibid.*, p. 73.

13. *Ibid.*, p. 75.

14. *Ibid.*, p. 82.

15. *Ibid.*, p. 82.

16. *Ibid.*, p. 72.

17. Paul McHugh, *Prostitution and Victorian Social Reform*, p. 139.

18. Report from the Select Committee on the Contagious Diseases Acts, *Parliamentary Papers*, Vol. 8 (1880), p. 33.

19. Ambrose King *et al.*, *Venereal Diseases*, p. 3.

20. Diane Beyer-Perett, *Ethics and Errors*, pp. 125–6.

21. Report of the Committee to Enquire into the Pathology and Treatment of the Venereal Disease, p. 247.

22. *Ibid.*, p. xx.

23. Compare this with Plymouth – 8.0 per cent; Liverpool – 4.3 per cent; Dublin – 10.4 per cent; Hamburg – 11.15 per cent; Copenhagen – 13.97 per

cent. See Report from the Select Committee on the Contagious Diseases Acts, p. 5.

24. *British Medical Journal*, Vol. 1 (1880), p. 344.
25. 'The Contagious Diseases Acts', *The Lancet*, Vol. 1 (1880), p. 302.
26. *British Medical Journal*, Vol. 1 (1880), p. 390.
27. J.T. Crissey and C.P. Lawrence, *The Dermatology and Syphilology of the Nineteenth Century*, p. 88.
28. Report of the Committee to Enquire into the Pathology and Treatment of the Venereal Disease, p. xiv.
29. *Ibid.*, p. xiv.
30. *Ibid.*, p. xv.
31. Langston Parker, *Modern Treatment of Syphilitic Diseases*, p. 269.
32. Report from the Select Committee on the Contagious Diseases Acts, pp. 2–3.
33. *Ibid.*, p. 4.
34. *Ibid.*, p. 5.
35. Richard L. Blanco, 'The Attempted Control of Venereal Disease in the Army of Mid-Victorian England', *Journal of the Society for Army Historical Research*, Vol. 45 (1967), p. 239.
36. Kenneth Ballhachet, *Sex, Death and Class under the Raj* (London, 1980), p. 162.
37. Cited in Richard L. Blanco, 'The Attempted Control of Venereal Disease, p. 239.
38. Frank Mort, *Dangerous Sexualities*, pp. 71–2.
39. Myna Trustram, *Daughters of the Regiment*, p. 1.
40. *Ibid.*, p. 26.
41. George L. Mosse, *Nationalism and Sexuality: Respectability and Abnormal Sexuality in Modern Europe* (New York, 1985), p. 13.
42. Report from the Select Committee on the Contagious Diseases Acts, p. 11.
43. *Ibid.*, p. 18.
44. *Ibid.*, p. 22.
45. *Ibid.*, p. 25.
46. Chancroid did not always respond to treatment and sometimes complications such as gangrene of the penis could develop. It is quite likely that such cases would be regarded as cases of syphilis when, in fact, they were chancroid. This disease was particularly prevalent in sea ports and was probably the disease that doctors such as Holmes Coote and Dr Gordon were describing in port towns in the 1850s. See Ivor Felstein, *Sexual Pollution* (London, 1974), pp. 135–6; Paul Redfern, *The Love Diseases* (London, 1979), p. 26.
47. F.B. Smith, 'The Contagious Diseases Acts Reconsidered', p. 217.
48. Report from the Select Committee on the Contagious Diseases Acts, p. 25.
49. *Ibid.*, p. 120.
50. *Ibid.*, p. 124.
51. See, for instance, *British Medical Journal*, Vol. 1 (1881), p. 444; 'S.C. on the C.D. Acts', *British Medical Journal*, Vol. 1 (1881), p. 482; 'S.C. on the C.D. Acts', *British Medical Journal*, Vol. 1 (1881), p. 862; 'The Contagious Diseases Acts', *The Lancet*, Vol. 1 (1880), p. 342; 'S.C. on the C.D. Acts', *British Medical Journal*, Vol. 1 (1881), p. 26.

52. Arthur Cooper, 'Review of Guyot', *London Medical Record* (15 December 1884), p. 546.
53. Report from the Select Committee on Contagious Diseases Acts, *Parliamentary Papers*, Vol. 9 (1882), p. 19.
54. Paul McHugh, *Prostitution and Victorian Social Reform*, p. 216.
55. *Ibid.*, pp. 216–18.
56. Judith Walkowitz, *Prostitution and Victorian Society*, p. 99.
57. 'The Contagious Diseases Acts', *British Medical Journal*, Vol. 2 (1883), p. 129.
58. 'The Contagious Diseases Acts', *British Medical Journal*, Vol. 2 (1883), p. 825.
59. 'The Contagious Diseases Acts', *British Medical Journal*, Vol. 2 (1883), p. 735.
60. Alfred Cooper, *Syphilis and Pseudo-Syphilis* (London, 1884), p. 12.
61. 'The Contagious Diseases Acts', *British Medical Journal*, Vol. 2 (1883), p. 834.
62. 'The Contagious Diseases Acts', *British Medical Journal*, Vol. 1 (1884), p. 1257.
63. H.C. French, *Syphilis in the Army* (London, 1907), p. 1. (His emphasis.)
64. Royal Commission on Venereal Disease, *Parliamentary Papers*, Commission and Reports (1916), p. 303.
65. *Ibid.*, p. 239.
66. *Ibid.*, p. 120.
67. Judith Walkowitz, *Prostitution in Victorian Society*, p. 230; F.B. Smith, 'The Contagious Diseases Acts Reconsidered'.

6 PATHOLOGIZING CHILDREN

1. Royal Commission regarding the Administration and Operation of the C.D. Acts, *Parliamentary Papers*, Vol. 19, House of Commons (1871), p. 425.
2. *Hansard Parliamentary Debates*, House of Lords, Third Series, Vol. 339 (1885), p. 1211.
3. *Ibid.*, p. 9.
4. Anne Stafford, The *Age of Consent* (London, 1964), p. 56.
5. R.L. Schultz, *Crusader in Babylon: W.T. Stead and the Pall Mall Gazette* (Lincoln, 1972), p. 28.
6. Ron Pearsall, *The Worm in the Bud*, p. 274.
7. *Ibid.*, p. 274.
8. Joseph Kestner, *Mythology and Misogyny* (Wisconsin, 1989), p. 3. Kestner suggests that there are several myths operative in the 'Maiden Tribute' but the myth controlling the entire series was that of Danae, imprisoned in a tower and impregnated by Zeus with gold. This transformation of semen into gold becomes the archetypal image of prostitution.
9. *Pall Mall Gazette* (6 July 1885), p. 1.
10. See F.B. Smith, 'Disease and Ethics'. Smith notes in this article that Labouchere, who went on to amend the Criminal Law Bill regarding homosexual acts between consenting and non-consenting men, had done this as

an attempt to prevent the Bill from passing. His antagonism towards Stead and social purity work in general is very important in this context.

11. Michael Pearson, *The Age of Consent*, pp. 13–14.
12. Ron Pearsall, *The Worm in the Bud*, p. 378.
13. Several works have been written dealing specifically with the campaign to pass this Act, including Charles Terot's *Traffic in Innocence* and Ann Stafford's *Age of Consent*: in these works Stead's mythic character remains intact. Ron Pearsall's *The Worm in the Bud* and Michael Pearson's *The Age of Consent* are highly critical of Stead and, indeed, anyone involved in the rescue of prostitutes. Their criticisms of Stead could be addressed to their own works which are largely based on anecdotal evidence and apocryphal detail.
14. See especially Judith Walkowitz,'The Politics of Prostitution', *Signs*, Vol. 6, No. 1 (1980); Judith Walkowitz, 'Male Vice and Female Virtue: Feminism and the Politics of Prostitution in Nineteenth Century Great Britain' in Ann Snitow, *et al.*, *Desire: The Politics of Sexuality* (London, 1984); Ellen Dubois and Linda Gordon, 'Seeking Ecstasy on the Battlefield: Danger and Pleasure in Nineteenth Century Feminist Thought' in Carole Vance (ed.), *Pleasure and Danger: Exploring Female Sexuality* (Boston, 1984); Deborah Gorham, 'The Maiden Tribute of Modern Babylon re-examined: Child Prostitution and the Idea of Childhood in Late Victorian England', *Victorian Studies*, Vol. 21 (1978).
15. Judith Walkowitz, 'Male Vice and Female Virtue', p. 48.
16. Judith Walkowitz, *Prostitution and Victorian Society*, p. 17.
17. Deborah Gorham,'The Maiden Tribute of Modern Babylon', p. 89.
18. Ellen Dubois and Linda Gordon, 'Seeking Ecstasy on the Battlefield', p. 38.
19. J.E. Mennell, 'The Politics of Frustration: The Maiden Tribute of Modern Babylon and the Morality Movement of 1885', *North Dakota Quarterly*, Vol. 49 (1981), p. 79.
20. *Ibid.*, p. 79.
21. Sheila Jeffreys, *The Spinster and Her Enemies: Feminism and Sexuality 1880–1930* (London, 1985), p. 56.
22. F.W. Lowdnes, 'Venereal Disease in Girls of Tender Age', *The Lancet* (22 January 1887), p. 168.
23. Antony E. Simpson, 'Vulnerability and the Age of Female Consent: Legal Innovation and Its Effect on Prosecutions for Rape in Eighteenth Century London' in E.R. Rosseau and Roy Porter (eds), *Sexual Undergrounds of the Enlightenment* (Chapel Hill, 1988), p. 193.
24. *Ibid.*, p. 193.
25. J.S. Caspar, *Pract. Hadbuch der Gerichtlichen Medicin*, Vol. 3 (Berlin, 1857), p. 103. See also F.B. Smith, *The People's Health*, p. 303. Smith claims that 'Quack Doctoresses' had kept special brothels in Liverpool for this purpose since 1827 to provide for this cure. While no doubt the practice was common, it would seem from the evidence that it was generally individual men rather than women who engaged in procuring children for this purpose.
26. Alfred Swaine Taylor, *The Principles and Practice of Medical Jurisprudence*, Vol. 3 (London, 1883), p. 427.
27. Antony E. Simpson, 'Vulnerability and the Age of Female Consent', pp. 193–4.

28.   *Ibid.*, pp. 193–4. Simpson argues that the place of children in the home in
       the metropolis made them especially vulnerable to sexual abuse. He argues
       that this was particularly true for child domestics. In his analysis of 189
       rape trials before the Old Bailey between 1730 and 1830, thirty-five in-
       volved allegations of abuse of servants by their masters, eight by workmates
       and thirty-five by other members of the household. Of the 141 cases of rape
       and attempted rape for the same period where the defendant's occupation
       is given, fifteen were gentlemen, eighteen were domestic servants, fifteen
       other servants and the rest were from occupations of the lower and middle
       classes. Similar evidence is presented by Anna Clark for the period 1800 to
       1845. In her study of rape trials in the Old Bailey for the period 1770 to
       1845, Clark found 20 per cent of cases involved masters and servants. From
       her study of newspapers for the period 1800 to 1845, of the ninety-three
       men accused of sexual assault on children in London where the occupation
       is given, 32 per cent came from the ranks of the labouring poor, 18 per cent
       were skilled artisans, 10 per cent were apprentices, 21 per cent were from
       the lower middle class and 18 per cent were gentlemen. Clark also found
       that in the rural north-east of England, for the period 1800–1845, skilled
       workers such as weavers, joiners, tailors and blacksmiths accounted for a
       disproportionate number of assaults on children – 83 per cent from the
       newspaper sample and 59 per cent in depositions from the North-east Assize.
       See Anna Clark, *Women's Silence, Men's Violence: Sexual Assault in Eng-
       land 1770–1845* (London, 1987), pp. 98–9. In one of the few contemporary
       descriptions of a man frequently using prostitutes from this period – the
       pornographic memoir *My Secret Life* – Walter, the author, often buys young
       girls or harasses young servants for sex because he fears catching 'the pox'.

29.   Dr Thomas Percival in his *Medical Ethics* (London, 1791). Percival re-
       corded this case as part of a text on medical ethics; the text was dedicated
       to his sons and is written for the most part like fatherly advice. In regard
       to this case Percival states, 'The preceding narrative may teach the young
       surgeon to act with great circumspection, when called upon to give an
       opinion in cases which are involved in any degree of obscurity. It behoves
       him to consider well the important duty he has to discharge both to an
       individual, and to the community' p. 223. For further discussion see Michael
       Ryan, *Medical Jurisprudence and State Medicine* (London, 1836), p. 316.

30.   Noma is a severe gangrenous process occurring predominantly in debili-
       tated and malnourished children. It typically begins as an ulcer inside the
       mouth that rapidly becomes necrotic and spreads to produce extensive de-
       struction of the tissues of the face, which may result in severe disfigurement
       and even death. Various bacteria have been implicated in its aetiology,
       including *Treponema vincenti* and *Bacteriodes melanomagenicus*. A very
       rare variation of this condition is noma of the genital area. Also known as
       cancrum oris and gangrenous stomatitis.

31.   T.W. Cooke, 'On Some Distressing Sequelae of the Diseases of Infancy:
       Purulent Discharges from the Aural, Nasal and Vaginal Passages', *The
       Lancet*, Vol. 2 (1850), p. 45.

32.   *Ibid.*, p. 46.

33.   Report of the Westminster Medical Society, 'Diseases in Children Simulat-
       ing Gonorrhoea', *The Lancet*, Vol. 1 (1837), p. 718.

34. T.W. Cooke, 'On Some distressing Sequelae of the Diseases of Infancy', p. 45.
35. 'Medical-Chirurgical Transactions', *Edinburgh Medical and Surgical Journal*, Vol. 13 (1817), p. 491.
36. *Ibid.*, p. 491.
37. Sir Astley Cooper, *Lectures on Surgery* (London, 1837), p. 541.
38. David Ferrier and William A. Guy, *Principles of Forensic Medicine* (London, 1888), p. 58.
39. Francis Ogston, *Lectures in Medical Jurisprudence* (London, 1878), p. 95.
40. *Ibid.*, p. 96.
41. Michael Ryan, *Medical Jurisprudence*, p. 315.
42. 'Well-Marked Syphilis in a Female Child Aged Ten Years', *The Lancet*, Vol. 2 (1860), p. 345.
43. See Anthony Wohl, 'Sex and the Single Room: Incest among the Victorian Working Classes' in Anthony Wohl (ed.), *The Victorian Family* (London, 1978).
44. From the Minutes of Evidence, Poor Law Commissioners on the Employment of Women and Children in Agriculture, *Parliamentary Papers*, Vol. 12 (1843).
45. *Ibid.*
46. Cited in Anthony Wohl, *The Eternal Slum* (London, 1977), p. 54.
47. Cited in W.R. Greg, 'Prostitution', p. 470.
48. Alfred Swaine Taylor, *The Principles and Practice of Medical Jurisprudence*, p. 429.
49. *Ibid.*, p. 434.
50. W.B. Kevesten, 'On the Evidence of Rape on Infants, with Remarks on the Case of Amos Greenwood', *Medical Times and Gazette* (9 April 1859), p. 362.
51. W.B. Wilde, 'Medico-Legal Observations upon the Case of Amos Greenwood', *Dublin Quarterly of Medicine & Science*, Vol. 27 (1858), p. 53.
52. *Ibid.*, p. 74.
53. *Ibid.*, p. 75.
54. *Ibid.*, p. 82.
55. *Ibid.*, p. 71.
56. *Ibid.*, p. 75.
57. *Ibid.*, p. 78.
58. *Ibid.*, p. 82.
59. J. Hudson, 'The Convict Hodges', *Medical Times and Gazette* (13 April 1861), p. 403.
60. *Ibid.*, p. 403.
61. *Ibid.*, p. 403.
62. Cited in Jeffrey Mousaieff Masson, *The Assault on Truth: Freud's Suppression of the Seduction Theory* (New York, 1985), p. 41.
63. *Ibid.*, p. 41.
64. It should be noted that the man agreed to pay money to the child's mother rather than be tried in court.
65. Francis Ogston, *Lectures in Medical Jurisprudence*, p. 92.
66. W.B. Kevesten, 'On the Evidence of Rape on Infants', p. 361.
67. Francis Ogston, *Lectures in Medical Jurisprudence*, p. 93.

68. Michael Ryan, *Medical Jurisprudence*, p. 311.
69. *Ibid.*, p. 311. For further discussion of this see Susan S.M. Edward, *Female Sexuality and the Law* (Oxford, 1981), pp. 100–8.
70. David Ferrier and William A. Guy, *Principles of Forensic Medicine*, p. 55.
71. Francis Ogston, *Lectures in Medical Jurisprudence*, p. 98.
72. The Hottentot apron was the name given to the 'extended pudenda' allegedly found in the indigenous women of the Cape of Good Hope. Voltaire and others claimed that this over-development signified hyper-sexuality in black women and used it as a device to argue against the plurality of the races. By the middle of the nineteenth century signs of hypersexuality, such as 'large breasts' and 'elongated' labia were being seen as signs of white women's innate depravity. See Johann Blumenbach, *Anthropological Treatises*, translated by Thomas Bendyshe, London, 1865. See also Londa Schiebinger, *Nature's Body*, p. 163; Sander L. Gilman, *Difference and Pathology*, p. 85; Mary Spongberg, 'Written on the Body: Reading Child Sexuality in Nineteenth Century Britain' *JIGS*, Vol. 1, 1995.
73. See Londa Schiebinger, *Nature's Body*, p. 163; Sander L. Gilman, *Difference and Pathology*, p. 85.
74. Francis Ogston, *Lectures in Medical Jurisprudence*, p. 98.
75. Technically this was a case of rape because for girls below the age of twelve it was held that consent cannot be given and that connection must therefore legally be considered involuntary.
76. 'Well-Marked Syphilis', p. 239.
77. Alfred Swaine Taylor, *The Practice and the Principles of Medical Jurisprudence*, p. 432.
78. *Ibid.*, p. 431.
79. *Ibid.*, p. 431.
80. *Ibid.*, p. 431.
81. Dr Chever, *Medical Jurisprudence of India* (London, 1857).
82. Cited in W.B. Kevesten, 'On the Evidence of Rape on Infants', p. 418.
83. Sander L. Gilman, *Difference and Pathology*, p. 44.
84. Caroline Conley, 'Rape and Justice in Victorian England', *Victorian Studies*, Vol. 29 (1986).
85. *Ibid.*, p. 92.

7 CHILD PROSTITUTION

1. Rev. R. Wardlaw, *Lectures on Prostitution*, p. 43.
2. *Ibid.*, p. 43.
3. *Ibid.*, p. 43.
4. William Tait, *Magdalenism: An Inquiry into the Extent, Causes and Consequences of Prostitution in Edinburgh* (Edinburgh, 1842), p. 102.
5. *Ibid.*, p. 102.
6. *Debates*, House of Lords, Vol. 75, 3rd. Series (1844), pp. 880–92.
7. According to the First Statute of Westminster of 1285 the female age of consent was twelve, which corresponded to the minimum age at which a woman could legally marry. Twelve was the stipulated age in canon law and was supported by the authority of the Talmud. An Act in 1576 changed

the violation of female children from a misdemeanour into a capital felony. In so doing, it took the significant step of redefining the age at which consent became an issue from twelve to ten. Thus, violation of girls under the age of ten, regardless of the issue of consent, became a capital offence, but only the First Statute continued to provide protection of female children between the ages of ten and twelve. Carnal knowledge of girls in this age group continued to be a misdemeanour. See Antony E. Simpson, 'Vulnerability and the Age of Female Consent', pp. 181–5.

8.   From the first report of the Associate Institute for Improving and Enforcing the Laws for the Protection of Women, cited in Judith Walkowitz, *Prostitution and Victorian Society*, p. 40.
9.   Edward Bristow, *Vice and Vigilance: Purity Movements in Britain since 1700* (Dublin, 1977), p. 61.
10.   W.R. Greg, 'Prostitution', p. 488. (His emphasis.)
11.   William Acton, *Prostitution*, p. 136.
12.   'Prostitution – the Signs of Reform', *The Lancet* (31 October 1857), p. 453.
13.   Erna Reiss, *The Rights and Duties of Englishwomen: A Study in Law and Public Opinion* (Manchester, 1934), p. 195.
14.   Sander Gilman reports that although the age of consent in Austria was twenty-one, it was the aim of the government to restrict all girls under sixteen from being registered to brothels but, in effect, only girls under fourteen were excluded. See Sander L. Gilman, *Difference and Pathology*, p. 42. In Italy the age of consent was also twenty-one. Yet when the Cavour Law introduced a system of regulation in 1863, 27 per cent of registered prostitutes were between the ages of sixteen and twenty. See Mary Gibson, *Prostitution and the State in Italy 1880–1915* (New Brunswick, 1986), p. 107. For the situation in Germany see R.J. Evans, 'Prostitution, State and Society in Imperial Germany', *Past and Present*, Vol. 70 (1976).
15.   Yves Guyot, *Prostitution under the Regulation System* (London, 1884), p. 226. See also Jill Harsin, *Policing Prostitution in Nineteenth Century Paris*.
16.   *The Shield* (18 April 1870), p. 1.
17.   *The Shield* (21 March 1870), p. 4.
18.   *The Shield* (7 March 1870), p. 1.
19.   'Licensing Prostitution', *Annual Report of the Rescue Society* (London, 1869), p. 9.
20.   Myna Trustram, *Daughters of the Regiment*, p. 1.
21.   Royal Commission Regarding the Administration and Operation of the CD Acts, p. 127.
22.   George Behlmer, *Child Abuse and Moral Reform in England 1870–1908* (Stanford, 1982), p. 5. See also Margaret May, 'Innocence and Experience: The Evolution of the Concept of Juvenile Delinquency in the Mid-nineteenth Century', *Victorian Studies*, Vol. 16 (1973).
23.   Rosa Waugh, *The Life of Benjamin Waugh* (London, 1913), p. 65.
24.   Royal Commission Regarding the Administration and Operation of the CD Acts, p. 425.
25.   *Ibid.*, p. 421.
26.   *Ibid.*, p. 453.
27.   *Ibid.*, p. 381.
28.   *Ibid.*, p. 240.

29.   Judith Walkowitz, *Prostitution and Victorian Society*, p. 95.
30.   *The Shield* (May 1st 1880), p. 64.
31.   *Ibid.*, p. 64. (Her emphasis.)
32.   Select Committee of the House of Lords on the Law relating to the Protection of Young Girls, *Parliamentary Papers*, Vol. 11 (1882), Question 264.
33.   *Ibid.*, Question 750.
34.   *Ibid.*, Question 718.
35.   Rev. R. Wardlaw, *Lectures on Prostitution*, p. 59.
36.   James Miller, *Prostitution Considered*, p. 6.
37.   Select Committee of the House of Lords on the Law relating to the Protection of Young Girls, Question 743.
38.   *Ibid.*, Question 865.

8   THE SINS OF THE FATHER

1.   See, for instance, Lucy Bland, '"Cleansing the Portals of Life": The Venereal Campaign in the Early Twentieth Century' in Mary Langan and Bill Schwarz, *Crises in the British State 1880–1930* (London, 1985).
2.   Theodore Rosebury, *Microbes and Morals: The Strange Story of Venereal Disease* (London, 1972), p. 104. Rosebury suggests that the quotations 'The Fathers have eaten a sour grape, and the children's teeth are set on edge' (Jeremiah, 31:29), 'He hath a flat nose' and is barred from the temple and 'one dead of whom the flesh is half consumed when he cometh out of his mother's womb' (Numbers, 12:12) could refer to the symptoms of congenital syphilis.
3.   *Ibid.*, pp. 9–11.
4.   James Handley, *Colloquia Chirurgica or the Art of Surgery Epitomiz'd and Made Easy* (London, 1743), p. 43.
5.   Nicholas Robinson, *A New Treatise on the Venereal Disease* (London, 1736), pp. 63–4.
6.   Anon., *Every Man is his Own Physician in Venereal Cases* (London, 1757), p. 3.
7.   John Hunter, *On the Venereal Disease*, pp. 20–80.
8.   Rudolph H. Kampmeier, 'John Hunter – A Man of Conviction', *Sexually Transmitted Diseases*, Vol. 4, No. 3 (1977), p. 115.
9.   David Nabarro, *Congenital Syphilis*, p. 12.
10.   For examples of this see Elizabeth Lomax, 'Infantile Syphilis, as an Example of the Nineteenth Century Belief in the Inheritance of Acquired Characteristics', *Journal of the History of Medicine*, Vol. 34, No. 1 (1979), p. 31.
11.   *Ibid.*, p. 284.
12.   Ambrose King *et al.*, *Venereal Disease*, p. 104.
13.   *Ibid.*, pp. 103–4.
14.   J.H.D. Widdess, 'William Wallace', *British Journal of Venereal Disease*, Vol. 41, No. 9 (1965), pp. 11–12.
15.   Allen M. Brandt, *No Magic Bullet* (Oxford, 1985), p. 10.
16.   Report of the Committee appointed to Enquire into the Pathology and Treatment of the Venereal Disease, Parliamentary Papers, Vol. 37 (1867), p. xv.

17. Thomas Ballard, 'What are the Signs of Congenital Syphilis?', *The Lancet*, Vol. 1 (1873), p. 736.

18. Jonathan Hutchinson, *Medical Times and Gazette* (1876), p. 643.

19. Cited in Robert Cory, 'On the Origin of Infantile Syphilis', *The Lancet*, Vol. 1 (1876), p. 886.

20. Allen M. Brandt, *No Magic Bullet*, p. 9.

21. See, for instance, Thomas Ballard, 'What are the Signs of Congenital Syphilis?', p. 737.

22. M.A. Waugh, 'Alfred Fournier, 1832–1914: His Influence on Venereology', *British Journal of Venereal Disease*, Vol. 50 (1974), p. 232.

23. Alfred Fournier, *Syphilis and Marriage* (London, 1881), pp. 34–5. (His emphasis.)

24. Cited in Robert Cory, 'On the Origin of Infantile Syphilis', *The Lancet*, Vol. 1 (1876), p. 885. Diday's idea that a syphilitic father could leave a syphilitic imprint in the mother's womb related to seventeenth- and eighteenth-century notions of heredity that dealt primarily with farm animals. Such ideas were taken up in the works of Zola and Taine, where the woman's first lover's image is printed on her and her children by other men. By the end of the nineteenth century, however, such ideas were generally dismissed and replaced by theories that stressed the moment of conception as the most important factor determining heredity. See Charles Rosenberg, 'The Bitter Fruit: Heredity, Disease and Social Thought in Nineteenth Century America', *Perspectives in American History*, Vol. 8 (1974). Such ideas were, however, to resurface in the twentieth century, particularly in Nazi racial theorists. Certain Nazi authors, such as Artur Dinter and Egon von Kapherr, used the idea of racial imprinting to promote anti-semitism. In these novels the plot usually revolved around a hapless but good Aryan man begetting children with a beautiful but shallow Aryan woman, only to find that the children resemble not their father, but a former lover of their mother, invariably a Jew. In Dinter's *Die Sunde wider das Blut* (The Sin against the Blood) one wicked Jew, Baron von Werhiem (alias Wertheim), has established a blonde brothel in order to systematically undermine the German race. The premise of these novels was not that Jews were cuckolding Aryan men but rather that they were leaving their racial imprint on Aryan women. Dinter claimed that in the woman of a higher race, a chemical change takes place through coitus with a lower race 'just as an indigo-coloured solution is turned red through a drop of acid'. It was such 'scientific anti-semitism' that was the intellectual source of the 'Aryan clause' and the first of the Nuremberg Laws 'For the Protection of German Blood and Honour'. See Gunter Hartung, 'Artur Dinter: A Successful Fascist Author in Pre-Fascist Germany', in John Milfull (ed.), *The Attractions of Fascism: Social Psychology and the Aesthetics of 'The Triumph of the Right'* (New York, 1990).

25. Alfred Fournier, *Syphilis and Marriage*, p. 35.

26. *Ibid.*, p. 27. (His emphasis.)

27. Jonathan Hutchinson, *Medical Times and Gazette* (1876), p. 643.

28. Prince Albert Morrow, *Social Disease and Marriage: Social Prophylaxis* (London, 1904), p. 193.

29. Alfred Fournier, *Syphilis and Marriage*, p. 30.

30. *Ibid.*, p. 24.

31. Prince Albert Morrow, *Social Disease and Marriage: Social Prophylaxis*, p. 193.
32. Alfred Fournier, *Syphilis and Marriage*, p. 43.
33. *Ibid.*, p. 59.
34. Charles Rosenberg, 'The Bitter Fruit: Heredity, Disease and Social Thought in Nineteenth Century America', p. 198.
35. Sander L. Gilman, *Difference and Pathology*, p. 218.
36. Cited in Claude Quétel, *The History of Syphilis*, pp. 168–9.
37. Alison Bashford, *'Breaking the Conspiracy of Silence': The Late Victorian and Edwardian Debate on Venereal Disease*, Honours Thesis (University of Sydney, 1990).
38. Jonathan Hutchinson, *Syphilis* (London, 1889), p. 68.
39. Elizabeth Lomax, 'Infantile Syphilis, as an Example of the Nineteenth Century Belief in the Inheritance of Acquired Characteristics', p. 31.
40. 'Syphilis and Marriage', *British Medical Journal*, Vol. 1 (1885), p. 875.
41. See G.H. Fleming, *Victorian Sex Goddess: Lady Colin Campbell and the Sensational Divorce Case of 1886* (Oxford, 1990), pp. 17–21.
42. Alfred Fournier, *Syphilis and Marriage*, p. viii.
43. *Ibid.*, p. viii.
44. Alison Bashford, *Breaking the Conspiracy of Silence*, p. 27.
45. F.W. Lowndes, 'Syphilis, and Marriage', *The Lancet*, Vol. 2 (1882), p. 8.
46. C.R. Drysdale, 'The Prognosis of Syphilis in Women and Children', *British Medical Journal*, Vol. 2 (1882), p. 395.
47. C.R. Drysdale, 'Syphilis, and Marriage', *British Medical Journal*, Vol. 1 (1885), p. 926.
48. 'Nottingham Medico-Chirurgical Society, *The Lancet*, Vol. 1 (1889), p. 1247.
49. See, for instance, J.A. Coutts, 'The Hunterian Lecture on Infantile Syphilis', *The Lancet*, Vol. 1 (1896), p. 467.
50. See, for instance, John A. Shaw-McKenzie, 'Maternal Syphilis', *The Lancet*, Vol. 1 (1896), p. 1457.
51. See, for instance, J.A. Coutts, *The Lancet*, Vol. 2 (1894), p. 164; George Ogilvie, 'Should a Healthy Mother Suckle Her Congenitally Syphilitic Child?', *The Lancet*, Vol. 1 (1896), p. 1791.
52. George F. Still, 'Congenital Syphilis' in D'arcy Power and J. Keogh Murphy, *A System of Syphilis* (Oxford, 1914), p. 483.
53. *Ibid.*, p. 484.
54. Cited in Frances Swiney, *The Bar of Isis* in Sheila Jeffreys (ed.), *The Sexuality Debates* (London, 1987), p. 474.
55. *Ibid.*, pp. 474–5.
56. See, for instance, David Mitchell, *Queen Christabel: A Biography of Christabel Pankhurst* (London, 1977); and Andrew Rosen, *Rise Up Women: The Militant Campaign of the Women's Social and Political Union 1903–1914* (London, 1974).
57. Tom Robinson, *The Lancet*, Vol. 2 (1895), p. 1165.
58. Alfred Fournier, *Syphilis Hérédetaire Tardive* (Paris, 1886), cited in Claude Quétel, *The History of Syphilis*, p. 167.
59. Elizabeth Lomax, 'Infantile Syphilis, as an Example of the Nineteenth Century Belief in the Inheritance of Acquired Characteristics', p. 34.

60. 'Syphilis and Nervous Disease in Children', *The Lancet*, Vol. 2 (1892), p. 1221.
61. Cited in T. Telford-Smith, 'Congenital Syphilis', *British Medical Journal*, Vol. 2 (1898), p. 1152.
62. J. Langdon-Down, *Mental Affections of Childhood and Youth* (London, 1887).
63. For a discussion of cretinism in the nineteenth century see Thomas Schlich, 'Changing Disease Identities: Cretinism, Surgery and Politics 1844–1892', *Medical History*, Vol. 38 (1994), pp. 421–43.
64. Daniel Pick, *Faces of Degeneration: A European Disorder, c.1848–1918* (Cambridge, 1989), p. 47.
65. George Rosen, *Madness in Society: Chapters in the Historical Sociology of Mental Illness* (Chicago, 1968), pp. 254–5.
66. Eric T. Carlson, 'Medicine and Degeneration: Theory and Praxis' in Edward J. Cunningham and Sander L. Gilman (eds), *Degeneration: The Dark Side of Progress* (New York, 1985), p. 122.
67. Daniel Pick, *Faces of Degeneration*, p. 203.
68. *Ibid.*, p. 203.
69. Janet Saunders, 'Quarantining the Weak-Minded: Psychiatric Definitions of Degeneracy and the Late-Victorian Asylum' in W.F. Bynum, Roy Porter and Michael Shepherd, *The Anatomy of Madness*, Vol. 3 (London, 1988), p. 277.
70. Claude Quétel, *The History of Syphilis*, p. 168.
71. George Rosen, *Madness in Society*, p. 254.
72. F.W. Mott, 'Syphilis of the Central Nervous System' in D'arcy Power and J. Keogh Murphy, *A System of Syphilis*, Vol. 4 (Oxford,1914), p. 238.
73. *Ibid.*, p. 237.
74. Margaret S. Thompson, 'The Wages of Sin: The Problem of Alcoholism and General-Paralysis in Nineteenth Century Edinburgh' in W.F. Bynum, Roy Porter and Michael Shepherd, *The Anatomy of Madness*, Vol. 3 (London, 1988), p. 326.
75. Jonathan Hutchinson, 'A Discussion on Some Aspects of Congenital Syphilis', *British Medical Journal*, Vol. 2 (1898), p. 1149.
76. See, for instance, Trevor Turner, 'Henry Maudsley: Psychiatrist, Philosopher, and Entrepreneur' in W.F. Bynum, Roy Porter and Michael Shepherd, *The Anatomy of Madness*, Vol. 3 (London, 1988), p. 164. See also Frederick A. Rhodes, *The Next Generation* (Boston, 1915), p. 95.
77. Sir Victor Horsley, Report of the Inter-Departmental Committee on Physical Degeneration, *Parliamentary Papers, Committees and Reports*, Vol. 1 (1904), p. 385.

9 THE SYPHILITIC AS MORAL DEGENERATE

1. Anna Davin, 'Imperialism and Motherhood', *History Workshop Journal*, No. 5 (1978), p. 10.
2. Mark B. Adams (ed.), *The Well Born Science: Eugenics in Germany, France, Brazil, and Russia* (Oxford, 1990), p. 3.
3. Daniel Pick, *Faces of Degeneration*; Lyndsay Andrew Farrall, *The Origin*

and Growth of the English Eugenics Movement 1865–1925 (New York, 1985).

4. Evelyn Hunt, 'The Cry of the Unborn', *Shafts* (2 October 1894), p. 344.

5. Ellis Ethelmer, 'The Contagious Diseases Acts: A Warning', *Westminster Review*, Vol. 147 (1897), p. 483. There is debate among scholars as to whether the pseudonym 'Ellis Ethelmer' was used by the feminist writer Elizabeth Wollstoneholme Elmy or by her husband, Benjamin Elmy.

6. See, for instance, Geoffrey Mortimer, 'Enforced Maternity', *Shafts* (14 January 1893), p. 167.

7. Geoffrey Mortimer, 'Immoral Marriage', *Shafts* (28 January 1893), p. 196.

8. 'Enforced Maternity', *Shafts* (18 February 1893), p. 251. (Emphasis in the original.)

9. Geoffrey Mortimer, 'Enforced Maternity' *Shafts* (14 January 1893), p. 196.

10. See, for instance, Samuel Hynes, *The Edwardian Turn of Mind* (Princeton, 1971); J.L. Wisenthal (ed.), *Shaw and Ibsen: The Quintessence of Shaw and Related Writings* (Toronto, 1979); Elaine Showalter, *Sexual Anarchy: Gender and Culture at the Fin de Siècle* (New York, 1990).

11. Elaine Showalter, *Sexual Anarchy*, p. 200.

12. Cited in Henrik Ibsen, *The Oxford Ibsen*, trans. James Walter McFarlane (New York, 1961), p. 482.

13. Sarah Grand, *The Heavenly Twins* (London, 1893), Vol. 1, p. 81.

14. *Ibid.*, Vol. 1, p. 220.

15. Emma Frances Brookes, *A Superfluous Woman* (London, 1894), p. 257.

16. *Ibid.*, p. 262.

17. *Ibid.*, p. 269.

18. See, for instance, Cicely Hamilton, *Marriage as a Trade* (London, 1981) (first published 1909) ; Lucy Bland, 'The Married Woman, the New Woman and the Feminist: Sexual Politics of the 1890s' in Jane Rendall (ed.), *Equal or Different: Women's Politics 1800–1914* (London, 1987); Lucy Bland, 'Marriage Laid Bare: Middle Class Women and Marital Sex *c.*1800–1914' in Jane Lewis (ed.), *Labour and Love: Women's Experience of Home and Family 1850–1940* (London, 1986).

19. Cicely Hamilton, *Marriage as Trade*, p. 54.

20. Laura Engelstein, '"Morality and the Wooden Spoon": Russian Doctors' View of Syphilis, Social Class and Sexual Behaviour, 1890–1905' in Thomas Laqueur and Catherine Gallagher, *The Making of the Modern Body*, (Berkeley, 1987), p. 169.

21. Prince Albert Morrow, *Social Disease and Marriage*, p. iii.

22. Allen M. Brandt, *No Magic Bullet*, p. 16.

23. Sander L. Gilman, *Difference and Pathology*, pp. 94–6.

24. Cited in Eugene S. Talbot, *Degeneracy: Its Causes, Signs and Results*, p. 319.

25. Cesare Lombroso and William Ferrero, *The Female Offender* (London, 1895), p. 112.

26. Cited in Lucia Zedner, *Women, Crime and Custody in Victorian England* (Oxford, 1991), p. 81.

27. Cesare Lombroso and William Ferrero, *The Female Offender*, p. 187.

28. Lucia Zedner, *Women, Crime and Custody*, p. 80.

29. Cited in Elaine Showalter, *The Female Malady* (London, 1985), p. 29.

30. *Ibid.*, p. 29. See also Michael J. Clark, ' "Morbid Introspection", Unsoundness of Mind, and British Psychological Medicine, *c*.1830–1900'; Trevor Turner, 'Henry Maudsley: Psychiatrist, Philosopher, and Entrepreneur' in W.F. Bynum, Roy Porter and Michael Shepherd, *The Anatomy of Madness*, Vol. 3 (London, 1988).
31. Elaine Showalter, *The Female Malady.*
32. Cited in F.W. Mott, 'Syphilis and the Central Nervous System', p. 244.
33. Eugene S. Talbot, *Degeneracy*, p. 322.
34. Anna Davin, 'Imperialism and Motherhood', p. 9.
35. Report of the Inter-Departmental Committee on Physical Degeneration, Great Britain, *Parliamentary Papers: Reports and Committees*, Vol. 1 (1904), p. 77.
36. *Ibid.*, pp. 77–8.
37. *Ibid.*, p. 150.
38. *Ibid.*, p. 385.
39. Richard Davenport-Hines, *Sex, Death and Punishment*, p. 217.
40. Report of the Inter-Departmental Committee on Physical Degeneration, p. 382.
41. *Ibid.*, p. 383.
42. Harvey G. Simmons, 'Explaining Social Policy: The English Mental Deficiency Act of 1913' *Journal of Social History*, Vol. 11, No. 3 (1978), p. 388.
43. *Ibid.*, p. 390.
44. See the evidence of Miss P.D. Townsend and Miss Jeffries. Royal Commission on the Care and Control of the Feeble-Minded, *Parliamentary Papers*, Vol. 1 (1904), p. 425.
45. *Ibid.*, Vol. 1, p. 100. (Her emphasis.)
46. *Ibid.*, Vol. 1, p. 470.
47. Robert Reid Rentoul, *Race Culture or Race Suicide?* (London, 1906), p. 42.
48. 'The Sterility of Prostitutes', *British Medical Journal*, Vol. 2 (1881), p. 656.
49. Robert Reid Rentoul, *Race Culture or Race Suicide?*, p. 42. See also F.A. Nyulasy, *The Intermarriage of Disease* (n.p.d., 1904); W.A. Chapple, *The Fertility of the Unfittest* (Melbourne, 1904); Charles Armstrong, *The Survival of the Unfittest* (London, 1927).
50. Harvey G. Simmons, 'Explaining Social Theory', p. 395.
51. Royal Commission on the Care and Control of the Feeble-Minded, *Parliamentary Papers*, Vol. 1 (1908), p. 497.
52. A.F. Tredgold, 'The Feeble-Minded – A Social Danger', *Eugenics Review*, Vol. 1 (1909), p. 101.
53. Cited in *Abstract Report of the Royal Commission on the Care and Control of the Feeble-Minded* (London, 1909), p. 295
54. A.F. Tredgold, 'The Feeble-Minded – A Social Danger', pp. 101–2.
55. Havelock Ellis, 'The Problem of the Feeble-Minded', *Journal of Heredity*, Vol. 5, No. 9 (1914), p. 509.
56. Arnold White, 'Eugenics and National Efficiency', *Eugenics Review*, Vol. 1 (1909), p. 110.
57. House of Commons *Debates* (1912), p. 1464. Cited in Harvey G. Simmons, 'Explaining Social Policy', p. 403.
58. Mr Chancellor speaking on 28 July 1913, *Hansard* (5th series), Vol. 56, cited in Lucia Zedner, *Women, Crime and Custody*, pp. 274–5.

59. *Ibid.*, p. 275.
60. See, for instance, Edward H. Beardsley, 'Allied Against Sin: American and British Responses to Venereal Disease in World War One', *Medical History*, Vol. 30 (1976); Lucy Bland, '"Cleansing the Portals of Life"; P.S. O'Connor, 'Venus and the Lonely Kiwi: The War Effort of Miss Ettie Rout', *New Zealand Journal of History*, Vol. 1, No. 1 (1967); Bridget A. Towers, 'Health Education Policy 1916–1926: Venereal Disease and the Prophylaxis Dilemma', *Medical History* Vol. 24 (1980).
61. Lucy Bland, '"Guardians of the Race" or "Vampires on the Nation's Health"? Female Sexuality and Its Regulation in Early Twentieth Century Britain' in Elizabeth Whitelegg *et al.* (eds), *The Changing Experience of Women* (Oxford, 1982); Arthur Marwick, *The Deluge: British Society and the First World War* (London, 1991).
62. Royal Commission on Venereal Disease, *Parliamentary Papers*, Commissions and Reports, 1916, p. 295.
63. *Ibid.*, p. 172.
64. Anne Campbell, *Girl Delinquents* (London, 1981), p. 44.
65. Lucy Bland, '"Cleansing the Portals of Life"', p. 132.
66. Harvey G. Simmons, 'Explaining Social Policy', p. 400.
67. Lucy Bland, '"In the Name of Protection": The Policing of Women in the First World War' in Carol Smart (ed.), *Sisters-in-Law* (London, 1985), p. 27.
68. E. Sylvia Pankhurst, *The Home Front: A Mirror of Life in England during the World War* (London, 1932), p. 102.
69. *Ibid.*, p. 104.
70. Lucy Bland, '"In the Name of Protection"', p. 31.
71. *Ibid.*, p. 32.
72. Arthur Marwick, *The Deluge*, p. 76.
73. Havelock Ellis, *Essays in Wartime* (London, 1917), p. 65. See also Bishop N. Harmon, *Staying the Plague* (London, 1917).
74. A. Maude Royden, *Downward Paths: An Inquiry into the Causes which Contribute to the Making of a Prostitute* (London, 1916), p. 57.
75. Havelock Ellis, *Essays in Wartime*, p. 127.
76. A. Maude Royden, *Downward Paths*, p. 10.
77. Richard Davenport-Hines, *Sex, Death and Punishment*, p. 248.
78. Parliamentary Committee on the Prevention of VD. See *Report & Evidence*, 1921, p. 43.
79. *Ibid.*, p. 43.
80. *Ibid.*, p. 44.
81. Richard Davenport-Hines, *Sex, Death and Punishment*, p. 248.
82. See Allen Brandt, *No Magic Bullet*; S. Gubar, '"This is My Rifle, This is My Gun": World War II and the Blitz on Women' in M.R. Higonnet *et al.*, *Behind the Lines: Gender and the Two World Wars* (Yale, 1987); R.R. Peirson, 'The Double Bind of the Double Standard: VD Control and the CWAV in World War II', *Canadian Historical Review*, Vol. 62, No. 1 (1981).
83. Louisa Martindale, *The Prevention of Venereal Disease* (London, 1945), p. 41.

10 TRAPPED IN A WOMAN'S BODY?

1. Sander L. Gilman, *Disease and Representation*, p. 254.
2. Simon Watney, *Policing Desire: Pornography, AIDS and the Media* (London, 1987), p. 9.
3. See, for instance, Sander L. Gilman, *Disease and Representation*; Paula Triechler, 'AIDS, Gender and Biomedical Discourse'; Elaine Showalter, *Sexual Anarchy*; Leo Bersani 'Is the Rectum a Grave?' *October*, No. 43 (1987); Douglas Crimp, *AIDS: Cultural Analysis, Cultural Activism* (Cambridge, Mass., 1988).
4. Simon Watney, 'The Spectacle of AIDS', *October*, No. 43 (1987), p. 47.
5. See, for instance, Michel Foucault, *The History of Sexuality*; Jeffrey Weeks, *Coming Out*; Richard Davenport-Hines, *Sex, Death and Punishment*; George Chauncey Jnr, ' "Christian Brotherhood or Sexual Perversion?" Homosexual Identities and the Construction of Sexual Boundaries in the World War One Era' in Martin Bauml Duberman, Martha Vicinus and George Chauncey Jnr (eds), *Hidden from History: Reclaiming the Gay and Lesbian Past* (New York, 1989).
6. Robert A. Nye, 'Sex Difference and Male Homosexuality in French Medical Discourse, 1830–1930', *Bulletin of the History of Medicine*, Vol. 63, No. 1 (1989), pp. 39–41.
7. Richard Davenport-Hines, *Sex, Death and Punishment*, pp. 108–9.
8. Jeffrey Weeks, *Coming Out*, p. 27.
9. R.D. Leach and H. Ellis, 'Carcinoma of the rectum in male homosexuals', *Journal of the Royal Society of Medicine*, Vol. 74 (1981), p. 491. See also Janet R. Daling *et al.*, 'Correlates of Homosexual Behavior and the Incidence of Anal Cancer' *Journal of the American Medical Association*, Vol. 247, No. 14 (1982), pp. 1988–90; P. Kondlapoodi, 'Anorectal Cancer and Homosexuality', *Journal of the American Medical Association*, Vol. 248, No. 17 (1982), p. 2114; Stephan J. Landis, 'Sexually Transmitted Disease among Homosexuals' *Canadian Medical Association Journal*, Vol. 130 (1984), pp. 370–2; Frederic P. Li *et al.*, 'Anorectal Squamous Carcinoma in Two Homosexual Men', *The Lancet*, Vol. 2 (1982), p. 391.
10. See also Gerald M. Oppenheimer, 'Causes, Cases, and Cohorts: The Role of Epidemiology in the Historical Construction of AIDS' in Elizabeth Fee and Daniel M. Fox, *AIDS: The Making of a Chronic Disease*; Cindy Patton, *Sex and Germs: The Politics of AIDS* (Montreal, 1986).
11. Kaye Wellings, 'Perceptions of Risk – Media Treatment of AIDS' in Peter Aggleton and Hilary Homans (eds), *Social Aspects of AIDS* (London, 1988), p. 67.
12. P. Ebbesen, *et al.*, *AIDS: A Basic Guide for Clinicians* (Copenhagen, 1984), p. 42.
13. Michael Lange *et al.*, 'Epidemiological Observations of Immunological Abnormalities in Men' in Pearl Ma and Donald Armstrong (eds), *The Acquired Immunodeficiency Syndrome and Other Infections of Homosexual Men* (New York, 1984), p. 358.
14. Joseph A. Sonnabend, 'Acquired Immunodeficiency – An explanation' in Pearl Ma and Donald Armstrong (eds), *The Acquired Immunodeficiency Syndrome and Other Infections of Homosexual Men*, p. 410.

15. Joseph A. Sonnabend, *et al.*, 'Acquired Immunodeficiency Syndrome, Opportunistic Infections and Malignancies in Male Homosexuals' *Journal of the American Medical Association*, Vol. 249, No. 17 (1983), p. 2371.

16. Randy Shilts, *And the Band Played On* (New York, 1987); Larry Kramer, *Letters from the Holocaust* (New York, 1988).

17. James A. Fletcher, 'Homosexuality: Kick and Kickback', *Southern Medical Journal*, Vol. 77 (1984), p. 150.

18. David T. Durack. 'Opportunistic Infections and Kaposi's Sarcoma in Homosexual Men', *New England Journal of Medicine*, Vol. 305, No. 2 (1981), p. 1466.

19. Margaret Fromer, *AIDS: Acquired Immune Deficiency Syndrome* (New York, 1983), p. 181.

20. Simon Watney, 'The Spectacle of AIDs'; Jeff Nunokawa, 'All the Sad Young Men: AIDS and the Work of Mourning' in Diana Fuss (ed.), *Inside/Out* (New York, 1992).

21. See, for instance, Hans H. Neumann, 'Letter to the Editor', *New England Journal of Medicine*, Vol. 306, No. 15 (1982), p. 935; Elismar M. Cortinho, 'Kaposi's Sarcoma and the Use of Oestrogen by Male Homosexuals', *The Lancet*, Vol. 1 (1982), p. 1362.

22. Carlos Navarro, *et al.*, 'Letter to the Editor', *New England Journal of Medicine*, Vol. 306, No. 15 (1982), p. 933.

23. Cited in Kaye Wellings, 'Perceptions of Risk – Media Treatment of AIDS', p. 65.

24. Anne Rompolo and H. Hunter Handsfield, 'An Overview of Sexually Transmitted Diseases in Homosexual Men' in Pearl Ma and Donald Armstrong (eds), *The Acquired Immunodeficiency Syndrome and Other Infections of Homosexual Men*, p. 3.

25. Yehudi M. Felman, 'Other Sexually Transmitted Diseases' in Pearl Ma and Donald Armstrong (eds), *The Acquired Immune Deficiency Syndrome and Other Infections of Homosexual Men*, p. 130.

26. See Paula Triechler, 'AIDS, Gender and Biomedical Discourse', p. 206.

27. Philippe Van De Perre *et al.*, 'Female Prostitutes: A Risk Group for Infection with Human T-Cell Lymphotropic Virus Type III', *The Lancet*, Vol. 2 (1985), p. 526.

28. Joyce Wallace, 'Acquired Immune Deficiency in Prostitutes' in Pearl Ma and Donald Armstrong (eds), *The Acquired Immune Deficiency Syndrome and Other Infections of Homosexual Men*, p. 253.

29. Cited in Paula A. Treichler, 'AIDS and HIV Infection in the Third World: A First World Chronicle', p. 34.

30. Judith Butler, *Bodies that Matter* (New York, 1994), p. 125.

Index